Electrifying Time

Telechron and GE Clocks, 1925-55

Jim Linz

Schiffer Publishing Ltd®

4880 Lower Valley Road, Atglen, PA 19310 USA

Dedication

In memory of John Rainbault, Ivan Bruce, Ray Patten, and the other designers and employees of the Warren Telechron Company.

Library of Congress Cataloging-in-Publication data

Linz, Jim.
    Electrifying time : Telechron and GE Clocks, 1925-55/ Jim Linz.
        p. cm.
    ISBN 0-7643-1190-5 (pbk.)
    1. Telechron, Inc. 2. Clocks and watches, Electric. I. Title
TS544.L56 2000
681.1'13-dc21
                                                    00-009618

ISBN: 0-7643-1190-5
Typeset in Kaufmann /Humanist 521

Printed in China
1 2 3 4

Published by Schiffer Publishing Ltd.
4880 Lower Valley Road
Atglen, PA 19310
Phone: (610) 593-1777; Fax: (610) 593-2002
e-mail: schifferbk@aol.com
Please visit our website catalog at
www.schifferbooks.com
or write for a free printed catalog.
This book may be purchased from the publisher.
Please include $3.95 for shipping.

In Europe, Schiffer books are distributed by
Bushwood Books
6 Marksbury Avenue
Kew Gardens
Surrey TW9 4JF England
Phone: 44 (0) 20 8392-8585; Fax: 44 (0) 20 8392-9876
e-mail: bushwd@aol.com

Please try your bookstore first.

We are interested in hearing from authors
with book ideas on related subjects.

Contents

Acknowledgments

This book would not have been possible without the cooperation and assistance of the Ashland Historical Society. A former employee of the Warren Telechron Company donated extensive records including catalogs, dealers' sales literature, service manuals, photographs, sales and shipping records, and an extensive collection of the *Telechronicle* and *Synchronuze*. These records provided the foundation for my research and are extensively pictured throughout this book, including photographs of individual clocks taken from catalogs and sales literature, covers and other promotional material from the *Telechronicle*, and historic photographs of Henry Warren and the Telechron plant. In addition, photographs of several of the clocks in the Ashland Historical Society's growing collection are included.

Although many individuals assisted in the preparation of this book, two—Dick Fannon and Jay Kennan—merit special recognition. Dick, like the other members of the Ashland Historical Society, is a volunteer. Although the Society is normally open to the public only on Wednesday evenings and Saturday mornings, Dick willingly gave up his own time to accommodate my almost monthly visits to Ashland. An Ashland native who worked at the Worcester plant during the early 1950s, Dick was also able to plug many of the gaps in my research.

In addition to allowing me to photograph his rapidly growing collection, Jay Kennan
- prepared Appendix I, sharing his experiences in repairing and restoring Telechron clocks;
- supplied many of the advertisements displayed in the book;
- scanned documents from the Ashland archives.
- provided valuable review comments and assistance in setting values;
- prepared the description of the Telechron rotors contained in Chapter 6;
- identified the "Massachusetts connection" in Telechron model names; and
- provided a valuable link to other Telechron collectors.

Other significant contributions include:

Mike Frost of Orsini & Frost, Inc., Manassas, Virginia, opened his archives, allowing me to photograph both catalog and repair manuals.

Sara Hassan allowed me to copy her 1930-31 General Electric Supply Corporation catalog and advertisements from her collection of vintage magazines.

Bob Merchant, Peter Scagnelli, Esther Cooperman, Sara Hassan, and Orsini & Frost, Inc. allowed me to photograph clocks from their collections.

Bob Merchant prepared artwork, including the drawing of the "Tuscan," researched the careers of the movie stars pictured in the *Telechronicle*, and searched through his extensive magazine collection for Telechron and General Electric advertisements.

Stephen Kruft, John and Judy McClain, and Alicia Petrainus submitted photographs from their collections.

Frank and Kay Powers guided me through the Ashland Historical Society archives.

John Anderson and the Hall of Electrical History, Schenectady Museum, supplied parts and repair manuals to assist in identifying models.

Beth Bisbano and the staff at the National Watch and Clock Museum Research Center and Library, Columbia, Pennsylvania assisted in my research. Several of the catalog photographs are from the library's collection.

Glen and Elaine Foster provided a copy of a Canadian General Electric catalog.

Thanks also to Peter Schiffer, Brandi Wright, Bruce Waters and the staff of Schiffer Publishing for guiding me through the book building process.

Introduction

Telechron—Time From a Distance

Henry Warren's 1916 invention of the self-starting synchronous electric clock motor and Warren Master Clock began a new era in timekeeping. The Warren Clock Company (renamed the Warren Telechron Company in 1926) switched from production of battery-operated clocks to production of synchronous electric clocks, choosing the tradename "Telechron" (initially spelled Telekron), meaning "time from a distance." This book looks at the timepieces manufactured by the Warren Telechron Company at just that—a distance of 45 to 75 years. I think that you will agree that the clocks that Warren built have stood the test of time.

Henry Warren essentially invented a product and then developed a market for it where none would otherwise have existed. Warren's synchronous electric clock had an Achilles heel—it could not tell time. Its motor essentially ran at the speed dictated by the frequency of current generated by the power station to which it was "attached." If the frequency generated by the power station fluctuated, the clock ran faster or slower. Like his earlier attempts at developing a battery-operated clock, the synchronous clock would be doomed to failure unless a means could be found to regulate the frequency of current generated by the power stations. In a few short months, Warren had developed and tested his Master Clock and, in so doing, created a market for his synchronous electric clocks.

Industrial giant General Electric, quick to recognize Warren's genius, purchased a 49 percent interest in the Warren Clock Company in 1917, before his inventions had even been patented. Initially, General Electric was a silent partner and clocks were sold only under the Telechron name. GE's Edison Electric Appliance Company did, however, produce some kitchen timers during the late 1920s using Telechron motors.

As power companies installed Warren Master clocks, the market for synchronous electric clocks rapidly expanded. The Warren Clock Company was not the only one to benefit. The power companies gained the ability to easily share electricity with adjoining utilities, eventually forming the "grid" that helps prevent brownouts in periods of peak demand or plant failures. The standardization of frequency, long a goal of appliance makers like Manning Bowman, made household appliances transportable. Previously, an appliance motor designed to work at the frequency generated by one power station might not work properly on the frequency generated by another station. Finally, other clock makers such as Hammond and Seth Thomas entered the market with their own electric clocks.

In the early years, the Warren Clock Company focused heavily on commercial installations, developing a wide range of models including post and tower clocks. It would install individual clocks or a central control system to link Telechron clocks throughout a factory or office building. The company estimated that 20 million people were "using" Telechron clocks by the mid-1920s. Although this book focuses primarily on consumer clocks, Appendix V shows

Cover of the June 1931 *Telechronicle*. The sketch of Henry Warren gracing the cover was sent in unsolicited by a reader of *Good Housekeeping*.

the range of commercial clocks available in 1931. Readers with access to the internet are urged to visit Pappy's Telechron Clock Page for a wider selection of commercial models.

Revere Rides Into The Picture

In 1925, the Herschede Hall Clock Company, the premier American manufacturer of tall case and chime clocks, uncertain about the reliability of electric clocks and unwilling to risk its reputation, established a separate company—the Revere Clock Company—to produce electric tall case and chime clocks. The exact nature of the relationship with the Warren Telechron Company is not clear, but the clocks used Telechron motors, Telechron and Revere promoted each other's clocks in their advertisements, and the two companies had a joint sales force. General Electric also became involved in the relationship around 1931, with Revere making the cases and chime movements for GE's tall case and chime clocks. Often the only difference between a GE and Revere model is the dial.

Herschede Hall's concerns about the reliability of Telechron motors proved unfounded and Revere clocks flourished. Perhaps the best gauge of the public's acceptance of the accuracy and reliability of Telechron clocks, however, is the failure of Telechron's own line of clocks with auxiliary spring-wound motors—the so-called "A" series clocks. Although a few models were included in the 1932 catalog, none of the clocks with auxiliary motors were big sellers making the "A" series clocks among the hardest to find. Apparently, the public did not see a need for the "safety net."

By the mid 1920s, Telechron was producing a small range of shelf and wall clocks aimed at consumers, most with wood or metal cases and "period" styling. Styles included Chippendale, Colonial, and Queen Anne. Sales were modest but encouraging. Then, in 1928, it made a bold move, introducing the Paul Frankl-designed "Modernique" in what has become known as the art deco style. It was followed in 1929 with the skyscraper-design "Electrolarm." Although traditional tambour models and period designs continued to be included in future Telechron catalogs, most of the new models introduced after 1932 featured art deco styling.

Around 1931, the General Electric name began to appear on dials, but as "General Electric Telechron" clocks. Some models, such as the "Electrolarm," were sold with both Telechron and General Electric Telechron dials. By 1934, however, the "Telechron" was dropped from most dials and the clocks became simply "General Electric." Most, however, continued to come off the same assembly lines as Telechron clocks.

Throughout the 1930s, Telechron introduced innovations from the illuminated alarm clock, to the set-and-forget 24-hour alarm, to the cyclometer clock. Henry Warren served as President of the Warren Telechron Company until 1943, at which time General Electric assumed control. General Electric continued to introduce innovations, including the clock radio (1946) and the snooze alarm (1956).

The distinct Telechron and General Electric brand names would continue into the mid 1950s at which time General Electric, which had gradually absorbed the former Warren Telechron Company into its corporate structure, once again began marketing clocks under the "General Electric Telechron" name. Slowly the Telechron name was allowed to disappear entirely. By the mid-1960s sales of General Electric clocks had started a steady decline and, one-by-one, plants were closed. In 1979, General Electric sold its only remaining clock manufacturing plant—the Homer Avenue plant in Ashland—to the Timex Corporation.

Just as the introduction of Henry Warren's synchronous electric clock contributed to the decline in manufacture of traditional pendulum and spring-wound clocks, the quartz movement and longer life batteries contributed to the decline in demand for synchronous motor electric clocks.

Design Makes Clocks Collectible

Although the Warren synchronous motor and other Telechron innovations were critical to the initial success of the Warren Telechron Company, the current value of Telechron and General Electric clocks is based primarily on their case designs. After all, many models share the same "innards."

Although Henry Warren was a "Master Clock" maker, he was not a Master Clockmaker. Initially, an Ashland carpentry shop made cases and the Warren Clock Company made the works and assembled the clocks. Both Warren Telechron and General Electric increasingly turned to their in-house design staff—including such long-forgotten designers as Leo Ivan Bruce, John P. Rainbault, and Raymond E. Patten—and freelance designers—like Paul Frankl, Walter Dorwin Teague, and Amos Northup—to develop new case designs. Rather than presenting "fresh" interpretations of period styles, they created their own expressions of the evolving art deco style. New materials, such as chromium and Bakelite were incorporated into many of the designs, not because of cost, but because of their beauty.

Art deco

The meaning of the term "art deco" is much debated. Bevis Hillier published the first English language book—Art Deco—on the subject in 1968, defining art deco as the decorative art of the 1920s and 1930s. Hillier coined the term art deco as a shorthand term for the influential 1925 Paris Exposition des Arts Décoratifs et Industriels Moderne. Scarcely a year later, however, Martin Battersby introduced the more refined "art déco" in his book, The Decorative Twenties. Unlike Hillier, Battersby used the term to describe the decorative arts during the period from 1910 to 1925. To Battersby, the 1925 Paris Exhibition "at once gave the style its name, demonstrated the culmination of the style and...saw its passing." According to Battersby, the term "art déco" was used as early as 1935 to describe the predominant style of the period leading up to the Paris Exhibition. That same year, authors David Gebhard and Harriette von Breton, in Kem Weber, used the term "moderne" to describe the style that predominated in America from 1920-1941. They used other terms, including "International Style," "Constructivist Machine Style," "Machine Expressionist Style," "Zig Zag Moderne," and "Streamlined Moderne" to explain different periods in the evolution.

Battersby took another shot at the definition in 1971 in The Decorative Thirties, describing the style of the 1930s as "modern-

Drawing of the Warren Telechron Company plant from the 1941 catalog.

ism." It is interesting to note, however, that plans were made in 1915 for an international exposition in Paris to promote the development of "modernism." The exposition was not held until 1925, however, because of World War I. In his own 1971 book, *The World of Art Deco*, Hillier discusses the varying definitions of "art deco." Defending his continued use of the term to refer generally to the decorative arts between the world wars, he argued that

> "Scholars may sub-divide the inter-war arts till they are blue in the face, and call the different morsels of the fricassée 'Inkpot style,' 'Dogfish manner,' 'Watermelon school' or what they please. For my part, I shall continue to emphasize the unifying, rather than the divisive aspects of—Art Deco."

Although terms such as "art moderne," "streamlined moderne," and "modernism" continue to be used to describe the style that evolved after the Paris Exhibition, art deco is commonly used today to encompass all of these movements. My only complaint is that the term "art deco" fails to capture the glamour, elegance, and excitement of the period. Maybe if we brought back the acute accent on the "é"!

Nor is the term "art deco" used exclusively to refer to buildings and items produced between the wars. Just as modern day interpretations of the "Colonial," "Louis XVI," and "Chippendale" styles are still produced, the flurry of interest in art deco during the 1970s and 1980s spawned a wide range of post-modern buildings and products in the art deco "style." Largely, however, these buildings and products are cheap imitations of the real thing. They are, however, a vast improvement over the "styles" that predominated in the 1970s—the wood-grained decade—in which every decorative item from a cardboard file folder to a blender received more than its share of woodgraining.

The Marriage of Art and Industrial Design

Somehow the real importance of the Paris Exposition is lost in the debate over the meaning of art deco. Because planning for the exposition had started 10 years earlier, most of the pavilions provided retrospectives of the style that had evolved in the ensuing years. Nice, but people do not go to expositions to celebrate the death of a style. They are attracted to an exposition, worlds fair, or auto show to catch a glimpse of the future. And that is what they got at the Pavilion de l'Esprit Nouveau. The pavilion displayed tubular chromium furniture and industrially designed objects by Le Corbusier and others, marking the evolution of a style that had previously been characterized by hand-crafted decorative items into a style characterized by mass production of machine-made items.

The Paris Exposition had little immediate impact on everyday America. Stores like Bloomingdales and Macys catering to a wealthy clientele held exhibitions of French art deco furniture and the works of emerging industrial designers like Walter Von Nessen, Paul Frankl, and Norman Bel Geddes, but their designs were intended for the upscale market. Between 1925 and the market crash in 1929, industrial designers directed their efforts toward a clientele who could afford the finest materials. For example, clock cases were generally made of solid mahogany, oak, or walnut or veneered with exotic woods.

With the onset of the Great Depression, however, cost became an overriding factor as the market for "luxury" goods dwindled. Companies scurrying to find ways to reduce costs turned to mass production. The Paris Exposition, however, demonstrated that machine-made items did not have to be devoid of style. Giftware manufacturers like Chase and Manning Bowman hired noted industrial designers to develop their product lines. Although these designers did not always have a firm understanding of the manufacturing process and what was feasible and cost-effective, what resulted was an almost perfect balance between the efficiency of machine production and the beauty of custom design.

The Warren Telechron and General Electric Companies were among the first American companies to embrace the art deco style. Just as giftware and household appliance manufacturer Manning Bowman had pioneered the use of chromium and Catalin in stunning streamlined coffee services and cocktail sets in the late 1920s, Telechron pioneered moderne clock designs with the introduction of the 1928 "Modernique" and 1929 "Electrolarm." Although the Telechron and General Electric catalogs would continue to feature predominantly traditional styles into the early 1930s, by 1933 the tide had turned and it was art moderne that predominated as new models were introduced. Perhaps more telling of the switch to art moderne styling is the number of traditional designs patented by Telechron between 1931-33 that did not enter production.

The balance between machine design and aesthetics was so perfect in the 1930s that the period became known as the "Design Decade."

Cost Shifts the Balance

Cost considerations quickly became the driving force in product design and manufacture after World War II and aesthetics became secondary. American companies faced increased pressure from foreign competitors with low labor and overhead costs. Although some companies relocated to the South in search of a non-union labor force, others, like General Electric, attempted to remain competitive by lowering the cost of raw materials. For example, newer, less expensive plastics like Plaskon™ replaced Bakelite in clock cases. Similarly, plastic often replaced glass in clock crystals and brass plating replaced solid brass. Similarly, plastic rotors often replaced metal. That is not to say that all GE and Telechron clocks of the 1950s lacked quality and style. For example, the Telechron designer line clocks introduced in 1955 were among the most distinctive—and most expensive—clocks produced during the 1950s. The public balked at the high prices, however, and the line was quickly discontinued. Today they are among the most collectible Telechron clocks.

The new, post World War II, plastics were molded into thinner, cheaper looking cases. The plastics themselves lacked the depth and richness that makes Bakelite so collectible today. By the 1950s, clocks, like so many consumer products, had largely become disposable. No longer would the owner take the clock to a clocksmith to have it repaired because repair costs would likely exceed the cost of a new clock. "Unbreakable" plastic crystals often yellowed or cracked. Unlike the glass crystals used in earlier clocks, the plastic crystals were often molded to fit a specific model. Once a model had been out of production for a few years, replacement crystals were no longer available and the clock often ended up in the trash.

Don't Blame GE

Several of the Telechron collectors and dealers I met in researching this book told me that they will not collect or sell General Electric clocks because of what General Electric did to Telechron. In my view, this is not a fair assessment of General Electric's involvement. Former Telechron engineer Dick Fannon noted that General Electric brought to its partnership with Telechron its sales and marketing expertise. Henry Warren was primarily an inventor and relied heavily on GE for management

A sample of the Telechron clocks available in the early 1950s.

support. For example, General Electric's corporate attorneys filed patent applications for Warren and the Telechron designers. Similarly, General Electric's corporate coffers made possible the construction of Telechron's Homer Avenue plant. The ultra modern Homer Avenue plant enabled the Warren Telechron Company to significantly lower production costs during the crucial depression years.

Some blame General Electric for the company's decline after Henry Warren retired in 1943. This, too, seems unfair because the years immediately following the end of World War II were among the most profitable in the company's history. General Electric seems to have correctly gauged the public's apparent loss of interest in style and insatiable demand for low cost consumer goods. While some companies entered or reentered the market after the war with stylish, high quality clocks, General Electric was quick to add new low cost models using cheaper plastics and plastic crystals. Therefore, sales soared to record levels.

Electrifying Time/Electrifying Times

Despite the Great Depression, American culture reached its pinnacle in the 1930s. With songwriters like Irving Berlin, the Gershwins, and Cole Porter, bandleaders like Gus Arnheim, Freddy Martin, and Vincent Lopez, and crooners like Crosby, Columbo, and Vallee, America danced and sang its way through the 1930s.

From the giftware designs of Kurt Rettich, Belle Kogan, and Russel Wright to the automotive designs of Walter Dorwin Teague, Amos Northup, and George Graff, art was applied to all aspects of industrial design. The 1930s were also the Golden Age of motion pictures. Stars like Alice Faye, Clark Gable, Myrna Loy, and Fred Astaire personified glamour and refinement. Comedians like Laurel and Hardy and Wheeler and Woolsey helped Americans forget their troubles and be happy. The Warren Telechron Company was an important part of these electrifying times. It both electrified timekeeping and produced some of the most electrifying designs of the art deco era.

The decline of the Warren Telechron Company in the ensuing decades is also consistent with the overall decline in American culture. Compare the awe-inspiring architecture of the Empire State and Chrysler buildings to the more recently designed World Trade and Sears Towers. Compare Radio City Music Hall to the Kennedy Center. Compare Michael Jackson's dancing to that of the Nicholas Brothers. Compare the design of the 1961 Dodge to that of the 1931 Dodge. Compare the cheap plastic cases and uninspired designs of most Telechron and General Electric clocks of the 1950s to the stunning 1930s designs of John Rainbault, Ivan Bruce, and Raymond Patten. Alas, General Electric gave the American public what it wanted.

Chapter 1
Electric Clocks:
On the Origin of the Species

Although electrical horology is generally considered to have begun around 1834 when Alexander Bain applied for a patent on the first electric clock system, its origins can actually be traced back thousands of years. It was, however, Henry Warren's development of the synchronous clock motor and Warren Master Clock that made electric clocks commercially viable.

Early Knowledge of Magnetism and Electricity

The Chinese are believed to have used the magnetic properties of lodestone, a naturally occurring magnetic oxide of iron, to locate the North Pole and guide journeys across China as early as 2600 BC. The first recorded knowledge of the magnetic properties of lodestone in the Western world was recorded by Thales of Miletus around 600 BC. Thales noticed that lodestone would attract small pieces of iron. Also credited with the first man-made electricity, Thales noticed that when a piece of amber (the fossil resin from ancient pine trees) is rubbed, it attracts light objects. Both the magnetic forces of lodestone and the static electricity produced by rubbing amber were, however, attributed to the presence of a soul.

Although the ancient Greeks and Romans observed the magnetic effects of lodestone, it was not until the 13th century AD that the direction indicating properties of lodestone were recorded by Peter Peregrinus. And it would be another 200-300 years before an attempt would be made to explain the nature of magnetism.

In 1600, Dr. William Gilbert, physician to Queen Elizabeth I, published his treatise "De Magnete." Among other things, Gilbert reported that the earth acts like a huge magnet, that magnets have two poles, that like poles reject while opposite poles attract, and that there are two distinct groups of substances—those that can be electrified and those that cannot. He called the magnetic effects caused by rubbing amber "electrics" from the Greek word signifying amber. Gilbert is considered the founder of the science of electricity and magnetism.

The first functional machine for producing electricity was invented in the 17th century by Baron Otto Von Guericke. Although he was able to produce electricity in greater quantity than heretofore possible, his machine produced static electricity. It was not until 1745 that Musschenbröek and Cuneus discovered the Leyden jar that allowed electrical energy to be stored. Their discovery, however, had no immediate practical application and was used primarily as a parlor trick. Electrical energy would be stored in a Leyden jar and up to 1,000 people would receive an electric shock when the energy was discharged through their bodies.

Around the same time, Stephen Gray became the first person to transmit electricity over a "long" distance. Under his experiments, electricity was conveyed several hundred yards along packthread. Gray also expanded on the work of Gilbert, finding that even substances that cannot be electrified can nevertheless conduct electric charges.

Understanding the Conventional Clock

In order to understand efforts to link increasing knowledge of electrical energy to timekeeping, it is important that the reader have a basic knowledge of how a conventional mechanical clock works. Mechanical clocks are composed of:

--the dial and hands which indicate time,
--a mechanism for driving the hands, and
--a means for regulating the speed of that mechanism.

In a conventional clock, either the falling of a weight or the uncoiling of a spring typically drives the hands. All early mechanical clocks were weight driven. An iron or lead weight would typically be suspended on a rope or chain with the other end wrapped around a barrel. A ratchet would be used to raise the weight as the rope was wrapped around the barrel. An escapement (a contrivance through which the energy of the weight is delivered to the pendulum or balance) would determine the rate at which the weight would fall.

A long strip of steel wound on an arbor drives spring clocks. The spring is wound by rotating the arbor. A ratchet and pawl prevent back motion during the winding process. After winding, the arbor remains stationary and the barrel rotates as the coil unwinds. Teeth cut into the periphery of the barrel allows its motion to drive the clock.

While weights and springs provide the power needed to drive mechanical clocks, without intervention, the weight would fall and the spring would unwind at increasing speeds, making time fly so to speak. The primary methods used to control the speed of the mechanical clock are the pendulum for weight driven clocks and the balance wheel for spring wound clocks.

A pendulum is merely a small heavy object (a "bob") suspended at the end of a thin wire, chain, or rod and attached at the other end to a pivot. When the pendulum is set in motion, it will swing to and fro at a rate determined entirely by the length of the wire. In other words, the time it takes the pendulum to complete its swing is not directly affected by the weight of the bob. In reality, however, several external factors, including air resistance, humidity, and temperature, affect the rate of swing.

An escapement links the pendulum to the hands, controlling the amount of power driving the clock hands. In the simplest terms, with each swing of the pendulum, the 'scape wheel moves forward one tooth and the pendulum receives an impulse to keep it in motion.

As the size of the timepiece decreases, it becomes impractical to use a pendulum to control speed. Small clocks, watches, and ship's clocks typically use a balance wheel instead of a pendulum. The to-and-fro motion of the balance wheel replaces the vibration of the pendulum. As in the pendulum clock, an escapement links the balance wheel to the hands and is kept in motion by an impulse from the spring.

Early Electrostatic Clocks

Around 1770, scientists began searching for ways to apply the increasing knowledge of magnetism and electricity to timekeeping. James Ferguson, in his 1770 treatise *An Introduction to Electricity*, described a clock driven by electrostatic electricity. Although he built models of his electrostatic clock, it was used for demonstration purposes only as there was no steady source of static electricity other than that which could be generated by hand-cranked machine. Somewhat impractical!

The discovery of the electric column by J. A. De Luc around 1809 made the development of electrostatic clocks more practical. The electric column generated static electricity and De Luc devised a pendulum driven by electrostatic forces rather than falling weights. By modifying De Luc's pendulum, England's Francis Ronalds, in 1814, constructed a "Galvanic Clock" run by static electricity.

Similar clocks were independently developed on the European continent at about the same time. One such electrostatic clock was displayed in a store window in Munich during the summer of 1815.

Although experiments with static electricity continued for the next 20 years or so, none of the electrostatic clocks proved to be commercially viable. Even as attempts were being made to harness static electricity to operate clocks, advances were being made in the understanding of the relationship between electricity and magnetism that would ultimately lead to the use of electromagnetic energy to power clocks.

A Turtle That Tells Time

One of the earliest applications of the principles of electricity to timekeeping was Grollier's mid-seventeenth century "turtle" clock. Grollier concealed a spring-wound clock mechanism beneath a shallow bowl of water. Attached to the movement was a small magnet so that the magnet rotated around the perimeter of the bowl every 12 hours. A small magnetic turtle floating on the surface of the water followed the magnet around the bowl, pointing to the hours marked on the edge of the bowl. Actual operation of this "mystery" clock was, however, unrelated to the use of magnets to display time.

A Frog Takes a Licking and Keeps on Kicking

Many a frog has given its life to science over the past 400 years, including those contributing to the development of electricity. As early as 1678, experimenters were using frogs to demonstrate the production of electric current. However, it would be another 100 years—and many generations of frogs—before the source of the electric current would be understood.

An inventor referred to in the literature simply as "Swammerdam" was able to induce contractions in a frog's muscle by wrapping a nerve in silver wire and holding it over a copper support. He found that when the silver wire was allowed to touch the copper support, the frog's muscle twitched. Over 100 years later, Luigi Galvani conducted similar experiments and found that dissected frog legs twitch in the vicinity of electric machines and that when two dissimilar metals are placed in contact with the nerve and muscle of a frog's leg, the muscle twitches when the metals are touched together. Galvani, however, attributed the effect to the production of electricity in the frog's leg.

Another Italian, Allesandro Volta, however, demonstrated that the electricity was generated not in the frog's leg but in the salty fluid in which the two metals were immersed. Volta developed the first battery—Volta's Piles—in 1800.

Development of the Electromagnet

Hans Christian Oersted published the first accounts of the magnetic effects of an electric current in 1819. Oersted demonstrated that an electric current would attract or deflect a compass needle. Around the same time, Andre Ampère demonstrated further effects caused by electric currents. He is best remembered, however, as the inventor of the solenoid—a spiral coil of wire that acts as a magnet when an electric current flows through it. Another Frenchman, Dominique Arago, and Englishman Humphrey Davy discovered independently that by placing a soft iron bar inside Ampere's solenoid the magnetic field could be increased significantly. In 1825, William Sturgeon used these discoveries to create the first electromagnet.

Another important advance occurred in 1826, when Germany's Georg Ohm explained the relationship between voltage, resistance, and current in an electric circuit, commonly referred to as Ohm's Law.

Ohm's and Sturgeon's discoveries had no immediate applications, however, because electric current could be supplied to an electromagnet for only short periods. Further progress in linking electromagnetic current and timekeeping would await the development of a longer lasting power source. Just such advancement occurred in 1838 when John Daniell invented the two-fluid "Daniell" cell. His invention created a "reliable," steady source of electric current.

The following year, Germany's Carl August Steinheil would use Daniell cells to send electric impulses from a master clock in Munich to a series of simple slave clocks. Each slave clock contained a magnet passing through a solenoid. When the solenoid in the slave clock received the electric impulse, it would move an anchor escapement, which in turn moved the hands. Little is known about the measure of success achieved by Steinheil's clock.

Alexander Bain's Pioneering Experiments in Electric Timekeeping

After attending lectures at the Adelaide Gallery and Polytechnic Institution in 1837 and marveling at the electromagnetic equipment in use at the facilities, young Scotsman Alexander Bain, a journeyman clockmaker in Clerkenwell, set out to find ways to apply electromagnetic energy to timekeeping and telegraphy.

Bain had, by July 1840, produced rough working models of both an electromagnetic clock and a printing telegraph. The editor of *Mechanics Magazine* arranged for Bain to meet Professor Charles Wheatstone in hopes of gaining the financial backing Bain needed to produce his inventions. In mid-August 1840, Bain took his models to Wheatstone. Bain was given 5 pounds with the promise of more when he produced models of the printing telegraph. Wheatstone advised Bain to suspend his work on the clock and not to mention it to anyone else.

Rather than help Bain produce his clock, however, Wheatstone stole his invention, having Bain's model copied and then presented as Wheatstone's own invention. Wheatstone presented "his" model of an electric clock before the Royal Society of London on November 26, 1840.

Unbeknownst to Wheatstone, however, John Barwise, a London chronometer maker, acting on behalf of Alexander Bain, had applied for the first patent for an electric clock on October 10 of the same year. In January 1841, Barwise, again acting on behalf of Bain, obtained an injunction preventing Wheatstone from displaying his clock model as his own invention. Shortly thereafter, Bain's model went on display at the Polytechnic Institution. Thus began a long-term feud between Bain and Wheatstone.

An Eye Towards the Future

Although Alexander Bain had no formal education, his patent, granted June 11, 1841, showed that he had a firm understanding of the importance of his invention. Bain foresaw most of the advances in electric timekeeping that would occur over the next 75 years. For example, Bain's patent covered the application of a pendulum having operating contacts to provide electric current to move other clocks, the use of electromagnets to drive clocks, and the use of a central clock to impulse, wind up, or set the hands of any number of other clocks. He also noted that his invention would allow the use of a central clock to regulate the pendulums of any number of other clocks and to set the hands of other clocks to agree with those of the central clock. Other developments foreseen in Bain's patent application included the (1) development of insulated electric cords to conduct electricity, (2) use of electricity to replace springs and weights as the driving force, (3) use of an electric current to strike a bell by means of an electromagnet, and (4) transmission of impulses from one clock to another in a series of clocks. As if that were not enough, Bain predicted that his system would enable uniform time distribution throughout the country.

Different Approaches to Electric Timekeeping

In the years following Alexander Bain's pioneering application of electromagnetic forces to timekeeping, hundreds of applications of this technology were developed. These applications fall into three basic approaches:

Tangential use of electricity in a conventional clock. Under this approach, electric impulses merely provide the power needed to operate the pendulum, springs, or weights. For example, a pendulum might be kept swinging by means of periodic electric impulses rather than a spring. Ordinary clock gearing continues to move the hands in response to the swinging pendulum.

Another example of the tangential use of electricity to operate an otherwise conventional clock is the use of an electric motor to periodically rewind the mainspring or weights. This approach was particularly useful in tower clocks, eliminating the need for a caretaker to climb the stairs to the tower and manually rewind the mechanism. Similarly, a magnet is used in automobile clocks to periodically rewind the mainspring.

A third example is the use of electricity to periodically lift a weighted lever. It is the falling of the weighted lever, however, that drives the clock.

Finally, the accuracy of a conventional spring-driven clock can be automatically regulated electrically. For example, an electromagnet placed at the 12 o'clock position might be energized once an hour, correcting any error by pulling the minute hand back to the 12. For such an approach to work, however, there must be some form of conventional master clock used to determine the frequency of the electric impulses.

Electrically-driven slave clocks. Under this approach, a conventional spring, weight, or pendulum-driven "master" clock is wired to a series of "slave" clocks whose gear trains are driven electrically by an impulse received from the master clock. Typically, the hands of the slave clock would move forward every minute.

Synchronous clocks. The synchronous clock motor is actually driven by alternating current, replacing conventional weights, springs, and pendulums. The synchronous motors' two magnetic poles are alternately activated as the current flows back and forth, causing the rotor (the first moving element of the motor) to re-volve at the same speed as the alternations in the current coming from the power station. In fact, all synchronous motor clocks deriving power from the same source maintain the same speed. A series of reduction gears allows the clock to display seconds, minutes, and hours.

Development of the Hipp Toggle

Working on the European continent at roughly the same time as Alexander Bain, Mattheus Hipp developed what has become known as the Hipp toggle. Basically, his invention consists of a toggle attached to a pendulum. The toggle passes freely over a notched block of steel until the swing of the pendulum falls below a certain arc at which time the toggle is caught in the notch. As the toggle depresses the steel block, the circuit is closed and the pendulum receives an impulse from the electromagnet. The first clocks using the Hipp toggle appeared in 1842. The Hipp toggle, and the multitude of imitators that followed, greatly improved the reliability of electrically impulsed pendulum clocks by depressing the contacts with greater force than had previously been achieved.

Electric Clocks Fall into Disrepute

As England developed plans for London's Great Exposition of 1851, planners decided that the most modern method of timekeeping should be employed. Two years earlier, Charles Shepherd had developed a clock in which an electromagnet raised a weighted arm that was released by the pendulum to give a constant impulse. Shepherd was chosen to install his clock system at the Exposition. Dials installed at the south, east, and west ends of the Exhibition Hall were to be controlled by an electric Master Clock placed among the other exhibits in the horology section of the Exposition. Unfortunately, Shepherd's clock did not function properly because of problems with the contacts and had to be replaced by a conventional clock.

With the dismal failure of Shepherd's clock, electric timekeeping fell into disrepute and little progress was made during the next 35 years. Referring to Shepherd's failure, Sir Edmund Beckett noted that

"...anyone who sets to work to invent an electric clock must start with the axiom that every now and then the electricity will fail to lift anything, however small, and if his clock does not provide for that it will fail too."

Efforts were largely redirected from developing electric clocks to developing electrical synchronizing systems that would correct mechanical clocks at periodic intervals.

The "Grim" Reaper

Following the failure of the electric clock at the Great Exposition of 1851, Lord Grimthorpe in his book *Clocks, Watches, and Bells,* commented that

"...these clocks never answered in any practical sense; nor would anything but the strongest evidence, independent of the inventor, convince me that any independent pendulum directly maintained by electricity can succeed in keeping good time for any considerable period."

Chester Pond Develops First Commercially-viable Electric Clock

In 1888, Chester Pond developed the first commercially viable clock rewound with an electric motor. His Self-Winding Clock

Company also developed an effective time correction system under which an hourly signal was sent over telegraph wires to every subscriber's clock. The signal impulsed a set of coils, setting in motion a mechanical correction. Pond's system was widely used by railroads and Western Union offices.

Invention of the Alternating Current Motor

In 1886, Nicola Tesla and Elihu Thompson discovered the "induction" motor that operated on alternating current. Previously, the motors ran only on direct current. Tesla and Thompson found that they could produce a rotating magnetic field in a stationary iron stator using poly phase alternating current. The motor was almost synchronous when operating freely, but when tasked with operating machinery, the speed dropped, the difference between the load and no-load speed being called the "slip." As improvements were made to the motors, they soon surpassed direct current motors in efficiency.

The induction motor was not suitable for clocks, however, for two reasons. First, they did not operate at a synchronous speed. Although there were induction motors capable of running at synchronous speed, they were much too cumbersome to be used in clocks and required both alternating and direct current to maintain synchronous speed. Second, the induction motor relied on poly phase alternating current whereas household clocks would have to run from a single phase electric supply.

Henry Warren as he appeared on the cover of the March 1930 *Telechronicle*.

Synchronome Clock System

The first high-precision electric clock system was developed by England's Frank Hope-Jones in 1895. Hope-Jones, in collaboration with G. B. Bowell, invented the Synchronome switch—an electrically reset gravity arm that drives a pendulum through an anchor escapement. This switch, which revolutionized electric timekeeping, allowed the pendulum to determine the time when the electrical contacts would operate without having to operate the contacts directly. While earlier clocks had proved unreliable because of problems with the opening and closing of the contacts, the Synchronome switch solved this problem by having the force provided by the falling of a massive gravity arm open the contacts while an electric impulse provided the force to raise the gravity arm. Hope-Jones' Master Clock was able to give a completely reliable electric time signal to secondary clocks on the system, advancing the clocks every half minute.

In the same year he introduced his Synchronome switch, Hope-Jones looked ahead and predicted a far different future for electric timekeeping. In the November 15, 1895 issue of *Lightning* (now the *Electrical Times*), Hope-Jones wrote, in reference to the opening of England's first power plant producing alternating rather than direct current, that

> "A standard clock may be placed in the engine-room at the central station of an alternating system, and with it a dial, the hands of which are rotated by a tiny synchronous alternating-current motor connected to the mains; the gearing between this dial and its motor being such that when the alternators are run at their normal frequency the hands progress at the proper rate, and thus any consumer who joins a similar dial across the mains will obtain the same result."

Development of the Synchronous Motor Clock

It would be another 20 years, however, before Hope-Jones' vision would become a reality. In 1915, Henry Warren invented the small, self-starting synchronous motor that would revolutionize timekeeping. After more than 10 years of experimentation, Warren obtained a patent for his synchronous motor in 1918. The motor, which ran on alternating current, could easily operate a gear train and clock hands. In fact, Warren's first synchronous motors had enough power to drive about 140 mechanical clock trains.

Alternating Current Prevails

Although Thomas Edison had warned against the dangers of alternating current, citing the electric chair as an example of the risks entailed in high voltage transmission, it is estimated that by 1916, 9 out of 10 homes and businesses in the United States were powered by alternating current. Direct current was found unsuitable for transmission over long distances because of energy losses. By contrast, high voltage transmission of alternating current minimized energy loss over transmission lines. Transformers at the receiving end lowered the voltage to safe levels for home use.

Although Warren's clocks ran accurately most of the time, at times the motor would run either fast or slow. In a 1936 interview with the *Boston Herald*, Warren recalled that

> "This first crude motor was connected by tiny gears to the hands of a clock which had a small dial. Then followed weeks of observation to determine the behavior of this clock, which was connected continuously to the Boston Edison system. It was off as much as ten to fifteen minutes per day."

Further experiments convinced Warren that the irregularity was not due to any problem with his motor but rather by variations in the current supplied by the Boston Edison Company. Although Boston Edison promised to provide 60-cycle alternating

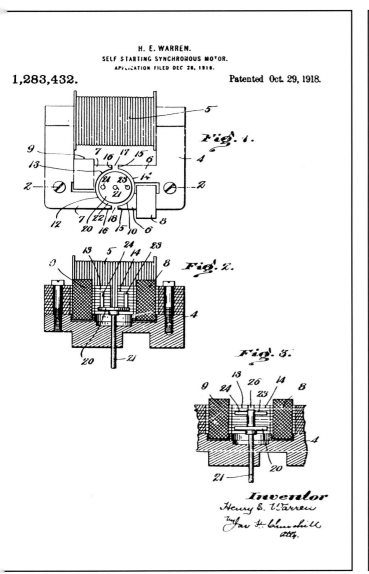

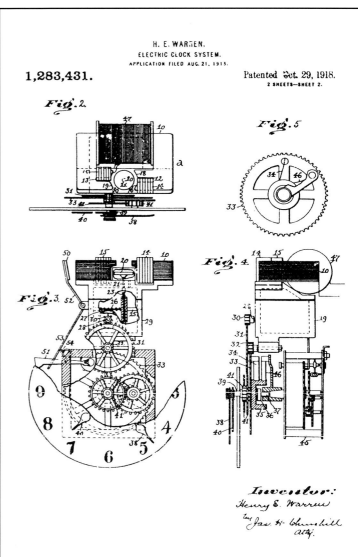

Henry's Warren's patent (No. 1,283,432) for a self-starting synchronous motor, awarded October 29, 1918. Warren filed the patent application in December 1916. This is one of three patents for synchronous motors awarded to Warren on the same day.

Henry Warren's patent (No. 1,283,431) for an electric clock system, awarded October 29, 1918. Warren applied for the patent August 21, 1916. Other Warren patents relating to the master clock include Nos. 1,409,502 and 1,502,493.

current, Warren found that the actual current was often above or below 60 cycles, causing his clocks to run either fast or slow.

Behind the Times

When Henry Warren demonstrated his synchronous clock motor in a speech before the Boston Clock Club on February 6, 1937, he had to bring his own power source. Unlike 90 percent of the country, central Boston still operated on direct current in the late 1930s. Warren had to use a portable alternating current generator to demonstrate the operation of his clock.

Development of the Master Clock

To make his new synchronous electric clocks commercially viable, Henry Warren needed to (1) develop a method to make electric current consistent and (2) convince power companies that they were not providing consistent current. Warren had little trouble addressing the first problem, developing a governor, known as a "Warren Master Clock," that could be used to regulate the current delivered by a power company.

The dial of the Warren Master Clock had two hands, one connected to an accurately adjusted pendulum clock and the other to one of his electrically driven synchronous clocks. As long as the

two hands revolved together, the power station was operating at exactly 60 cycles per second. If the hand attached to the synchronous clock fell behind, however, then the speed of the generators was increased to bring the frequency back to 60 cycles per second. Similarly, if the hand attached to the synchronous clock moved ahead of the hand attached to the conventional clock, then the generators were slowed. All synchronous clocks receiving power from the power station would thus run at the same speed.

The second problem—convincing Boston Edison that it needed his Master Clock--proved more formidable. Boston Edison had just installed a new, state-of-the-art generator and was convinced that it was providing uniform 60-cycle current.

After months of meetings with Boston Edison engineers and officials, Warren was finally given permission to install the Warren Master Clock at Boston Edison on an experimental basis. Warren agreed to promptly remove the clock if it did not perform exactly as he predicted. The Master Clock was installed on October 16, 1916, and activated on the 23rd. Later that day, Warren sent the following telegram to his partner Homer Loring:

"Frequency control apparatus started in Edison station three hours ago. Results fully equal expectations. Local officials pleased. Think that a hard fight has been won."

In a February 22, 1932, radio broadcast with Lowell Thomas, Henry Warren explained his invention of synchronous timekeeping:

"Perhaps the easiest way to tell you the principle of operation of the new electric clocks would be to draw on your imagination…Now the electric current which supplies the light, heat and power in your home is made up of waves in miniature like the ocean waves; but there is this difference, we can control the regularity of the electric waves. What I did was to build a clock with a substitute for a pendulum that would respond to these electric waves and then provide another instrument which could be used by the power companies to make the waves perfectly regular in their rate."

With his Master Clock in place, Warren's synchronous clocks achieved astonishing accuracy. The master clock at the power station was corrected twice a day by comparison with time signals received from the Naval Observatory near Washington, DC. Just as the Naval Observatory time signals ensured that the accuracy of the master clock was within one second per day, so too were all of the synchronous clocks linked to the power station.

By 1925, about 400 of Warren's original floor model Master Clocks (Type A) had been installed in power stations. In addition, many other power stations had installed the slightly less accurate wall model Master Clock (Type B).

With the frequency of much of the nation's power supply regulated by Warren Master Clocks, the stage was set for the explosive growth of electric timekeeping in the late 1920s and 1930s. Sales of electric clocks increased from about 87,000 in 1927 to almost 4.3 million in 1937. There was a corresponding decrease in sales of spring-wound clocks from 2.4 million to about 1.5 million over the same time frame. The only area in which spring wound clocks held their own was alarm clocks. Sales of spring-wound alarm clocks increased slightly, from 10.5 to 10.6 million during the 10 year period.

Benefits of the Warren Master Clock Extend Beyond Timekeeping

The Warren Master Clock had far reaching benefits outside the realm of timekeeping, essentially transforming the entire electrical supply system in the United States. Before the development of the Warren Master Clock, the transfer of energy between power stations was cumbersome and expensive. Transfer could be accomplished in two ways. First, alternating current from the supplying power station could be converted to direct current and then converted back to alternating current at the receiving station. Second, a frequency-converting machine could be purchased to facilitate the transfer. Such machines, however, were expensive.

Two power stations regulated with Warren Master Clocks, however, could easily exchange electrical energy because they could be adjusted to operate at the same constant frequency.

The standardization of average frequency brought about by installation of Warren Master Clocks also:

 --provided more uniform speed to motor-driven machinery, improving efficiency,
 --lowered power companies maintenance costs by enabling them to use synchronous motors in their maximum demand meters and graphic recorders, and
 --facilitated the development of consumer electric appliances by making it possible to standardize the frequency of electric current throughout the country.

This last benefit cannot be overstated. Without standardization, the efficiency of household electric appliances varied depending on the power source. More important, there was no guarantee that the appliance would work if the consumer moved and plugged it into a new power supply. A group of manufacturers, led by Manning-Bowman's Reginald P. Tracy, sought legislation to establish a uniform 60-cycle electric service in the United States. Implementation of the legislation was made possible by the installation of Warren Master Clocks in most power stations. It was estimated that in 1947, Warren Master Clocks regulated over 95 percent of the electric lines in the United States.

Presentation of a Warren Master Clock to the Smithsonian Institution. *Courtesy of Ashland Historical Society.*

"Next to Edison's electric light, Mr. Warren's clock will be most universally remembered."
-Attributed to "an important national authority."

Chapter 2

Henry Warren —
"The Father of Electric Time"

Born May 21, 1872, in the Roxbury section of Boston, Henry E. Warren would live almost his entire life within 50 miles of his birthplace. His parents, Henry and Adelaide Louisa (Ellis) Warren, remained in Roxbury for several years following the birth of Henry and his sister Louise (1874). In 1880, as Roxbury's population soared, his parents decided to move to the suburbs—Newton Centre. Newton Centre is about 8 miles southwest of Boston. Henry's maternal grandfather, Rowland Ellis, lived with the family and is credited with developing young Henry's mechanical abilities. Rowland Ellis was a leader in Boston community affairs, including service as a member of the legislature. Henry Warren, like his grandfather, would play an active role in community service for over 60 years.

Early Signs of Inventiveness

Even as a young child, Warren showed signs of future genius. For example, he devised a way to feed his chickens without hav-

ing to get out of bed on cold mornings. He rigged up a mechanism that allowed him to push a button by his bed and tip over a bucket of feed in the chicken coop. Similarly, he refitted his mother's old foot-powered sewing machine to run on electricity.

Concerned that their son was sickly and not strong enough to attend public school, his parents enrolled him at the Allen School in West Newton. For six years, young Henry rode the three miles to and from school on his bicycle. After graduating from the Newton School in 1889 at age 18, Henry and a friend embarked, in July 1890, on a walking tour of rural Vermont and New Hampshire. Using skills developed during his early teens, Henry and his companion paid their way by taking photographs of the homes they passed on their journey and selling copies to the owners. They developed their negatives in streams along the way.

As a child, Warren made frequent journeys to northern New England on his bicycle. Although he later substituted a saddle horse for the bicycle, Warren continued to vacation in New England, particularly Mt. Monadnock in southwestern New Hampshire, for the rest of his life.

Henry Warren chose to pursue his education at the Massachusetts Institute of Technology (MIT), studying electrical engineering. Warren continued to live with his parents in Newton Centre, commuting to classes in Cambridge. He graduated with a Bachelor of Science degree in 1894.

At the urging of their pastor, Henry and his second cousin, Homer Loring, founded a Young People's Society at the Unitarian

Left: Henry Warren in front of his house on Chestnut Street in Ashland, Massachusetts. *Courtesy of Ashland Historical Society.*

Above: Henry Warren's home on Chestnut Street, Ashland, Massachusetts. The home now belongs to Northeastern University. *Courtesy of Ashland Historical Society.*

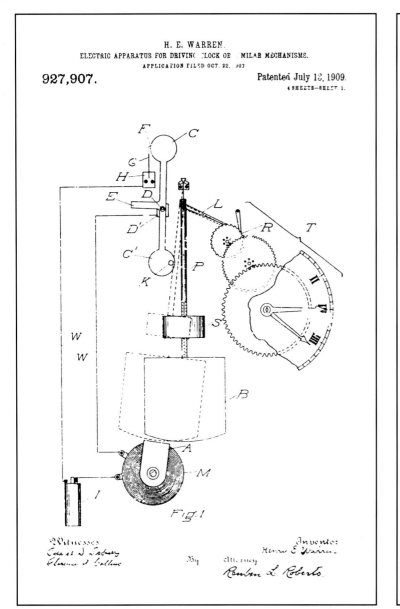

H. E. WARREN.
ELECTRIC APPARATUS FOR DRIVING CLOCK OR SIMILAR MECHANISMS.
APPLICATION FILED OCT. 22, 1908.

927,907.

Patented July 13, 1909.
4 SHEETS—SHEET 1.

Fig.1

WITNESSES
Inventor:
Henry E. Warren.
By
Attorney
Reuben L. Roberts.

H. E. WARREN.
ELECTRIC APPARATUS FOR DRIVING CLOCKS OR SIMILAR MECHANISM
APPLICATION FILED DEC. 23 1909.

1,089,886.

Patented Mar. 10, 1914.
6 SHEETS—SHEET 1.

Fig. 1.

WITNESSES:
Charles J. Woodbury
Florence A. Collins

INVENTOR.
Henry E. Warren.
BY
Reuben L. Roberts.
ATTORNEY.

Henry Warren received his first patent for an electric clock on July 12, 1909. The application for the battery driven clock was filed in October 1908.

Henry Warren received a second patent for a battery-operated clock on May 10, 1914. Application for the patent had been filed 5 years earlier, in December 1909.

church. It was through the society, named the Hale Union after Unitarian clergyman and writer Edward Everett Hale, that Henry met his future wife, Edith Smith, secretary of the society. It was, however, to be a long courtship. Henry and Edith did not marry until 1907.

While still a student at MIT, Warren applied for his first U.S. patent. A friend, George Whipple, who was an expert in water purification, sought Warren's help in developing an instrument that could take temperatures in inaccessible locations. In May 1895, Warren and Whipple were granted a patent for an electrical instrument they named a "Thermophone" that could measure temperatures from a distance. The "Thermophone" was a commercial success; installations included the US Capitol and the Derwentwater Reservoir in England.

After graduating from MIT, Warren, in 1897, accepted a position as an electrical engineer in Saginaw, Michigan, helping rehabilitate the Saginaw Valley Traction Company. A Boston syndicate, which included among its members Homer Loring's father, had acquired the streetcar company following its bankruptcy. The syndicate hired Homer Loring and his long-time friend Henry Warren to breathe new life into the failing business. Loring was able to greatly expand ridership by building an amusement park at one

end of the streetcar line. Warren, for his part, developed a method for using the excess steam generated by the plant to efficiently extract underground salt deposits. Steam from the streetcar plant was conducted underground to the salt deposits, liquefying the deposits and forcing them to the surface.

Having restored the Saginaw Valley Traction Company to profitability, Loring and Warren returned to Newton Centre in 1902. Initially, Warren became involved in land development, buying 11 acres of land near his parents' home. After building five houses along an existing road running along one edge of the property, Warren built additional roads through the property, including Westminster Road, named after his father's birthplace—Westminster, Massachusetts. Rather than developing the lots along the new roads, Warren sold the remaining land to other developers.

That same year, Warren would again join forces with his long-time friend Homer Loring. The same syndicate that had hired Loring and Warren to turn around the Saginaw Valley Traction Company, bought the Lombard Governor Company of Boston and installed Homer Loring as president. Warren assumed the position of superintendent and engineer, quickly inventing an electric generator for waterwheels. The company's plant in Boston's Roxbury Crossing area lacked a good water supply for testing new

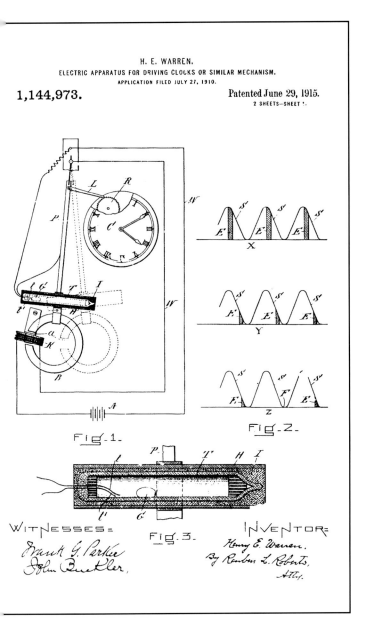

H. E. WARREN.
ELECTRIC APPARATUS FOR DRIVING CLOCKS OR SIMILAR MECHANISM.
APPLICATION FILED JULY 27, 1910.

1,144,973.

Patented June 29, 1915.
2 SHEETS—SHEET 1.

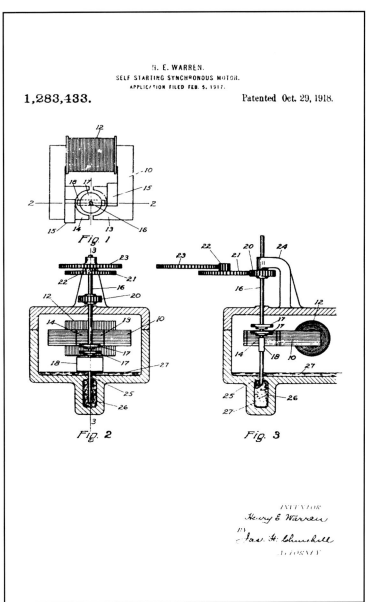

H. E. WARREN.
SELF STARTING SYNCHRONOUS MOTOR.
APPLICATION FILED FEB. 5, 1917.

1,283,433.

Patented Oct. 29, 1918.

A third Warren patent for a battery-operated clock was awarded on July 29, 1915, almost 5 years to the day from when the application was filed.

Henry Warren received three patents for self-starting synchronous motors on October 29, 1918. Application for this patent was made in February 1917.

waterwheel generators and, at Warren's urging, a suitable location was sought for a new plant. Warren conducted a search for a site within 25 miles of Boston, finally settling on Ashland.

At the time, Ashland was in a state of economic decline. Once a thriving mill town, the city had a number of available industrial buildings along the headwaters of the Sudbury River and over 100 empty houses. The Lombard Governor Company's 1904 move to Ashland breathed new life into the community. Within 10 years, the company had built and installed more than 3,000 of Warren's electric waterwheel generators at water power plants throughout the United States and in many other countries.

After the Lombard Governor Company moved to Ashland, Warren initially commuted on horseback from Newton Centre, a round-trip distance of 36 miles. Eventually, however, he apparently grew tired of the commute and began boarding in Ashland during the week and returning to Newton Centre on the weekends. It was not until 1907, when he married Edith Smith, that Warren moved to Ashland.

Warren and his new bride rented half of a double house on a 30 acre farm on Chestnut Street, high on a hill overlooking a lake and the town. He later bought the house and an additional 45 acres of land. He quickly converted a barn on the property into a machine shop.

Finding it hard to find reliable gears, Warren invented new production techniques that yielded a higher quality gear. As commercial demand increased, Warren established the Warren Gear Works. By 1917, the company employed eight people. The company, however, continued to be primarily a diversion as Warren continued to work full time at the Lombard Governor Company.

Early Attempts at Developing Reliable Electric Clocks

At the same time, Warren turned his attention to his lifetime fascination with timekeeping. After completing a days work as Superintendent of the Lombard Governor Company, Warren would return to his Chestnut Street farm and the small shop he had established to conduct experiments with electric motors. His initial attempt at developing a reliable electric clock centered on the use of battery power. Around 1908, Warren converted an old banjo clock to run on a 1.5 volt battery. Warren kept records showing the fall of battery power over time. He applied for his first patent for a battery operated clock in 1908 and the patent (No. 927,907) was granted in 1909. Three years later he organized the Warren Clock Company to produce battery operated clocks. When the company was incorporated in 1914, Warren was again teamed with Homer Loring, a stockholder and director of the new company.

These clocks were not successful, however, because they would run slower as the battery weakened. In the days before the development of mercury and then alkaline batteries, battery life was measured in hours or days rather than months. Just as the development of commercially viable electric cars has been limited by battery technology, so too was the commercial potential of battery driven clocks limited. It was not until the development of the mercury battery in the mid-1960s that battery operated clocks became commercially viable.

Development of Synchronous Electric Clock and Warren Master Clock

With battery power proving unreliable, Warren turned his sights toward harnessing alternating current. By 1916, he had developed and applied for a patent on a small, self-starting, synchronous motor to run on alternating current.

Warren found, however, that variations in the current supplied by the Boston Edison Company caused his clocks to be unreliable. He quickly developed a governor, known as a "Master Clock," capable of controlling the current delivered by a power company. Despite original reluctance, Boston Edison agreed to test the Master Clock. The test was successful and the Master Clock was per-

manently installed. Henry Warren received payment for the clock, however, only when he threatened to have it removed.

The General Electric Company, which had been struggling to gain widespread acceptance of alternating current as an alternative to Thomas Edison's advocacy of direct current, quickly recognized the importance of Warren's invention and, with Warren's blessing, purchased a 49 percent interest in the Warren Clock Company in 1919. Henry Warren continued as president.

During World War I, Warren designed hydraulically operated machines used in the production of heavy shells and also developed a new form of fire control mechanism.

With the final obstacle to development of commercially viable electric clocks overcome, Warren resigned his position at the Lombard Governor Company in 1920 in order to devote his full attention to his clocks. He sold his interest in the Warren Telechron Company to General Electric in 1943.

Other Business Interests

Around 1932, Warren again dabbled in real estate development, purchasing a 17 acre tract now known as "Ashland Heights." Warren built three streets through the property, including Warren Road, and sold lots to people seeking to build substantial homes.

Henry Warren with one of his inventions.
Courtesy of Ashland Historical Society.

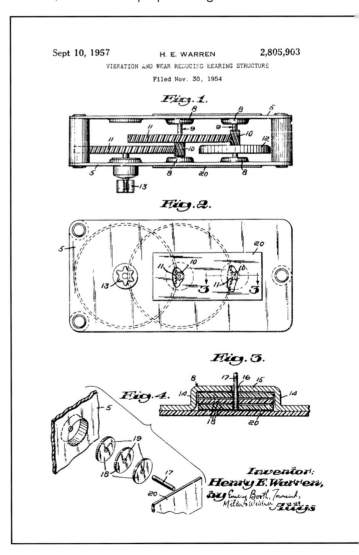

Henry Warren's final patent was awarded September 10, 1957, 11 days before his death. Application for the patent had been filed November 30, 1954, when Warren was only 82.

Warren again became associated with the Lombard Governor Company in 1937, purchasing the company following the death of the owner. For the next 20 years—until his own death in 1957—Henry Warren managed the renamed Lombard Governor Corporation and served as its President. After his departure in 1920, the company had diversified into other fields. Warren refocused the company on the production of governors and directed efforts to expand and retool to support the war effort during World War II. As part of this effort, the Navy was allowed to construct and equip a new state-of-the-art manufacturing facility adjacent to the Lombard factory. In 1943, the Lombard Governor Company was the first Ashland plant to receive the Army-Navy "E" for outstanding performance in support of the war effort. Following the war, Lombard purchased the plant from the Navy.

During Henry Warren's leadership, the Lombard Governor Corporation produced the first efficient hydraulic speed governor and the first hydraulically operated relief valve. The company also produced chain saws and large plastic molding machines.

Among Warren's 135 plus inventions was a time standard used to operate the motors rotating giant telescopes tracking a certain star. Among the telescopes using Warren's time standard is the 200 inch telescope at Mt. Palomar. In addition, the control consoles incorporating these devices that are installed at the U.S. Naval Observatory at Flagstaff, Arizona, were designed by Henry Warren and built by Lombard.

Just one year after acquiring Lombard, Warren, in 1938, became a founder of Fenwal, Inc. He was a stockholder and director of the company, which made temperature controls, until 1946. Fenwal is currently one of the nation's largest manufacturers of fire extinguishers.

During World War II, Warren again established an experimental shop in a house on his farm. Although he employed 14 men, Warren also spent many hours conducting experiments on his own. Among his inventions during this period was a self-starting synchronous motor that would run without oil.

Warren remained vigorous and active up until the time of his death, receiving his last patent on September 10, 1957, just 11 days before his death, September 21, 1957, in his beloved home.

Henry Warren in Print and On the Air

Henry Warren wrote numerous articles for technical journals and other publications, and frequently lectured at the Massachusetts Institute of Technology, the American Institute of Electrical Engineers, and scientific societies. In addition, he was a frequent guest on radio programs, the most memorable of which was a 1932 appearance on the *Literary Digest* radio program hosted by Lowell Thomas.

Although Warren typically wrote and lectured about his inventions, he also wrote poetry, displaying his love of nature.

Warren Active in the Community

Almost from the moment he moved to Ashland in 1904, Henry Warren assumed an active role in the community. His community service took many forms. First, he was active in civic affairs. For example, Henry Warren served as

- Chairman and Member of the Ashland Board of Selectmen from 1907 to 1909.
- Member and later Chairman of the Ashland Board of Water Commissioners during the crucial period when the public water system was installed (1910-1917).
- Founder and trustee of the Algonquin Council of the Boy Scouts of America. Warren also established a scholarship fund to benefit Ashland area boy scouts.

- Trustee of the Middlesex County Extension Service from 1936 to 1953, serving as president from 1945-53. During his tenure, the 4-H camp at Ashby, Massachusetts was established.
- Trustee of the Framingham Union Hospital, the Salvation Army, and the New England Forestry Association.

Warren's love of nature led him to ensure that development would not destroy the small town character of Ashland. He was influential in establishing Stone Park on 15 acres donated to the city. Similarly, he was instrumental in establishing the 500 acre Ashland Town Forest near Winter Street.

Henry and Edith Warren had no children of their own, but were part of the "village" that raised the children of Ashland. Henry was instrumental in forming a Boy Scout troop in Ashland and was among the founders of the Algonquin Council of Boy Scouts. Similarly, as a trustee in the Middlesex County Extension Service from 1936-53, Henry Warren worked closely with the community's young 4-H members. He regularly attended sporting events at Ashland High School and later endowed a scholarship fund at the school. Scholarship funds were also endowed for the Algonquin Council and several colleges. In his will, Henry Warren provided for the establishment of a Warren Benevolent Fund to provide scholarship aid to students from the Ashland vicinity.

Edith Warren shared her husband's philanthropic interests, serving as secretary of the Ashland Chapter of the American Red Cross and the Ashland Public Health Nurse Board. She also ran the annual Christmas Seal drive and was director of the Massachusetts Tuberculosis League for 3 years. Like her husband, Mrs. Warren was fond of tennis, skiing, and other outdoor activities. She donated 40 acres of land to Northeastern University for the establishment of the Warren Center for Physical Education.

Henry Warren on the Importance of Open Space

Although Henry Warren had no children of his own, he nevertheless had strong convictions about the proper environment for raising children. In arguing for the establishment of what is now Stone Park, Warren commented that:

"Thoughtful fathers and mothers are beginning to understand the importance of natural surroundings for their children, and are learning that healthy men and women cannot be developed amidst the artificial restrictions of modern city apartment buildings."

Multiple Awards Conferred on Henry Warren

Henry Warren's inventive genius was recognized through a number of prestigious awards. These include:

- The John Price Wetherill medal awarded by Philadelphia's prestigious Franklin Institute in 1935 in recognition of Warren's development of the Telechron motor. Also receiving the Wetherill medal at the same ceremony was Albert Einstein.
- The 1935 Lammé Medal awarded by the American Institute of Electrical Engineers for "meritorious achievement in the development of electrical appliances for machines."
- Selection in 1940 as a "Modern Pioneer on the Frontier of American Industry" by the Associated Industries of Massa-

Henry Warren was instrumental in obtaining funds for construction of the Ashland Post Office. Postmaster Anna L. Cavanaugh paid tribute to Warren when the building's cornerstone was laid January 8, 1940:

"There is no question as to whom Ashland's good fortune to have this honor should be given. There is among her citizens one who, besides being the head of Ashland's largest industry with over 1,000 employees, has been instrumental in procuring this building for the town and has devoted his entire life for this town and its welfare. This man is respected with the fondest admiration by his townspeople and is famed throughout the country, yet he is never too busy to lend his energies and abilities for the good of Ashland. So with affectionate gratitude I hand the trowel to Ashland's No. I citizen, Henry E. Warren."

chusetts, in conjunction with the National Association of Manufacturers.

• A nationwide radio broadcast sponsored by the Associated Electric Companies to commemorate the 30th anniversary of Warren's invention of the synchronous electric clock.

• An honorary Doctor of Science degree conferred on Warren in 1950 by Rutgers University.

An Engineer with "Inventive Genius"

In conferring an honorary Doctor of Science degree on Henry Warren in 1950, Rutgers University noted in the citation that:

"As an engineer whose inventive genius has been documented through the granting of scores of patents by our own and by foreign governments; as the inventor of the synchronous electric clock making possible the interconnection of vast electric power systems; as an industrialist whose initiative and organizational skill have created a great and thriving industry; as a humanitarian whose influence for good has been felt in many fields; you enter today the honorary fellowship of the University with the grateful appreciation of your friends and admirers everywhere."

Perhaps none of the honors were as meaningful to Warren, however, as the tribute paid to him by the Warren Telechron employees. As part of Ashland's 1946 centennial celebration, Telechron employees planted a hemlock tree in the Murphy Square. The tree was planted as a living memorial to Henry Warren. Sadly, the tree did not survive.

Blazed Trails by Henry Warren

Where'er we go by earth or sea or air,
In forest dark, cross wildest waves, in starlit sky
In Cavern deep, on mountain slope, in thoughts profound
We find the works of those who went before.

The marks we know or quickly learn
A broken twig, a pile of stones, a notch in bark
A beam of light, a special sound, a map, a compass true
The lightning's voice, momentum's laws,
the place of stars above.

These guides are true, we shall not fail
to reach our journey's end
If we but follow them,
They serve to mark the path of all who choose to pass that way
For good or ill.

We reach their goal and pass beyond,
thanks to the strength we've saved.
A debt to them we owe, when at the end
we scan the way o'er which we passed.
Our silent prayer is uttered there
God bless the men who blazed the trail.

"Life outdoors in the beautiful country half way between Boston and Worcester in the town of Ashland is the nearest approach to heaven that I know."

-Henry Warren, circa 1952

Chapter 3

A Brief History of Warren Telechron, General Electric, Herschede Hall, and Revere

Warren Telechron

The Warren Clock Company was established in Ashland, Massachusetts in 1912 to produce a line of battery-driven clocks invented by Henry Warren. Initially, the company operated out of a barn on Warren's farm while Henry Warren continued his full-time employment as superintendent of the Lombard Governor Company. Two years later, the company was incorporated with Warren's second cousin, boss, and close friend, Homer Loring, serving as a director and stockholder.

By 1915, the business had been moved from Warren's farm to space rented from the Lombard Governor Company in the center of town. The Warren Clock Company's initial effort to sell clocks, however, proved unsuccessful. Because battery life was short and power would gradually decrease over the life of the battery, the clocks proved unreliable. Although not a commercial success, many of the features found in Warren's earliest clocks were incorporated into later models.

Continuing his experiments with electric timekeeping, Warren invented a small, self-starting synchronous motor that would revolutionize timekeeping. After more than 10 years of experimentation, Warren obtained a patent for his synchronous motor in 1918. The motor, which ran on alternating current, could easily operate a gear train and clock hands. Sadly, however, the clock did not keep accurate time.

After determining that his clocks were not accurate because of fluctuations in the frequency of current produced by Boston Edison, Warren set out to develop an instrument that could eliminate such fluctuations and thus make his clocks accurate. After the installation of his "Warren Master Clock" at Boston Edison proved successful, other power companies installed Warren Master Clocks.

Warren's synchronous motor and Master Clock quickly drew the attention of the General Electric Company, one of a number of manufacturers pushing for the adoption of alternating current as a standard throughout the United States.

Although General Electric acquired a half interest in the Warren Clock Company in 1917, Henry Warren remained as President. Under the arrangement, General Electric was able to use Telechron motors in its own clocks and appliances. Other clock and instrument manufacturers could use Telechron motors under license to the Warren Clock Co.

Perfect Timing

Cover to circa 1931 Telechron catalog.

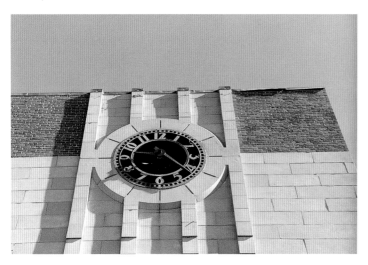

The clock tower at the Homer Ave. plant.

All that remains of one of the tower clocks at the original Homer Ave. plant.

The remains of a clock tower from the closed Homer Ave. plant.

Workers at the Telechron factory.
Courtesy of Ashland Historical Society.

With Warren Master Clocks installed in increasing numbers of power stations throughout the country, the way had been paved for the introduction of commercially-viable electric clocks. Initial production focused heavily on installations in office buildings, factories, and stores. These commercial installations allowed the Warren Clock Company to claim that an estimated 20 million people were "using" Telechron electric clocks by the mid-1920s.

In 1926, the Warren Clock Company was renamed the Warren Telechron Company. The following year, construction of a new plant on Ashland's Homer Avenue was started, funded in part by General Electric. Built in sections, construction of the plant was completed in 1937. As demand for Telechron clocks increased, a second factory building in Ashland was purchased, followed by three buildings in Worcester, 20 miles west of Ashland.

Workers at the Telechron factory. *Courtesy of Ashland Historical Society.*

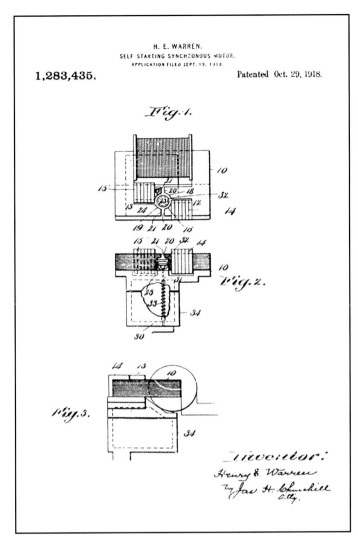

Henry Warren's third patent (1,283,435) for a self-starting synchronous motor awarded October 29, 1918. The application for this patent was filed on September 19, 1918.

Many radio stations aired Telechron time signals, one of the ways in which Telechron clocks were promoted.

The Red Dot

One "advantage" of "spin-to-start" electric clocks was that they stopped working when there was a power outage and would not begin running when the power was restored. By contrast, Telechron and General Electric clocks would re-start as soon as the power was restored. This created the risk that owners would not realize that there had been a power outage and therefore would not know to reset their clocks.

The Warren Telechron Company solved this problem by adding a power loss indicator to the dial. The indicator drops and shows a red "flag" when there is a power outage. When power is restored, the clock restarts, but the red flag continues to show on the dial to alert the owner that the clock needs to be reset. As soon as the clock is reset, the red indicator disappears.

In the 1920s and early 1930s, a large portion of the company's business centered on commercial installations. These ranged from individual clocks for indoor or outdoor installations to massive systems of clocks developed for such buildings as the Bullocks Wilshire department store in Los Angeles and the Internal Revenue Service headquarters in Washington, DC. Although this book is focused primarily on clocks developed for home use, Appendix V pictures many of the commercial styles available in 1931.

Around 1929, Telechron entered into a cooperative agreement with the Miller Company of Meriden, Connecticut to supply Telechron clocks for use in a new line of electric table lamps. The Miller Company, established in 1844, was a leading lamp manufacturer with nationwide distribution. The company's ads for the new line of lamps prominently featured the inclusion of Telechron clocks.

The Warren Telechron Company continued to introduce new developments in electric clocks throughout the 1930s, many of which were invented by Henry Warren. These innovations include the

• Current interruption indicator, that familiar red dot found on the dial of Telechron, GE, and Revere clocks.

• An auxiliary electrically wound movement that enables a synchronous movement clock to continue operating during power outages. The synchronous motor furnishes the power to operate the clock, winds up the ordinary spring driven clock movement when it is unwound, and permits the spring to unwind and drive the clock whenever the electric motor stops. Henry Warren developed the auxiliary movement in 1926, but the patent was not granted until 1931. Although Telechron marketed a few clocks with the auxiliary movements in the early 1930s, they were not popular. Clocks with auxiliary movements have an "A" between the series and model numbers.

• Illuminated clock, invented by Henry Warren in 1929. Warren developed a switch that allowed the lamp to be turned on and off without interfering with the operation of the clock.

• Cyclometer clock invented by Edgar Bourquin in 1933. Although the most famous cyclometer clocks were those introduced later in the 1930s by Lawson, with KEM Weber designs, and Pennwood Numechron, with Peter Muller Munk designs, Bourquin both developed the technology and designed the cases for the first GE and Telechron models. Walter Dorwin Teague designed some of the Telechron and GE cyclometer clocks.

• Clock radio introduced by Telechron in 1946. Although Telechron tried to interest major radio manufacturers in its invention, it decided to produce the "Musalarm" itself when the radio manufacturers showed little interest.

• Repeating alarm timer invented by Henry Warren in 1937. Rather than sounding a single alarm, the repeating alarm timer continues to sound its alarm until shut off by deenergization of the timing motor.

Henry Warren sold his interest in the Warren Telechron Company to General Electric in 1943, giving GE full ownership. With Henry Warren's retirement, long-time employee Irwin Kokins became President. In addition to serving as General Manager during the 1930s, Kokins was credited with the design of two clocks

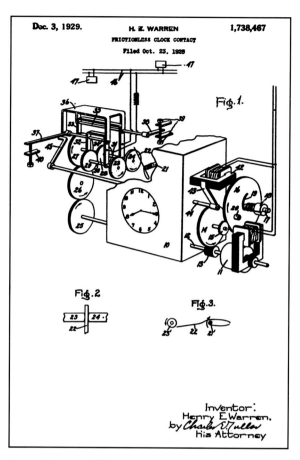

Henry Warren's 1929 patent for a frictionless clock contact.

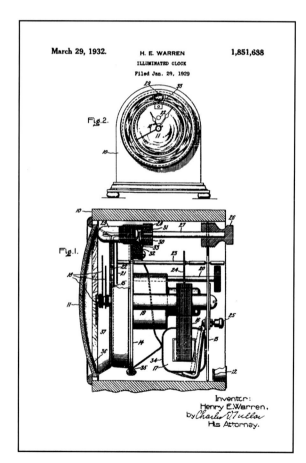

Henry Warren was awarded a patent (No. 1,851,688) for an electrically illuminated clock on March 29, 1932. The application had been filed in January 1929, and such clocks had been marketed for over two years before the patent was granted.

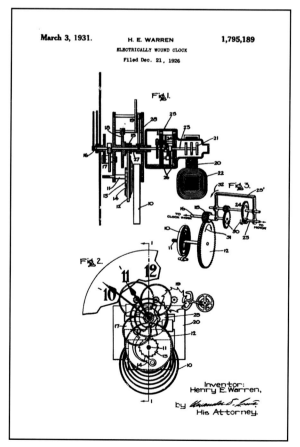

Henry Warren was awarded a patent (No. 1,795,189) for an electrically wound clock on March 3, 1931.

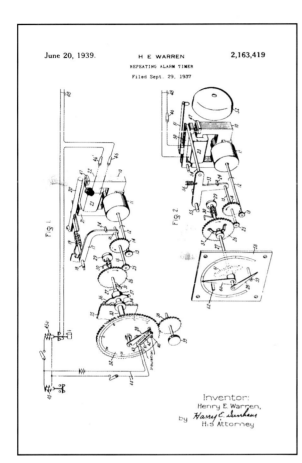

Henry Warren was awarded a patent for a repeating alarm timer on June 30, 1939. The application was filed September 29, 1937.

What's in a name?

Although I have presented dates for the progression of company names, there is some confusion as to the exact dates and there is some overlap in name usage. For example, the 1926 Telechron catalog uses "Warren Clock Company" and "Warren Telechron Company" on opposite pages of the same catalog. Similarly, "Telechron, Inc." has been found on some documents prepared years before the "official" name change.

Telechron management as portrayed in the *Telechronicle*. In addition to Henry Warren, top managers were Irwin W. Kokins, General Manager; C. E. Davis, Sales Manager; and R. M. Chase, Factory Superintendent.

Miller Lamps with Telechron clocks were offered in "700 cities coast to coast where the electric light company supplies 'regulated' current." Unlike Revere advertisements, which noted that the clocks were "Telechron motored," Miller clearly notes that its lamps contain Telechron clocks. (*House & Garden*, April 1929)

Telechron People You Ought to Know

President HENRY E. WARREN . . . . Inventor of the Telechron Master Clock and Telechron self-starting, synchronous motor. A worker first, last and always. Hobby? Hiking . . . *not* golf!

General Manager I. W. KOKINS . . . genial, enterprising, far-seeing. Hobby? Music and art.

Sales Manager C. E. DAVIS . . . always alert to build even greater markets for Authorized Dealers of Telechron Clocks. Hobby? Squash and dogs.

Factory Superintendent R. M. CHASE . . . a man of few words but much action. Hobby? Golf . . . *not* hiking!

◄ 13 ►

After obtaining controlling interest in the Warren Telechron Company in 1943, General Electric gradually absorbed the company. Initially, this was a subtle change—dropping Henry Warren's name from the company in 1946. From 1946 to 1951 the company was known as Telechron, Inc. and continued to produce separate lines of Telechron and General Electric clocks. In 1951 (some sources say 1948), however, the company lost its separate identity and became simply the "Telechron Department," the clock and timer division of the General Electric Co. Eventually, even the "Telechron Department" apparently disappeared becoming the "Clock and Timer Division" of the "Housewares Department."

In 1947, Telechron, Inc. operated five plants and employed about 3,100 people, almost half at the Homer Ave. plant in Ashland. In addition to the administrative offices, the Homer Ave. plant was used for parts and assembly. A smaller Ashland plant employing about 100 people was also used for parts and assembly. The two plants in Worcester, one responsible for producing the motor coils and a second used for assembly, had 350 and 750 employees respectively. A third Worcester plant was being brought online. Finally, commercial clocks were being produced at a plant in Lowell, Massachusetts, employing about 400 people.

During the 1950s, employment dropped to about 2,800 workers spread across 5 plants—two in Ashland, two in Worcester, and one in Lowell. The Clock and Timer Division, however, began a rapid decline in the 1960s as foreign competition and cordless clocks with quartz movements chipped away at sales. As production costs increased, due in part to higher salaries and benefits negotiated through union contracts, the Telechron Department was unable to remain competitive with Japanese and other foreign manufacturers able to lower production costs through "sweatshop" type operations and hourly wages measured in cents rather than dollars.

During the 1960s, General Electric consolidated the operations of the "Clock and Timer Division," closing all but the Homer Ave. plant.

In 1979, GE sold the "Clock and Timer Division" to Timex. Timex, in turn, sold the company to a group of local investors in 1983. The new company, once again known as Telechron, Inc. continued to operate the Homer Ave. plant until December 1992, primarily producing timers. As plans to close the Ashland factory developed, General Electric briefly reentered the picture, purchasing the watch motor assembly equipment and shipping it to a

GE plant in Carol, Iowa. At that time the plant was closed and operations transferred to Leland, North Carolina. The company remains in operation today, but no longer produces clocks.

Keepin' Time

A group of Telechron employees put together their own dance band—the Telechron Timesters—to entertain at social gatherings of the Telechron "Home Folks."

Keepin' Time

THE Telechron Home Folks maintain one whale of a good little orchestra— The "Telechron Timesters"—employees of the Warren Telechron Company.

Such an organization does wonders toward making the occasional Home Folks' social gatherings a complete and wholesome success. It is an old and well-known adage that "all work and no play makes Jack a dull boy" and all "Telechronland" fully appreciates and takes pride in this very efficient group of musicians.

A group of Warren Telechron employees put together their own orchestra, the "Telechron Timesters," to entertain at social functions.

General Electric

On October 15, 1878, a group of investors put together $50,000 and founded the Edison Electric Light Company to support Thomas Alva Edison's experiments with incandescent lighting. Scarcely a year later, on October 19, 1879, Edison tested a light bulb with a hair thin cotton thread filament. The bulb burned for 40 hours. Edison's patent application for the incandescent light bulb was approved in 1880.

Although the press was skeptical of the new invention and some even questioned whether the demonstration had been staged, gas company stocks quickly plummeted while stock in the Edison Electric Light Company soared to $3,500 a share. Not bad for an initial investment totaling only $50,000.

The first major installation of incandescent lighting would follow when Edison, in 1882, wired the area around New York City's Pearl Street Station. About 14,000 incandescent lights illuminated approximately 900 buildings.

As new uses for electricity were rapidly invented (including the electric chair in 1890 and the electric elevator in 1895), a fundamental difference of opinion surfaced as to the type of current that should be generated by power plants. Edison believed that direct current, that is, current that flows in only one direction, was safer and should be used. Others, however, believed that alternating current—an electrical current that changes direction at regular intervals—offered significant advantages over direct current. Alternating current was, in Edison's view, dangerous. The tide began to turn in favor of alternating current, however, when, in 1893, George Westinghouse was awarded a contract to develop a power plant at Niagara Falls using alternating current.

In 1899, the Edison Electric Light Company was consolidated with several of Edison's other ventures to form the Edison General Electric Company. Three years later, Edison General Electric merged with its principal rival—Thompson Houston—creating the General Electric Company. Edison's involvement in the company essentially ended at that time. Although he was on the Board of Directors for the next 10 years, he reportedly attended only one board meeting. In addition, he sold all of his stock in the new company in 1894, only two years after the merger.

Following the consolidation, Charles Coffin served as president of General Electric for 30 years, refocusing the company into a supplier and consumer products manufacturer. He sold "Edison General Electric" public utility companies in New York, Boston, Detroit, and other cities to avoid antitrust actions similar to those taken against the railroad and telegraph industries. With the sell-offs, GE became a non-regulated supplier to the utilities.

In 1900, Coffin was instrumental in establishing a formal research and development department. Initially, the R&D laboratory was set up in a barn behind the Schenectady, New York, home of Charles Proteus Steinmetz. Steinmetz, a hunchbacked German immigrant, was affectionately known as "the wizard of electricity."

As research and development efforts expanded, General Electric was able to attract some of the nation's top researchers. For example, General Electric lured William D. Coolidge away from an academic position at the Massachusetts Institute of Technology. Coolidge's experiments led to the development of the tungsten filament light bulb, still the most widely used form of incandescent lighting.

Another top researcher who joined the General Electric Research and Development Department was Irving Langmuir. Langmuir's improvements in vacuum tubes paved the way for radio, television, and other electronics. He was awarded the 1932 Nobel Prize in chemistry.

Although the research and development department experimented with electric stoves and refrigerators, General Electric was initially slow to enter the field of consumer appliances. Most of its early consumer products were developed by other firms and introduced as GE products through mergers and acquisitions. For example, the General Electric "Hot Point" electric iron was invented by Earl Richardson in response to his wife's need for an iron that would effectively iron around buttons and collars. Richardson invented an iron whose heating elements converged around the tip—the hot point—and set up the Pacific Electric Heating Company to produce the irons. The company became the leading producer of flat irons in the United States. Similarly,

George Alexander Hughes invented the electric range in 1910, establishing the Hughes Electric Company in Chicago to manufacture the ranges. The first six ranges were shipped to Billings, Montana where their arrival was greeted by a brass band. Perhaps the most shocking aspect of the Hughes stove was its color—white. Up until the introduction of the clean burning electric stove, ranges had typically been black to hide the soot.

Both the iron and stove became General Electric products when the Pacific Electric Heating Company and the Hughes Electric Company were acquired through merger. A new company, the Edison General Electric Appliance Company, was formed to produce and market a series of Hotpoint electric appliances including—in addition to irons and stoves— radiant heaters, percolators, foot warmers, and sewing machines.

During the teens and early 1920s, consumer products continued to be only a small part of General Electric's product line. Under the leadership of Edwin Rice, GE president from 1913 to 1922, the company continued to focus primarily on the production of electrical apparatus for industrial use. Although General Electric sales grew from $12 million in 1894 to $243 million in 1922, three-fourths of the sales were of capital goods equipment. Incandescent lamps, fans, and small electric appliances accounted for most of the consumer production. Sales of stoves and refrigerators were primarily limited to the wealthy.

When Gerald Swope assumed the presidency in 1922, however, he quickly set out to increase General Electric's focus on consumer products. Swope and Chairman of the Board Owen D. Young saw unlimited potential for reliable, inexpensive household electric products. The 1927 introduction of the "monitor top" refrigerator, proved Swope and Owen to be visionaries. Within a year, over one million had been sold.

In 1928, General Electric hired industrial designer Raymond E. Patten to head its in-house design operations. During the Depression, General Electric introduced a succession of new home electric appliances including food mixers, vacuum cleaners, clothes washers, dishwashers, air conditioners, radios, and disposals, many of which were designed by Patten. GE's motto became "More Goods for More People at Less Cost."

Much as it had moved into consumer production of irons and stoves through acquisition and merger, General Electric, in 1917, moved into the production of electric clocks when it acquired a 49 percent interest in the Warren Clock Company. Initially, clocks were not produced under the General Electric brand name. Clock timers sold as accessories for stoves produced by its subsidiary Edison General Electric Appliance Company were marketed under the Hotpoint™ trade name. Its earliest stove timers were not even electric; they used spring-wound movements produced by the Lux Clock Company of Waterbury, Connecticut. Later Hotpoint timers were fitted with Telechron movements. Like Revere clocks, the dials were generally labeled "Telechron motored." It is not clear who manufactured the cases.

Although GE had acquired a strong financial interest in the Warren Clock Company in 1917, it was not until sometime in 1930 or 1931 that clocks bearing the General Electric brand were introduced. Initially, a number of models previously sold as Telechron models were transferred to General Electric. Others became available as both GE and Telechron models, the only difference being the dial. The models with General Electric dials were given an "AB" prefix in the model number. The dials typically placed the words "General Electric" in the upper portion of the dial and "Telechron" on the bottom portion. They were marketed as "General Electric Telechron" clocks. By the mid 1930s, however,

"Telechron" was dropped from the dial and the clocks were marketed simply as "General Electric" clocks. They continued to roll off the same assembly lines as Telechron clocks.

In 1940, Charles Wilson succeeded Swope as president, serving until 1952. During the early years of Wilson's presidency, consumer production was halted to support the war effort. In addition to production of aircraft engines and radar equipment, General Electric became involved in the nuclear energy and aerospace industries.

With the retirement of Henry Warren in 1943, General Electric acquired controlling interest in the Warren Telechron Company. During the postwar boom, General Electric introduced an automatic clothes dryer and television in 1947. By 1950, General Electric had 183,000 employees, 117 plants, and $1.96 billion in sales.

In 1950, Ralph Cordiner succeeded Charles Wilson as president, serving until 1958. "B" movie star Ronald Reagan was hired as the company's new spokesman in 1953. Reagan served as host of "GE Theatre" on CBS, where the 50s slogan "At GE Progress is our Most Important Product" was introduced. The microwave oven was introduced in 1950. Other products introduced during the 1950s included toaster ovens, portable hair dryers, table top broilers, and pocket radios.

Cordiner is best remembered, however, for the manufacturing plant constructed near Louisville, Kentucky. General Electric built six huge manufacturing buildings and a warehouse with 4

Cover to a General Electric clock catalog for 1936.

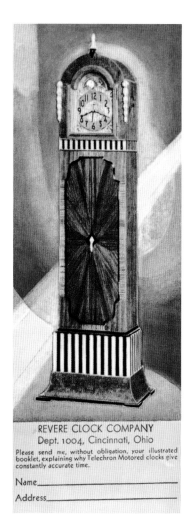

A Revere art moderne tall case clock from the late 1920s.

million square feet on 942 acres. The buildings themselves covered 93 acres. One building was the size of 15 football fields. The facility included 20 miles of paved roads and had its own police force, fire department, taxi service, railroad, and newspaper. Employment totaled about 12,000.

In 1979, General Electric sold its only remaining clock manufacturing plant—the Homer Ave. plant in Ashland, Massachusetts—to the Timex Corporation.

Herschede Hall and Revere Clock Companies

In 1873, 16-year-old Frank Herschede went to work as an apprentice clock and watch repairman to Charles Cook at a Cincinnati jewelry store. Four years later, he opened his own shop, catering to the jewelry trade. As his jewelry business expanded and moved to larger quarters, Herschede began, in 1885, to import English clock movements to be used in cases manufactured by a nearby cabinet shop. The clock business was successful and, in 1900, Herschede bought the cabinet-maker's shop. The following year, Herschede's hall clocks won a gold metal at a Charleston, South Carolina exposition.

Herschede's son Walter joined the firm in 1902 after his high school graduation. Later that year, Frank Herschede formally incorporated the firm as the Herschede Hall Clock Company. Frank's younger brother, John, became the firm's first president.

The Company continued to win awards for its clocks, including several at the 1904 Louisiana Purchase Exposition in St. Louis. As sales increased, the company moved to larger quarters in 1903. Six years later, the company decided to manufacture its own movements and purchased an adjoining building to assemble the movements. The first movement was assembled and passed inspection January 10, 1911. Initially the movements played the Whittington and Westminster chimes, but in 1913 the "Canterbury Chimes" were added. The Canterbury Chimes were composed by Charles Eisen specifically for Herschede.

By the early 1920s the company had opened branch offices in New York, Chicago, and San Francisco and the company was the premier American manufacturer of chime hall clocks and mantel clocks. Following Frank Herschede's death in 1922, his son Walter became company president.

By this time, interest in electric clocks was increasing and Walter Herschede began working with Henry Warren on the development of an electric movement chime clock. To protect the good name of his company in the event the electric clock proved unreliable, Herschede set up a new firm, the Revere Clock Company, to market the electric chime clocks. The new firm's factory, however, was located in the Herschede Hall plant.

The dials on Revere clocks are clearly labeled "Telechron-motored" and the two companies had a combined sales force and complimentary advertising campaigns. In other words, ads for Revere clocks typically promoted Telechron clocks and visa versa. It has also been reported that Revere manufactured some parts and cases for the Warren Telechron Company. Most of the Revere line was composed of mantel and boudoir models although Revere also produced a few hall clocks with auxiliary spring mechanisms to keep the clocks running in case of power failure.

With the new Revere line a success, Walter Herschede quickly added electrically-driven Herschede floor clocks to the company's product line. It also entered into an agreement to produce chime and hall clocks for General Electric. General Electric quickly became Herschede's biggest customer. Just as many early Warren Telechron clocks were produced with both Telechron and General Electric/Telechron dials, so too were Herschede models produced with a variety of dials, including Herschede, Revere, General Electric, and in at least a few cases, Telechron.

Revere and Telechron Share Display

At an Exposition held by the Cincinnati Edison Electric Company in October 1929, Telechron and Revere shared a 10 by 20 foot display. In reporting on the Exposition, the November 1929 *Telechronicle* stated that

"To help Mr. and Mrs. Public realize that clock cases are not carved with a jack-knife, a work-bench was introduced into the exhibit, at which a Revere clock-case craftsman displayed his skill in manipulating the many different knives so necessary in fine hand carving. Mr. and Mrs. Public were eager to learn something about hand carving and this craftsman certainly attracted a large audience at all times.

"The next logical step on the part of Mr. and Mrs. Public was into the booth to learn 'what makes the hands go around'."

By 1929, company sales had reached $1.2 million and the firm employed 300 workers. Following the stock market crash, however, sales of Herschede clocks tumbled dramatically. Even the introduction of a full line of electric clocks under the Herschede name could not stem the slide. In 1933, sales totaled only $187,000. With the market for luxury clocks all but gone, Herschede introduced a line of inexpensive electric clocks—Crown Clocks—in 1933. Even the new line, however, failed and was quickly discontinued. Making matters worse, the Warren Telechron Company expanded its production capacity in 1934 and stopped purchasing parts from Herschede. An increase in sales to General Electric, however, helped offset the loss of the Telechron sales.

With its clock business reeling, Herschede signed contracts with the Parkrite and Karpark companies to produce parking meters. Herschede acquired the Karpark Corporation in 1938. Karpark, in turn, absorbed Parkrite.

World War II brought a temporary end to the production of both clocks and parking meters. During the war, a new firm, Panocular Corporation, was established to produce optical lenses and equipment to support the war effort. Returning to consumer production after the war, Herschede initially found high demand for clocks. The company resumed supplying clocks to General Electric and also had contracts to make striking clocks for Telechron (now controlled by GE).

Herschede's fortunes quickly faded, however, as a 20 percent excise tax was imposed on luxury items, including many of its clocks, and profit margins dwindled in the parking meter industry because of fierce competition. Adding to the problems were increased labor costs after the company signed its first union contract in 1946.

The Panocular Corporation was reactivated during the Korean War, but the company's other products faced increasingly fierce foreign competition during the 1950s. Herschede began importing clock mechanisms and eventually entire clocks bearing the Herschede name. In a last ditch effort to improve its financial position, Herschede acquired another faltering company—Rookwood Pottery—in 1959. Rookwood, perhaps America's finest and most collectible pottery, was also located in Cincinnati.

Herschede and its associated companies, by now including Panocular, Karpark, and Rookwood, relocated to Starkville, Mississippi in 1960 in a search for lower labor and production costs. The company continued to have financial difficulties following the move, and, in 1967 was sold to a group of local Starkville businessmen, ending over 80 years of family ownership. Five years later, the Herschede Hall Clock Company merged with Howard Furniture and Briarwood Lamps to form Arnold Industries, Inc. Production of clocks was discontinued at that time.

Telechron Crosses the Atlantic

Although the battle between direct and alternating current had been all but settled by 1918 in the United States, direct current continued to be the norm in Great Britain well into the 1920s. In 1927, however, Great Britain set up the Central Electricity Board and charged it with coordinating the nation's electric supply by means of a "Grid." The Board adopted alternating current as the standard for the whole country, setting 50 cycles per second as the uniform "periodicity" for the whole country. Under the variance allowed (+/- 2-1/2 percent), however, a clock could gain or lose about a half-hour a day, making electrical timekeeping impractical.

In order for electric timekeeping to become practical in the United Kingdom, the variance needed to be eliminated. Everett, Edgcumbe & Co., under license from the Warren Telechron Company, introduced the Warren Master Clock in the United Kingdom under the tradename "Synclock." They also introduced the first synchronous motor clocks in the United Kingdom, also under the trade name "Synclock." Their company, Synclocks, Ltd., produced the motors under license from the Warren Telechron Company.

Herschede Hall floor clocks from the May and Halas Distributors' catalog for 1942.

Revere chime clocks from the May and Halas Distributors' catalog for 1942. Note that the use of Telechron motors is still prominently featured.

Chapter 4
Marketing & Promotion

The *Telechronicle*

In September 1927, the Warren Telechron Company launched a new monthly magazine—the *Telechronicle*—aimed at jewelry stores and other retailers. The *Telechronicle* contained announcements of new models and special promotions, and helpful ideas and products for window and counter displays. They also contained information on the combined Telechron and Revere sales force. Frequently, they contained a poem by Gladys Knowlton or another Warren Telechron employee, always with a Telechron theme. By the early 1930s, the *Telechronicle* had taken on a new appearance, often with Hollywood stars plugging their latest film. In addition, they often used cartoons to promote special campaigns.

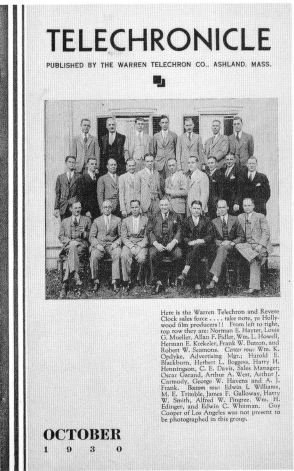

Above: The combined Warren Telechron and Revere sales force. (*Telechronicle*, October 1930)

Right: Cover to an early issue of the *Telechronicle*. Initially, the same cover was used for every issue. On the cover is a drawing of the sundial at England's Christ College with the inscription:
"Time Passes Silently Away
By minutes, hours, and then the day."

More Stars than There are in Heaven™: Celebrity Endorsements

Metro-Goldwyn-Mayer's popular slogan "More Stars than there are in Heaven" seems an apt description of Telechron's advertising approach during the early 1930s. Covers of the *Telechronicle* routinely featured film stars with their favorite Telechron clock. Although stars from all of the major studios made appearances, the Warren Telechron Company appears to have forged a special alliance with Radio-Keith-Orpheum (RKO) pictures. Covers of the *Telechronicle* were often graced by "stills" from forthcoming Radio pictures portraying a scene of the star with a Telechron clock in the background. Both companies benefited: RKO from the publicity generated for its new films; Telechron from the "free" advertising generated by putting Telechron clocks on the big screen in front of millions of moviegoers. The focus on soon-to-be-released films helped ensure that an adoring audience, eager to learn about their favorite stars, would stop by their Telechron dealer to learn about "coming attractions" and hopefully pick up a new Telechron at the same time.

In addition to film stars, the *Telechronicle* also featured bandleaders like Paul Ash and sports celebrities like Amos Alonso Stagg.

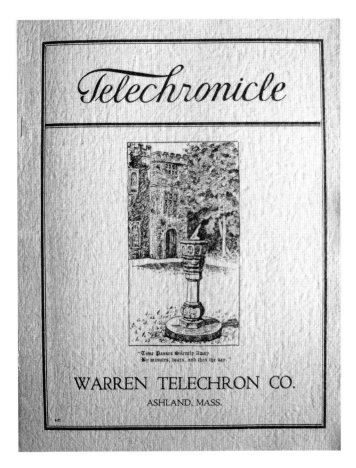

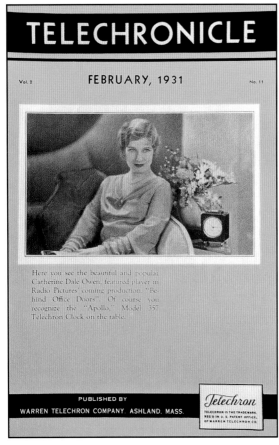

Popular stage actress Catherine Dale Owen (1903-1965) appeared in Radio Pictures' 1931 film "Behind Office Doors." Shown in the February 1931 *Telechronicle* with the Telechron "Apollo."

Purnell Pratt and Constance Cummings, featured players in Radio Pictures' production "TRAVELING HUSBANDS", shown with a Telechron Clock.

Purnell Pratt (1886-1941) and Constance Cummings from Radio Pictures' "Traveling Husband." Pratt appeared in countless character roles throughout the 1930s often playing tough city editors or frustrated police chiefs.
Beautiful and charming Constance Cummings had a long and successful career in Hollywood and found even greater success in England. Among her more notable roles were leading lady opposite Harold Lloyd in "Movie Crazy" (1931) and as Rex Harrison's bewildered second wife in "Blythe Spirit."

The cover of the July 1931 *Telechronicle* featured film star Laura La Plante gazing at a Telechron motored Revere clock. Ms. La Plante had a long and varied film career. From leading lady in silent and early talking pictures in both Hollywood and England, she eventually became a character actress of no little charm.

Dorothy Lee (1911-1999), pictured with the "Apollo," was a cute little thing who could add a bit of sparkle to any Wheeler and Woolsey movie. And that was just about all she did in a picture career that lasted 10 years.

Bert Wheeler (1895-1968) and Robert Woolsey (1890-1938) kick off Telechron's new year in style with the "Modernique."
This comedy team was hugely successful from 1930 to 1937 in a series of pictures made at Radio. Only recently, thanks to cable television, has this long forgotten duo had a minor renaissance.

Rochelle Hudson (1914-1972), pictured on the cover of the November 1931 *Telechronicle* with the "Apollo," is perhaps best remembered as "Lilums" in the 1934 picture "Harold Teen" (A MUST SEE!). She also played Shirley Temple's older sister in "Curly Top" (1935) and W.C. Fields' daughter in "Poppy."

Vol. 5   APRIL-MAY, 1935   No. 1

TELECHRONICLE

"My, isn't Telechron's 'Pharaoh' model clock a beauty?" The young lady with the look of admiration is none other than June Knight, popular motion picture star.

The following please note and pass on to:

RETURN TO:

June Knight (1913-1987), was a popular star in numerous Broadway plays and some films. Among her costars were Russ Columbo (better than Sinatra), Robert Taylor, and Buddy Rogers. She is pictured in the April-May *Telechronicle* with the Telechron "Pharaoh."

TELECHRONICLE
PUBLISHED BY THE WARREN TELECHRON CO., ASHLAND, MASS.

Edwina Booth . . . leading Lady in the "Trader Horn" film expedition sent to Africa by Metro-Goldwyn-Mayer, won't have to worry about the time of day on the dark continent . . . . She took her Telechron Electric Clock along with her.

AUGUST
1 9 3 0

Edwina Booth (1905-1991), featured on the cover of the August 1930 *Telechronicle*, is a rather obscure actress in early talkies. Among her roles as a leading lady was the ill-fated white goddess in "Trader Horn."

Ah-h-h-h! None other than the famous movie pair—LAUREL AND HARDY—Hal Roach stellar comedians. Oh!!—them eyes—them expressions, as they cast eudemonistic (deliciae humani generis) faces upon Telechron's "Minitmaster" model!

1992.32.9 ap

Stan Laurel (1891-1965) and Oliver Hardy (1892-1957) plug the Telechron "Minitmaster," the first cyclometer clock. Perhaps the greatest comedy team of all time, their films and shorts still enjoy a wide audience.

WELL, well, well . . . "Behind Office Doors" is going to be a great picture! Here's another "shot" from it (the movie people call this a "still") showing Ricardo Cortez and Mary Astor, stars, discussing that all-important element known as "time" and you can see that they selected the "Apollo" model Telechron Clock to give them the real "low-down" in this particular scene. We've got some big things almost ready for you, Mr. Authorized Telechron Dealer . . . . watch for coming announcements.

2-32-9w

The popular and beautiful Mary Astor, featured player in Radio Pictures' coming big production "Private Secretary" is here shown probably turning back the hands of time because she (the private secretary) no doubt thinks a great deal of the boss (who will be Robert Ames). Watch for future announcements concerning the part YOU are to play in this outstanding film of the year!

1992-32-9w

Far left: The "Apollo" appears again in this still from "Behind Office Doors" starring Ricardo Cortez (1900-1977) and Mary Astor. Born Jack Kranze, the studio thought that "Ricardo Cortez" was a name better suited for cashing in on the "Latin Lover" craze started by Valentino in the 1920s. It seems to have worked as Cortez made countless films during the 1930s, starring opposite such stars as Kay Frances and Irene Dunne.

Left: Mary Astor (1906-1987) is pictured with a massive Telechron commercial wall clock. This talented actress was in pictures for many decades, from the 1926 silent classic "Don Juan" opposite John Barrymore to the very forgettable 1961 "Return to Peyton Place." She is best remembered, however, for roles in "Dodsworth" (1936) and "The Maltese Falcon" (1941). She is pictured here plugging her upcoming film "Private Secretary."

Right: Obscure film and stage star Sam Hardy (1883-1935) helps introduce the "Minitmaster" in the March-April 1933 Telechronicle.

Far right: Telechron and Revere frequently had joint advertisements. Here Mary Astor plugs the Telechron "Cathedral" and "Modernique" and the Revere "Lafayette" tall case clock.

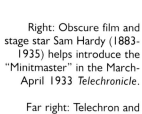

Vol. 4　　MARCH-APRIL, 1933　　No. 4

TELECHRONICLE

SAM HARDY, of movie and stage fame, says the new Telechron "MINITMASTER" is a knockout. This photo air-mailed from Hollywood. See Page 5.

WARREN *Telechron* COMPANY

$9.95 CATHEDRAL with Moulded Case

Model 370 $20

Mary Astor
STAR OF RADIO PICTURES

becomes one of the most popular actresses of the day. Little wonder! . . . for she, like Telechron motored Electric Clocks, achieved stardom through modern up-to-the-minute personality.

Simply plug any Telechron Clock into an electric outlet. The electricity keeps them correct. Models for every room . . . for every purse . . . for every purpose.

No winding, oiling or regulating. See our complete line on display.

Telechron and Revere

Self-starting, Synchronous Electric Clocks

YOUR NAME
and Your Address

LAFAYETTE with Westminster Chimes 197 with Time Movement Only 165

Mat 8100

MODERNIQUE $50 (Enamled finish) $55 (Gold finish) Designed by Paul T. Frankl

SMARTLY MODERN

Telechron Clocks are "as modern as the next minute". There are many interesting models for every room in the home or office . . . moderately priced from $9.75 to $55 for the silent clocks, and $30 to $1000 for charming strike and chime models.

Simply plug them into the nearest electric outlet—the electricity keeps them correct.

Only about 10 cents a month to run.

Telechron
Self-starting, Synchronous Electric Clocks

YOUR NAME
and Your Address

Mat 8104

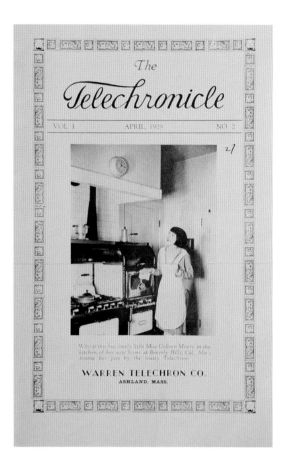

Far left: Colleen Moore (1903-1988) is shown "timing her pies" by her Telechron clock in the April 1929 *Telechronicle*. Colleen Moore was a mega-star during the 1920s and continued in films until 1934.

Left: Here is the Telechron "Modernique" making an appearance in the RKO film "Fanny Foley Herself" starring Edna May Oliver. One of the most popular and caricatured actresses of the 1930s, Oliver (1883-1942) played everything from old maid school teacher detectives to cranky old dowagers. The September 1931 *Telechronicle* notes that the "'Modernique' is a great favorite of moviedom...they like its originality."

Right: Paul Ash—the Radio Rajah of Jazz—is featured on the April 1930 *Telechronicle* with the "Modernique." Ash, whose name is sometimes spelled "Ashe," led one of the most popular dance bands of the 1920s and took to the air in the 1930s for Pabst Blue Ribbon™ Beer. He recorded prolifically for Columbia Records.

Far right: Not all of Telechron's stars came from Hollywood. Here legendary college football coach Amos Alonzo Stagg is pictured receiving a Revere chiming banjo clock. This is another indication of the close working relationship that existed between Revere and Telechron.

The Grinch That Sold Telechrons

In 1932, the *Telechronicle* began to feature the adventures of Gus and Gussie Guess created by Theodore Seuss Geisel, better known as Dr. Seuss.

Gus and Gussie Guess were formed as anagrams of "Seuss Geisel." Although the cartoons appeared in the *Telechronicle*, I found no evidence of a national advertising campaign featuring Gus and Gussie and they were soon forgotten. By contrast, Dr. Seuss produced comic ads for the insecticide "Flit" for 17 years. His ad phrase "Quick Henry, the Flit" survived long after the product disappeared.

Theodore Seuss Geisel

Theodore Seuss Geisel (1902-1991), a native of Springfield, Massachusetts, attended Dartmouth College and Oxford University. Returning from England in 1927, Dr. Seuss began his career drawing cartoons and writing humorous articles for *Judge*. His early cartoons also appeared in *Life*, *Vanity Fair*, and *Liberty*.

During World War II, Dr. Seuss joined the Army, serving in Hollywood under famed movie director Frank Capra. His wartime service won him Academy Awards for the documentaries *Hitler Lives* and *Design for Death* and for the cartoon *Gerald McBoing-Boing*.

Although Dr. Seuss' first book, *And to Think That I Saw It on Mulberry Street*, was published in 1937, he is best remembered for the string of children's classics published between the mid-1950s and mid-1980s. These include *The Cat in the Hat* (1957) and *The Grinch That Stole Christmas* (1957). One of his books, *Green Eggs and Ham*, uses only 50 words.

"Mad Moments" with Dr. Seuss' Gus and Gussie Guess. (*Telechronicle*, February-March 1932)

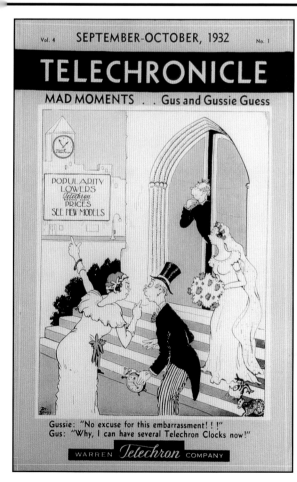

Gus and Gussie Guess plug Telechron's new models and lower prices in the September-October 1932 *Telechronicle*.

Gus and Gussie plug Telechrons in this January-February 1933 *Telechronicle*.

Gus and Gussie Guess announce a special campaign in which Telechron will give $1 for any clock as a trade-in on a Telechron.

Humor continued to be an important form of advertisement for Telechron in 1934. The NRA eagle, denotes that the Warren Telechron Company was doing its part to pull the nation out of the Great Depression.

Magazine Advertisements

Both Telechron and General Electric advertised prolifically in magazines. For example, in the first six months of 1930, Telechron advertisements appeared in the *Saturday Evening Post*, *Literary Digest*, *Time*, *Good Housekeeping*, *Ladies Home Journal*, *Delineator*, *Vogue*, *Vanity Fair*, and *House and Garden*. Advertisements also appeared in *House Beautiful*, *World's Work*, *Country Life*, *New Yorker*, *Town and Country*, and *National Geographic*. Throughout the 1930s-1950s, Telechron clocks continued to be advertised prolifically in the *Saturday Evening Post* and other leading magazines.

General Electric also made effective use of magazine advertising beginning with the introduction of its own line of electric clocks in 1931. Its early advertisements emphasized the accuracy of its clocks "regulated by comparison with National Observatory Radio Time Signals" and the fact that they were powered with the "well-known Telechron motor." General Electric advertisements featured both clocks made at the Warren Telechron plant in Ashland and at the Revere/Herschede Hall plant in Cincinnati. General Electric frequently placed full-page color advertisements in *American Home*.

Examples of Telechron and General Electric advertisements are interspersed throughout this book.

The *Telechronicle* also gave dealers information on national magazine advertisements for Telechron clocks, this one's from 1930.

By 1941, the Warren Telechron Company had narrowed its national advertising campaign to *Life*, *Look*, *Colliers*, *The Saturday Evening Post*, and *Better Homes and Gardens*.

It was often difficult to determine which company was advertising— Revere or Telechron. In this case, it appears to be a Revere advertisement, but Telechron clocks get equal billing. (*National Geographic*, May 1929)

Sales Helps

Another frequent topic in the *Telechronicle* were the numerous "sales helps," including elaborate store and window displays, available to retailers. Among the items available were a 12-1/2" x 5-1/4" "imitation bronze" sign identifying the retailer as an "Authorized Dealer" for "Telechron Springless Clocks." Another "imitation bronze" sign intended for display in the window or on a counter read simply "Correct Electric Time by Telechron." Retailers were also promised the "Scoop for Telechron Authorized Dealers," a portfolio containing details of upcoming sales campaigns.

One of the most impressive sales helps was the patented "Flasherad" sign. This seven color sign, approximately 13" x 30", displayed the model 355 but, when lit, displayed a power station behind the clock. It was available to dealers for only $2.50 postpaid. Both Telechron and General Electric also made available to their dealers a variety of display racks.

Telechron supplied a variety of sales brochures to its dealers at no cost. These included a full line brochure detailing all models and specialized brochures featuring low cost models, new models, and business models. Dealers were encouraged to place the brochures on the counter and to include the specialized brochure in bills mailed to their customers.

The *Telechronicle* also showed a variety of suggested window displays using Telechron clocks and display pieces available from the Warren Telechron Company.

Advertisement for General Electric clocks, circa 1931. Note that two of the clocks are chime clocks with "R" catalog numbers meaning they were produced by Revere.

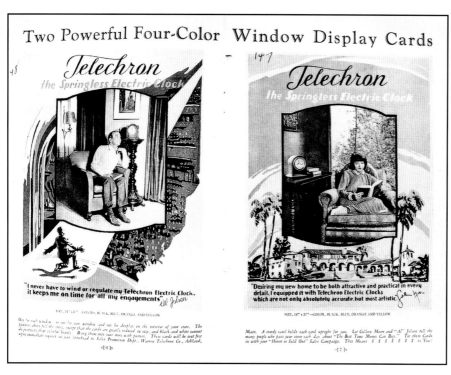

Two Powerful Four-Color Window Display Cards

The "stars" also made appearances in four-color window display cards. Here Al Jolson and Colleen Moore are shown at home with their Telechron clocks.

A *Telechronicle* display of "dealer helps."

Telechron
DIRECT MAIL PIECES

Telechron offered authorized dealers a variety of direct mail pieces that could be imprinted with the dealer's name and mailed to potential customers.

Telechron
SUGGESTED WINDOW DISPLAYS

The *Telechronicle* contained suggested window displays of Telechron clocks.

The Telechron Electric "Flasherad Display Sign"

Another of the Telechron dealer helps was the "Flasherad Display Sign."

SALES — HELPS

FOR

TELECHRON DEALERS

Form No. 720

Form No. 721

A new circular featuring the low-priced models. Provision for dealer's imprint. Free copies upon request.

Form No. 722

A new circular selecting one or more leading models of the different groups. Provision for dealer's imprint.

Form No. 701-A

Presenting all Telechron standard commercial models. "Time for Business." Provision for dealer's imprint.

(Requests for This Free Material Should Be Made to Your Telechron Distributer)

This business-getting material is yours FREE, in reasonable quantities for the asking. (Be sure you refer to respective Form Numbers.) Put the "Full-Line" folder on your counters and display tables; mail the circulars with your bills at no extra postage expense.

CORRECT ELECTRIC TIME BY Telechron

Form No. 707. A green and silver plaque to hang or stand near a Telechron Standard Commercial Model. 4¼" x 14".

Page Five

The *Telechronicle* told dealers about the wide array of available "sales—helps."

Telechron continued to offer a wide array of "Dealer Helps" in 1941. A variety of displays were offered, each prominently featuring "Father Telechron."

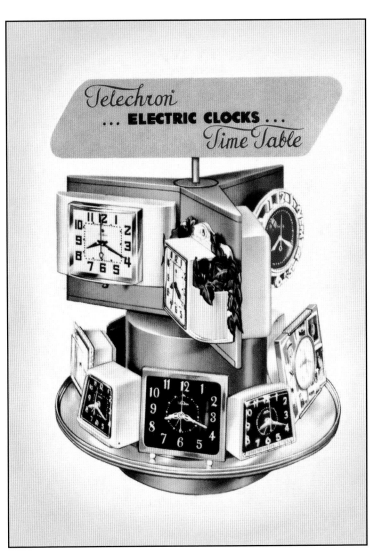

The 1951 Telechron "Time Table."

A General Electric Deluxe Clock Shop from the early 1950s.

Special Campaigns and Promotions

The *Telechronicle* was also used to advertise special sales campaigns and promotions. These included special models (clocks with model numbers beginning with "CF" or "CH"), "trade-in" specials when an old clock would be worth $1 in trade on a new Telechron, and special colors or dials offered on production models. General Electric also produced Special Campaign Models but they are usually designated by the "X" appearing in the middle of the model number.

These campaigns often featured a sales slogan, such as "Put a Telechron Under Every Tree," "Modernize Your Time," and "Telechron Plays to a Full House."

Because they were available for short periods, the Special Campaign Models are generally harder to find than clocks that entered general production. There were, however, also Special Campaign Models that subsequently entered regular production.

Cover to the November 1930 *Telechronicle* announcing the beginning of the Christmas campaign "Put a Telechron Clock in Another Room This Christmas." Dealers were offered the colorful 8" x 16" counter or window display card reproduced on the cover.

March 1934 *Telechronicle* announcing the new models.

Telechron's new Spring Song—"Modernize Your Time."

Cover to the Fall, 1934 *Telechronicle* announcing the new campaign.

TELECHRONICLE

PUBLISHED BY THE WARREN TELECHRON CO., ASHLAND, MASS.

This is the season for June Brides
. . . . . and Telechron Electric
Clocks . . . . . Thousands of
couples will be given this most
appropriate of all gifts which will
enable them to start life on time.

MAY-JUNE
1 9 3 0

Cover to the May-June 1930 *Telechronicle*. The copy reads: "This is the season for June Brides….. and Telechron Electric clocks….. Thousands of couples will be given this most appropriate of all gifts which will enable them to start life on time."

Miss Telechron
At Gimbel Brothers Pageant

A new theme to symbolize time was utilized by the Clock Department of Gimbel Bros., New York, in the recent Store Pageant, celebrating the 88th Anniversary of Gimbel Bros. in business.

This pageant is an annual event with the store and a prize is awarded to the Department producing the most unique costume.

This year Father Time lost his job in the character of Time and in his stead, gaily stepped Miss C. Chrystal as the TELECHRON GIRL. In her modern array she won all kinds of attention for her department and quite naturally brought Telechrons before her co-workers in a most fitting manner.

Miss Chrystal devotes a great deal of her time to the sale of Telechrons and her enthusiasm prompted her to request Miss Lee, in charge of Gimbel's Clock Department, to permit her to appear in the pageant as the Telechron Girl.

Isn't this an idea for your store . . . . . during the Christmas buying season? Why not establish a "Miss Telechron" either in your store or city . . . . . such unique features as this will do much to bring your stock of Telechron Clocks to your public's attention.

After Gimbel's, New York, introduced "Miss Telechron" at the pageant celebrating the department store's 88th anniversary, the Warren Telechron Company was quick to encourage other stores and communities to follow suit.

Promotion of Telechron Clocks in Canada

Telechron and Revere frequently had joint advertisements in U. S. magazines in which models from both companies would be featured. At the bottom of the advertisement, under the Warren Telechron and Revere addresses, would appear the statement "In Canada, Canadian General Electric Company, Toronto, Ontario."

The 1931 General Electric Telechron clock catalog published by the Canadian General Electric Company details extensive advertising and promotional efforts, noting that "Canadian General Electric advertising is so extensive that it literally blankets Canada." Unlike the advertising campaigns in the United States, which focused on magazine advertisements, Canadian General Electric focused its advertising efforts on newspapers. In addition, advertisements were placed on streetcars, in trade journals and magazines, and on the weekly Canadian General Electric radio broadcast.

The marketing campaign in Canada very clearly focused on the "acceptance" of the General Electric name as the reason for dealers to market General Electric Telechron clocks. Potential dealers are advised in the 1931 catalog that

"An intensive national advertising campaign for General Electric Telechron Clocks will commence as soon as dealer distribution is completed. Large space newspaper advertisements will stir up interest in General Electric Telechron Clocks all over the Dominion—in your community.

"Dealers will be supplied with a liberal amount of display material, folders, sales literature…and a ready prepared ad. Service for their local advertising will be available.

"Every dealer has at his disposal the facilities of the Advertising Department, Canadian General Electric Co., Limited, to assist him in the preparation of sales letters…special advertisements…and other such plans."

An
Electric Clock
supported by the
tremendous profit
possibilities
of the name » »

GENERAL
ELECTRIC

**All C.G.E. Sales Literature helps sell
General Electric Telechron Clocks**

Hundreds of thousands of booklets, folders, calendars, direct-mail broadsides and other such C.G.E. sales literature which carries the name "General Electric", are distributed each year. Here, indeed, is a name that is known everywhere . . . and that is associated with products of unquestioned superiority. Think of the profit possibilities this name "General Electric" brings to General Electric Telechron Clocks!

Page Eleven

SELL GENERAL ELECTRIC TELECHRON CLOCKS

Everybody knows . . .
GENERAL ⓖⓔ ELECTRIC

GENERAL ELECTRIC . . .
whose name everywhere stands for
reliability in everything electrical . .
now offers to

CENTRAL STATIONS
    ELECTRICAL DEALERS
        JEWELLERS and
BETTER CLASS HARDWARE DEALERS

a new . . . dependable profit maker

GENERAL ⓖⓔ ELECTRIC
TELECHRON CLOCK

Page Four

PROFIT BY GENERAL ELECTRIC PRESTIGE

44

Chapter 5

Selected Designers

Both Telechron and General Electric used in-house designers to develop the bulk of their clock cases during the 1930s-1950s. These designers—particularly Leo Ivan Bruce for Telechron and Ray Patten and John Rainbault for General Electric—are largely forgotten today. Many of their designs, however, meet or exceed those created by the "big name" designers like Walter Dorwin Teague. In fact, Rainbault's designs were so exceptional that they are widely "attributed to" Rockwell Kent, Gilbert Rohde, Teague, or Russel Wright. The work of other "company men," like George Graff of the Dura Corporation and Amos Northup of the Murray Corporation, who contributed designs to GE and Telechron, are easily recognized by automobile enthusiasts but largely ignored in retrospectives of industrial design in the 1930s. Such design retrospectives typically tout the futuristic automotive designs of Norman Bel Geddes that never entered production, but ignore the string of production vehicles designed by Amos Northup during the golden age of the automobile, including the Reo Royale, Graham Blue Streak, and several Hupmobiles.

Over 30 individuals were awarded design patents for Telechron or General Electric clocks. While some, like Patten, Bruce, and Rainbault have multiple patents, others designed only one or two clocks but had active design careers in other fields. For still others, however, the clock they designed for General Electric or Telechron is their only design credit. It should not be assumed, however, that the absence of design patents necessarily means that the individual did not do additional work. Many firms did not bother to patent their designs. For example, the Chase Brass and Copper Company generally patented the designs submitted by big name freelance designers, but not those of its Director of Design—Harry Laylon. Anyone with additional biographical information on the designers is encouraged to contact the author so that it can be incorporated in future editions.

A complete listing of design patents for production models appears in appendix II. Appendix III contains design patents assigned to the Warren Telechron Company that do not appear to have entered production.

Jacques Martial Bars

Jacques Bars (1895-1987) was awarded 12 design patents between 1934 and 1941, all but one assigned to Telechron or General Electric. Although his first clock design apparently did not enter production, his other 10 clock designs all entered production, including the 1935 "Tempo" (3F61), the 1935 "Luxor," and the 1936 "Gendarme." His designs include several mantel and strike clocks. In addition to his clock designs, Bars was awarded a design patent in 1940 for a combined handle and holder for safety razors. Originally from New York City, Bars later relocated to Great Neck, New York and, at the time of his death, December 2, 1987, was living in Tracy, California.

Jacques Bars' clock designs included the "Radio Traveler" (No. 8B52). (D104,013, awarded April 13, 1937)

Edgar Bourquin

Edgar Bourquin (1893-1972) both invented and designed the first cyclometer clocks, companion models sold under the Telechron and General Electric brand names. An employee of the Warren Telechron Company, Bourquin lived in nearby Framingham, Massachusetts. Although he applied for a patent on his invention on July 6, 1933, the patent was not awarded until February 12, 1935. Bourquin's patent also included a perpetual calendar. He was awarded separate design patents for two clock cases incorporating the perpetual calendar but the clocks were never produced.

Bourquin also designed one of the most successful kitchen clocks ever produced—the "Hostess" and "New Hostess"—in almost continual production from 1930 to the early 1950s. In addition to the "Hostess," Bourquin designed the 1932-39 "Consort" (2F01).

Bourquin's other inventions include an advertising clock in which a train races around the perimeter of the clock (1937) and a rotating dial clock (1938). Although rights to both patents were

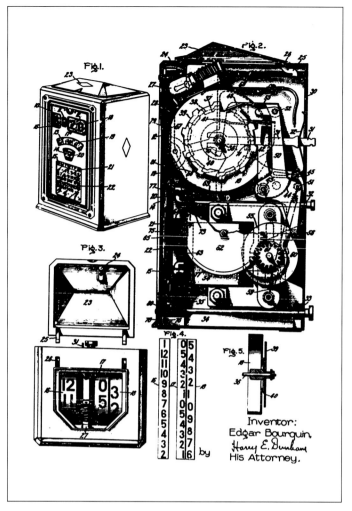

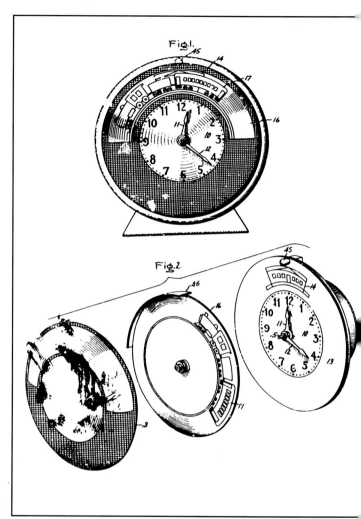

Edgar Bourquin's patent for the first commercially viable cyclometer clock. (No. 1,991,241, filed July 6, 1933 and awarded Feb. 12, 1935)

Edgar Bourquin's patent for a novel advertising clock in which a train travels around the dial. (No.- 2,082,612, filed Oct. 20, 1936 and awarded June 1, 1937)

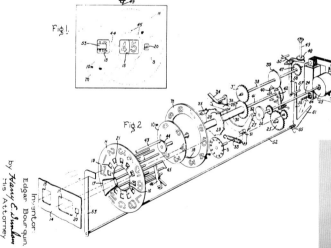

Above: Edgar Bourquin's patent for a rotating dial numeral clock (No. 2,130,873, filed Feb. 23, 1938 and awarded Sept. 20, 1938). Although the patent rights were assigned to the Warren Tele-chron Company, the Winslow Manufacturing Co. introduced the rotating numeral clock.

Right: Winslow Manufacturing Company's rotating dial clock. Highly sought after by collectors, these clocks often have stress cracks in the catalin cases caused by the pressure exerted by the movement.

assigned to the Warren Telechron Company, a rotating dial clock based on Bourquin's invention was produced by the Winslow Manufacturing Company.

The only other patent I identified for Edgar Bourquin was awarded in 1947 for invention of a time outlet permitting clocks to be installed in supporting walls essentially flush with the wall. By this time, Bourquin had relocated to Los Angeles where he would remain for the remainder of his life. He died in the Los Angeles suburb of La Crescenta in October 1972.

Leo Ivan Bruce

Leo Ivan Bruce (1911-1973) was the principal designer for the Warren Telechron Company from 1937 to 1955, having been awarded almost 60 design patents. Among his most notable designs were the 1937-53 "Buffet," and the series of "Telalarm" models (also known as the "Secretary" and "Cordial") based on his 1939 design. Perhaps his best design work, however, was a pre-war group of onyx clocks, the "Shoreham" (4B151), "Barclay" (4B153), "Hampshire" (4B155), and "Harwich" (4B07). Introduced in August 1940, sales of the four models languished because of their high prices ($22.50 to $35.00) compared to other models typically selling for $5 to $10. Excellent design and rarity (fewer than 1,000 of each model was sold) combine to make the four models among the most sought after Telechron models. Although Bruce contributed some awful designs in the early 1950s, he is also responsible for design of two of the ill-fated 1954-55 Designer Line clocks, the "Outline" (No. 5H65) and the "Showpiece" (No. 5H67). The Designer Line was one of the few attempts General Electric made in the postwar years to match innovative designs with quality workmanship. Unlike most of the everyday clocks, the Designer Line clocks had the look and feel of quality that largely disappeared in the postwar era. These classic designs are bound to increase in value as nostalgia for 1950s designs continues to explode. Like the prewar designer series, however, sales of the 1950s designer line were slow adding to their current value.

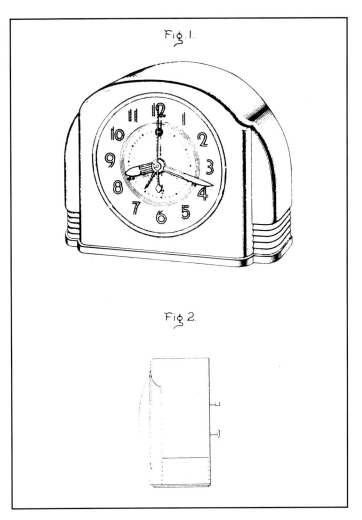

Among Leo Ivan Bruce's clock designs was the Special Campaign Model "Semester" (No. CH7111). (D131,802, awarded March 31, 1942)

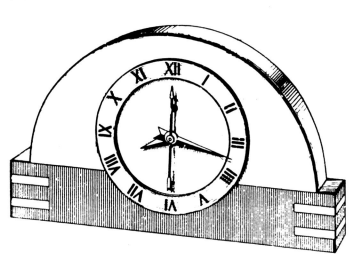

Among Leo Ivan Bruce's most distinctive designs were four onyx clocks introduced in 1940. Shown here is the "Harwich" (No. 4B07). (D124,830, awarded Jan. 28, 1941)

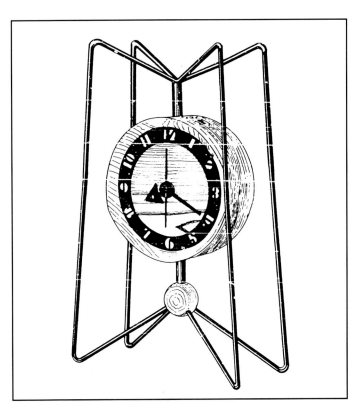

Leo Ivan Bruce was awarded a design patent for the 1954-55 "Outline," one of the most distinctive Telechron clocks of the 1950s. (D173,142, awarded Oct. 5, 1954)

Francesco Collura

Francesco Collura (1913-1991) counts three Telechron timers and the world's first clock radio among his 24 patents. His Telechron patents, awarded in 1946, were for the "Musalarm" (8H59), "Selector" (8H55), "Lite Call" (8H57), and "Switch-alarm" (8H61).

In addition to his brief work for Telechron, Collura did design work for a wide range of companies. His designs include: a lettering scriber (Keuffel & Easer Co.), a fan propeller (Torrington Manufacturing Co.), cuff links, hand and power tools (Miller Falls Co.), a padlock (Eagle Lock Co.), a canasta card tray, a pressure cooker (General Mills), an adjustable optician's chair (American Optical Co.), and an iron. His mechanical inventions include a centrifugal pump, an infant walker, and a push button mechanical pencil.

Although he was originally from Ohio, Collura was living in New York City at the time of his death in January 1991.

Simon DeVaulchier

New Yorker Simon DeVaulchier (1893-1971) is perhaps best remembered as the designer of the Colgate Palmolive toothpaste tube. In addition to the toothpaste tube, DeVaulchier designed a number of bottle and face powder boxes for the cosmetic firm Pinaud, Inc. and other firms. For Telechron he designed the immensely popular "Airlux" (4F55) and its related models as well as the more distinctive but less successful 1934-36 "Starman" (4F57). It was a design for Telechron competitor Westclox™, however, that earned DeVaulchier a place in the 1934 Museum of Modern Art Exhibit *Machine Art*. A Bakelite handbag watch designed by DeVaulchier & Blow was one of only three timepieces included in the exhibit.

Paul T. Frankl

Paul Theodore Frankl (1886-1958) was born in Vienna, Austria on October 14, 1886. He studied in Vienna, Paris, Munich, and Berlin before moving to the United States in 1914. Frankl is best remembered for his "skyscraper" bookcase designs during the late 1920s. His furniture designs, which included desks and wardrobes as well as the famous bookcases, were custom-made by the Frankl Galleries, Inc. Although his furniture was not known either for the quality of the materials or finish when compared to French designs and craftsmanship, they were immensely popular. Never known for his modesty, Frankl bragged that the 1925 Paris Exposition would have been markedly different had he been able to display his skyscraper designs. Frankl's designs caught the imagination of the American public and his style was often copied by other designers and applied to all forms of industrial design. It was during this period that Frankl designed the most famous of Telechron clocks—the "Modernique"—which sadly was also the only clock he apparently designed. Although the "Electrolarm" is almost universally attributed to Frankl, he did not receive a patent for the design, and I found no evidence to suggest that he had a role in its design.

While in New York, Frankl helped set up Macys's 1927 "Art in Trade" exhibition, both displaying his own furniture designs and lecturing on "The Skyscraper in Decoration." He also worked for the Celluloid Corporation designing dresser sets, receiving seven patents for his designs in 1929.

By the early 1930s, however, Frankl had moved from the vertical skyscraper designs of his bookcases to more horizontal streamlined designs. In the late 1930s and 1940s, he designed furniture for the Johnson Furniture Company, often using cork veneers.

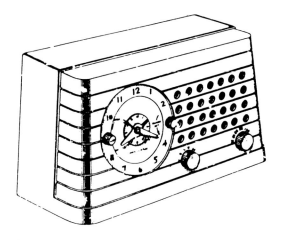

Among Francesco Collura's designs was the first clock radio. (D145,996, awarded Dec. 3, 1946)

Frankl was a leading advocate of the modern style in the late 1920s and 1930s, writing and lecturing prolifically. By 1940, he had relocated to Los Angeles, with offices at 3281 Wilshire Boulevard. His entry in *Who's Who in American Art 1940-1941* notes that he is the author of *Machine-made Leisure, Form and Re-form* (1930), *New Dimensions: The Decorative Arts of Today in Words & Pictures* (1928), and *Space for Living: Creative Interior Decoration and Design* (1938).

Frankl was instrumental in the formation of the American Designers Gallery in 1928 and the American Union of Decorative Artists and Craftsmen in 1930. In addition, he was a member of the American Institute of Designers.

George R. Graff

George Graff (1894-1966) designed a wide range of products in the art moderne style during the 1930s including clock cases, battery operated candles, fountain pen holders and display boxes, ashtrays, electric fans, and automobile heaters and hardware. He was awarded over 40 design patents,

During the early 1930s, Graff worked for the Dura Corporation of Toledo, Ohio, a major supplier to the automotive industry that also dabbled in consumer products. It was during this period that he designed the cases for what would become the Telechron 1931-36 "Telalarm" (Nos. 711 & 715) and the General Electric "Alarm Lite" (Nos. 712 & 716). Graff assigned the rights to his design patents to Dura, and I suspect that Dura produced the clock cases for the Warren Telechron Company much as they manufactured parts for the leading automobile manufacturers. Some of Graff's other clock designs were put into production by Westclox. Graff also designed a number of clock dials while at Dura.

Graff's designs for Dura also included a series of battery-operated electric candles and a fountain pen holder. Throughout the 1930s, however, Graff continued to focus primarily on automobile heaters, first for Dura and then for John E. Goerlich, also of Toledo. He also designed fans for Samson-United and Wagner Electric. By 1940, Graff had turned his talents towards household products, designing sewing and toilet article cases for the Henkel-Clauss Company of Fremont, Ohio and display boxes for the Parker Pen Company of Janesville, Wisconsin.

Graff's last design patent, for a detergent mixing device, was awarded November 21, 1951.

George Graff designed this Eveready battery-operated candle. Notice the use of the stepped motif on both the base and top of the lens. (D84,077, filed Sept. 6,1930 and awarded May 5, 1931.) Graff also designed the "Telalarm" in the photo.

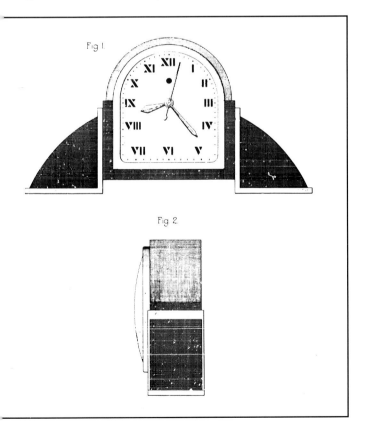

Belle Kogan designed the "Brandon" (No. 5F03). (D93,228, awarded Sept. 4, 1934)

Belle Kogan

Belle Kogan was born in Russia on June 26, 1905. She was trained at the Winold Reiss Art School, the Pratt Institute, and the Kunstgewerbe Schule of Phorzheim in Baden, Germany. In addition to her clock case designs for the Warren Telechron Company, Ms. Kogan designed sterling silver hollow-ware for Reed and Barton, dinnerware for Ebeling and Reuss, electric appliances for Samson United, glassware for the Federal Glass Company, pottery for Red Wing Potteries, brushes for the National Brush Co., and silverware for Kirk & Sons. Ms. Kogan had a studio at 362 Fifth Ave., New York, New York. She is listed in the 1940 edition of *Who's Who in American Art*.

Belle Kogan was awarded five design patents for clocks, all of which were assigned to the Warren Telechron Company. Her most notable design was for the "Smug" (8F01) and "Quacker" (7F63), one of Telechron's few ventures into novelty designs. Kogan also designed a variation with a shorter beak, but it was not produced. Another of Kogan's designs entered production as the "Brandon" (5F03) and "Doric" (5F51). The "Doric" is basically the center section of the "Brandon." Although Belle Kogan designed only five Telechron clocks, her designs are, in the author's opinion, more inspiring than those of the more widely known Walter Dorwin Teague.

Irwin Kokins

Irwin Kokins (1886-1966) of Framingham, Massachusetts was a long-time employee of the Warren Telechron Company. During most of the 1930s and early 1940s, he was Telechron's General Manager. He became president in 1943 following Henry Warren's retirement. He was described in the *Telechronicle* as "genial, enterprising, farseeing." His hobbies were music and art. Kokins

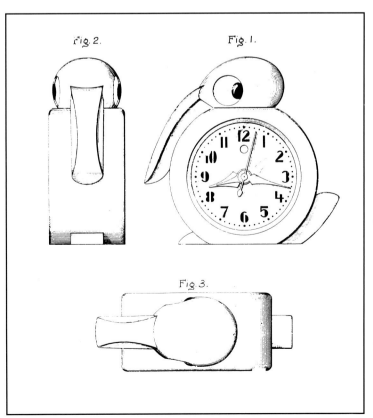

Belle Kogan's best known design was for the "Quacker" (No. 7F63) and "Smug" (No. 8F01). (D93,662, awarded Oct. 23, 1934)

managed to find the time to design two clocks, the 1933-36 "Telebell" (7F53) and the 1935-37 "Deputy" and "Aladdin" (7F65). Kokins' 1934 design for the "Telebell" appears to be an adaptation of a design patented two years earlier by another Telechron employee—Emma Thomas—that was not produced.

Eugene Lux

Eugene Lux (1887-1963) was a very prolific designer, holding over 25 design and mechanical patents including designs for four Telechron clocks: the "Kitchenguide" (2F03), "Esquire" (3F03), "Vassal" (3H97), and "Traymore" (4F69). Lux began his career in New York City, but later moved to Norwalk, Connecticut. Among his other designs are watch boxes and displays for both the Bulova and Gruen watch companies, toilet accessories containers for leading cosmetics manufacturer Harriet Hubbard Ayer, and a wide range of vanity items for the Columbia Protektosite Company, Inc. His designs for Columbia Protektosite included vanity furniture and a toy bathtub and vanity. In addition to his design patents, Lux also obtained mechanical patents for a suspension hook and a combination comb and sheath handle designed for Columbia Protektosite.

Jacques Martial

Jacques Martial of Great Neck, New York, designed only one clock which was marketed under three names—the "Ballard" (4H78), "New Ballard" (4H92) with a redesigned dial, and "Informer" (7H122). Perhaps Martial's most successful design, however, was a combination ink well and fountain pen holder for the Esterbrook Pen Company. Although Martial is a largely forgotten designer, the fountain pen holder was immensely popular and is readily found in antique shops. Most of Martial's design patents were awarded in the years immediately following World War II when he designed a number of radio and radio/record player cabinets for the Viewtone Company of New York. In addition to his design work, Martial also holds a mechanical patent for his invention of a razor blade ejector pack.

Amos Northup

Another "company man" largely ignored in industrial design retrospectives of the past 25 years, Amos Northup is well known and revered by classic automobile enthusiasts. For it was Northup, not Bel Geddes, Teague, or Loewy, whose designs set the stage for the streamlined automobiles of the 1930s. As the chief designer for the Murray Corporation of America, Amos Northup designed many landmark automobiles including the 1931 Reo Royale, 1932 Graham Blue Streak, 1933 Willys 77, the 1938 sharknose Graham, the 1930 Hudson club sedan, the Ford A/B 400s, and several Hupmobiles.

Prior to joining the Murray Corporation, Northup designed the 1924 Wills Ste. Claire and was the chief designer for the Willys-Overland Corporation, designing the 1929 Great Six Series 66B Plaidside Roadster that took the New York auto show by storm. In its review of the show, *Autobody* noted that

"The Northup design for the new Willys-Knight series was the most revolutionary of any that has lately appeared for a production car...The new Willys-Knight 66B series was noteworthy for its high degree of originality and the pleasing effects obtained exteriorly with the use of line and proportion and in the interior with the restrained use of a modernistic motif..."

"The interior of these closed models were pleasing examples of the application of modernistic treatment in keep-

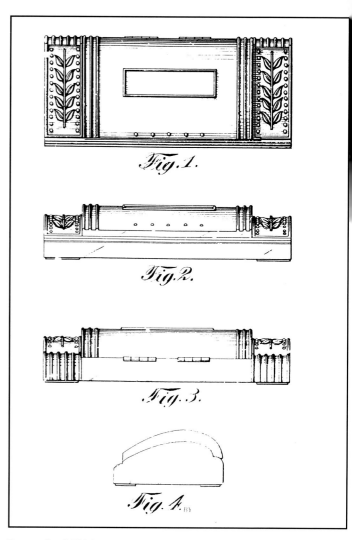

Eugene Lux' 1936 design of a watchcase (D100,869, awarded Aug. 18, 1936). Lux designed cases for both Gruen and Bulova watches.

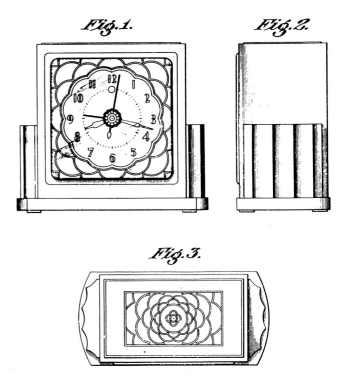

Amos Northup's only clock design was the "Lumalarm" (No. 7F58). (D97,204, awarded Oct. 15, 1935)

ing with our machine age. The elaborate and complicated forms of the Gothic and Renaissance periods are omitted, and the simpler straight-line motifs of the present are employed."

When it was introduced in late 1930 as a 1931 model, *Automobile Industries* described the Reo Royale as "the most radical departure in lines that has been made in some time." Another leading publication of the time wrote that "Reo…commissioned [Northup] to begin at the beginning and design a car not out of the past but into the future." Walter Robinson explained this departure in a 1978 issue of *Special-Interest Autos*:

> "The Royale led the styling revolution that totally changed the shapes of cars during the 1930s….This handsomest of Reos had a consistency of design, a harmony, a unified dignity, and the look of substantiality that no other car had captured before. Before the Royale, form had followed function in its simplest terms. In other words, a car's hood had been a little metal house to keep rain and snow off the engine. Fenders were curved sheets of steel to keep splatter off the main body section. The body itself was another wood-and-metal house to contain the passengers. The gas tank looked like a modified barrel. The radiator stood up front, sometimes with a partial cover but usually with its tubes, fins, or honeycombs exposed."

In a stunning departure from the past, Northup and his assistant, Julio Andrade (later an assistant to Harley Earl at General Motors), designed a streamlined car with "vee" grille shell, upswept fenders, and "duck-tailed" rear end. Although the Royale was not "streamlined" in the same manner currently used by automakers, wind tunnel tests were used to identify ways to reduce wind resistance. These tests led to the elimination of the external visor, the rounding of the fenders, and the concealment of the radiator cap under the hood.

Northup's next design, the 1932 Graham Blue Streak would also be a style setter. While using many of the styling innovations introduced in the Reo Royale, such as the "vee" grille, the Blue Streak introduced the "skirted fender" a design innovation quickly copied by Ford, Chevrolet, Nash, Terraplane, and others.

Northup was awarded numerous design and mechanical patents for his work with the Murray Corporation. His career came to a tragic end around 1937 when he slipped on an icy sidewalk in front of his Pleasant Ridge, Michigan home and cracked his skull.

Although most of his work was in automotive design, he was awarded a design patent for a washing machine assigned to the Bendix Corporation and a design patent for a clock—the "Lumalarm" (7F58)—assigned to General Electric.

Reo is short for Ransom E. Olds, the founder
of both Reo and Oldsmobile.

Amos Northup on the Future of Automotive Design

In a paper presented before the Society of Automotive Engineers in New York on November 15, 1928, Amos Northup predicted the future direction of motor car design. Among his predictions was the switch to front wheel drive, introduced by E. L. Cord about a year later, but largely ignored in this country until Oldsmobile brought it back in the 1970s Toronado.

Northup also saw the need to update the interiors of automobiles, noting that it was hard to tell the difference between the interior of 1918 and 1928 automobiles. He called for the application of modern art, with its straight lines and planes, to automobile interiors, urging designers to apply modern design to all aspects of automobile interiors without waiting for the public to demand such change.

Finally, Northup called for a unified design concept for the automobile similar to that used by architects in the design of skyscrapers.

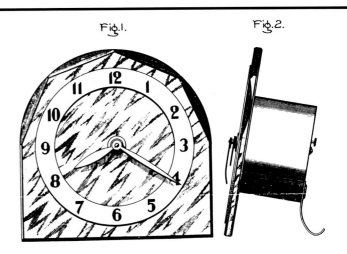

John Rainbault's designs included the "Blue Night" series of mirrored glass clocks. (D104,046, awarded Apr. 13, 1937)

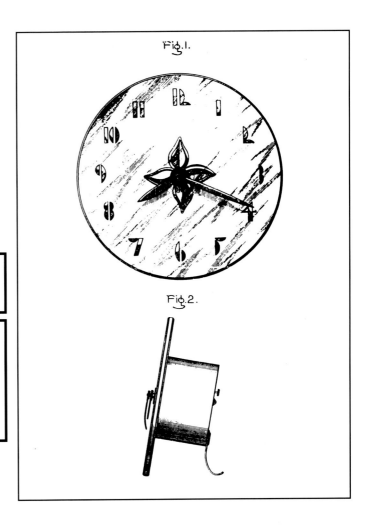

John Rainbault designed the "Mirage" (No. 5F58). (D104,049, awarded Apr. 13, 1937)

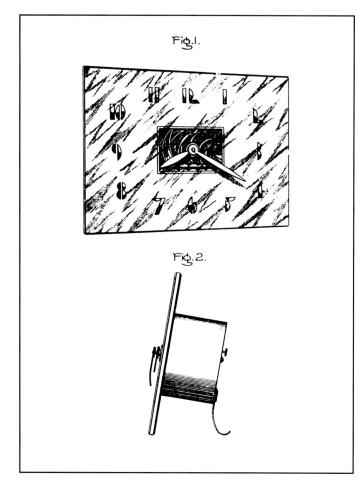

John Rainbault also designed the dial used on the "Soiree" (No. 5F56) and "Salon" (No. 5F54). (D-105,714, awarded Aug. 17, 1937)

The stunning design of the 5F50 "Mirage" has been attributed to Rockwell Kent, Russel Wright, and Walter Dorwin Teague among others, but the design patent was awarded to John Rainbault. (D104,048, awarded Apr. 13, 1937)

Raymond E. Patten

Raymond Patten is one of the most under appreciated industrial designers of the art deco period. He began his career in the late 1920s with the Edison General Electric Company in Chicago, living at the time in Oak Park, Illinois. His early designs included a number of small household appliances such as coffeepots and waffle irons. He also designed a number of stove clock/timers, including the stunning Model TM-8, a true design classic and perhaps the most collectible stove timer ever produced.

After becoming the head of design for General Electric, Patten relocated to company offices in Bridgeport, Connecticut. He continued to design many of General Electric's products ranging from simple control knobs and escutcheon plates for radios to locomotives, from coffeepots to washing machines and refrigerators, and from industrial timers to alarm clocks.

Patten's designs are always among the best in their field. His 1931 toaster design with a leaping gazelle is arguably the most beautiful toaster ever produced and sells for upwards of $400-$600. Similarly, his 1937 design for a coffee urn compares favorably to designs by Jay Ackerman for Manning Bowman and Alphonso Iannelli for Sunbeam. Finally, his clock designs compare very favorably to the rather bland and unimaginative designs Walter Dorwin Teague developed for Telechron and General Electric.

Patten's clock designs include the "Chef" (2F04), "Kitchen Hostess" (2F06), "Vogue" (3F56), "Lotus" (4F58), "Dictator" (4F60), "Vedette" (7F56), and "Select-O-Switch" (8F50).

Patten's final design work was also his biggest project—the design of a locomotive body.

John P. Rainbault

John Rainbault was the leading designer of General Electric clocks in the 1930s yet little is known about him. U.S. Patent Office records show that he lived in New York City in the early 1930s but by 1940 had moved to Bridgeport, Connecticut. He received 22 clock design patents between 1933 and 1941, all of which were assigned to General Electric. Thus, it appears likely that he was a staff designer working for Ray Patten. There are currently no Rainbault's listed in U.S. telephone directories and no Social Security records of a John Rainbault. Nor was John Rainbault among the World War II casualties from either New York or Connecticut.

Some of Rainbault's designs are so extraordinary that the clocks are typically "attributed to" Russel Wright, Walter Dorwin Teague, Gilbert Rohde, or Rockwell Kent. These clocks include the "Mirage" (5F50), "Mirage" (5F52), "Salon" (5F54), and "Soiree" (5F56). Although the designs of the "Alencon" (6B02), "Circe" (7H92) and "Breton" (4H72) were not patented, the numerals and central motif are clearly Rainbault designs. Similarly, Rainbault designed the "Blue Night" series (4F62, 4F64, and 4F66).

As a staff designer, Rainbault was likely involved in the design of many other General Electric clocks that were not patented. For example, he was awarded a design patent for the 7F74 "Heralder" but not the 7F72 "Heralder" with the same case design but with a different base and dial. The dial design on the 7F72, however, appears to be based on an earlier Rainbault design. While Rainbault appears to be the most likely designer, a definitive determination cannot be made without substantiating evidence.

Kurt Rettich

Kurt Rettich (1885-1964) of Toledo, Ohio, was a prolific designer who counted among his designs the "Duke" (3F51), his only clock design. Like George Graff, Rettich's early work was for the Dura Corporation, a leading supplier to the automobile industry. His work for Dura, however, appears to have been limited to consumer products, namely bottle cap removers. Rettich quickly moved on to design work for the Reynolds Spring Metal Company of Jackson, Michigan. Between 1932 and 1933, he designed a number of novelty bar accessories, ashtrays, cigarette boxes, and picture frames for Reynolds. It was during this period that he also designed the "Duke," assigning the patent rights to the Warren Telechron Company.

Rettich appears to have spent the rest of his career designing art moderne cabinet and appliance hardware for the Keeler Brass Company of Grand Rapids, Michigan. With the exception of an inkwell designed in 1937 for the Terry Penfiller Company of Janesville, Michigan, all of Rettich's design patents after 1934 were assigned to Keeler Brass. His final design patent, for a stove handle, was awarded in 1950.

Walter Dorwin Teague, Sr.

Walter Dorwin Teague, Sr. (1883-1960) was one of America's most influential industrial designers. Teague studied at New York's Art Students' League and began his career with the New York advertising agency, Calkins and Holden in 1908. Three years later, he opened his own studio. In addition to advertising campaigns for Phoenix Hosiery and Community Plate, the firm was involved in book designs. The firm soon expanded its focus and Teague designed piano cases for Steinway and packaging for a variety of consumer products.

Teague's big break came, however, when he landed a contract to design cameras for Eastman Kodak in the late 1920s. His firm's association with Kodak would continue for more than 30 years. Despite his relationship with Kodak, however, Teague also designed the Polaroid Land Camera.

Teague's designs during the 1930s included the 1930 Marmon automobile, the 1936 *Baby Brownie* camera, Texaco service stations, vases and bowls for Corning Glassworks' Steuben Division, and a Ford Showroom in New York. Five of Teague's designs for Steuben were included in the Museum of Modern Art's 1934 Exhibit *Machine Art*. His designs also included Pullman coaches for the New Haven Railroad and the 1952 Scripto ball-point pen.

In 1937-38 Teague was awarded design patents for seven clocks. Although rights to all of the patents were assigned to the Warren Telechron Company, one of the designs, for the "New Executive" (8B04) was produced as a General Electric model. The other Teague designs include the "Baron" (8B07), "Tribute" (8B09), "Organizer" (8B53), "Explorer" (8F03), "Clarion" (7F03), and "Meadowlark" (7F73). Teague's clock designs, other than the "New Executive," are not among the firm's most creative work and Teague-designed Telechron's do not generally attract a premium price. Instead, it is the innovative designs of Raymond Patten and John Rainbault—often incorrectly credited to Teague or Rockwell Kent—which are among the most collectible General Electric and Telechron models.

It should be kept in mind too that Walter Dorwin Teague was not personally involved in all of the designs that bear his name. For example, his son, Walter Dorwin Teague, Jr. later claimed that it was he, rather than his father, who designed the Marmon 16. Teague, Jr.'s claim should be viewed with some skepticism, however, as he was just beginning his studies at the Massachusetts Institute of Technology when the Marmon 16 was designed.

Findley Williams

Findley Williams (1906-1992) had a distinguished design career that included work for the Warren Telechron Company, Fostoria Glass Company, and the Bissell Carpet Sweeper Company. His earliest design credits are for candlesticks, bowls, dishes, a cocktail shaker top, and a centerpiece for Fostoria from 1935-37. Beginning in 1937, Williams designed a series of carpet sweepers for Bissell, continuing his association with Bissell until 1940. It was during this period that he designed the "Stewardess" (2H09)

and "Kendall" (4H95) for Telechron. The "Stewardess" is one of the most collectible kitchen clocks because of its distinctive styling. Williams also designed store displays for W. L. Stensgaard & Associates during this period. Near the end of World War II, Williams designed a series of "kiddie" cars in the shape of military vehicles.

In addition to his design work, Findley Williams was awarded a mechanical patent in 1940 for a pebbled surface developed to reflect and diffuse light. Patent rights were assigned to the Certain-teed Products Corporation of New York. His invention appears to be a form of suspended acoustic ceiling that took America by storm after World War II.

Russel Wright

Although Russel Wright (1904-1976) was one of the most prominent designers of the art deco period, his first and only known design for General Electric was the 1954 "Ceramic" (No. 2H48) kitchen clock, designed near the end of his career. Wright began his career in the mid 1920s, working as a set designer for Norman Bel Geddes. His first entry into the decorative arts occurred in 1927 when he began making miniature versions of his stage sets.

Like Bel Geddes, Wright soon moved away from set design and, by 1930, was designing and producing giftware items in spun aluminum. Having established his own workshop in New York, Wright began producing a wide range of metalwork, including sterling silver flatware. His early design efforts drew heavily on the work of European designers such as Jean Puiforcat and Josef Hoffman.

Russel Wright was one of the first of the new breed of "industrial designers" to have his name mentioned in advertisements for giftware items. Among his early work were designs for chromium giftware for the Chase Brass and Copper Company of Waterbury, Connecticut. His 13 designs, including the Pancake and Corn Set (No. 28003), are among the most collectible Chase items. One of Wright's designs, a set of wood salad and berry bowls, was included in the 1934 Museum of Modern Art Exhibit *Machine Art*.

Wright's other designs include a 60 piece collection of Heywood Wakefield furniture (1934), Conant Ball's *Modern Living* furniture line (1935), Steubenville Pottery's *American Modern* dinnerware (1939), Iroquois' *Casual China* (1946), Stratton's Easier Living furniture (1950), Samsonite™ furniture (1950s), Melmac™ dinnerware (1946), and glassware for Century Metalcraft and others.

After the mid 1950s, Wright put his design talents to work for both the U. S. State Department and the National Park Service. As a consultant to the State Department, Wright developed ideas for cottage industries in Southeast Asia and designed more than 100 products to be manufactured in Japan. After abandoning most of his design activities in 1967, Wright consulted with the National Park Service on programming and planning.

Other Designers

Rudolph M. Babel (1924-1976) of Providence, Rhode Island, was awarded five clock design patents between 1951 and 1955, all of which were assigned to the General Electric Company. His designs include the "Butler" (2H41), "Panorama" (5H71), "Dorm" (7H211), "Guest" (7H169), and "Tribute" (7H179). General Electric did not obtain any clock design patents in 1956 or 1957 and it is not clear whether Babel continued to design clocks after 1955.

Robert O. Fletcher of Ashland, Massachusetts was awarded five clock design patents in 1955, four of which entered production. Fletcher designed the "Swirl" (2H45), "Telecrat" (7H217), "Turnabout" (7H221), and "Illumitime" (5H69). I found no record

Errol W. Goff designed the Tudor (No. 356). (D-82,424, awarded Nov. 4, 1930)

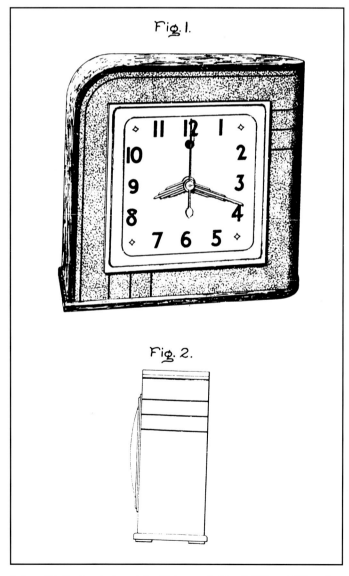

Fig. 1.

Fig. 2.

Robert W. Goulet designed the "Advocate" (No. 3H77) and "Guest" (No. 7H89). (D115,620, awarded July 11, 1939)

of Fletcher's fifth design, a recessed kitchen wall clock, having entered production. General Electric did not obtain any clock design patents in 1956 or 1957 and is not clear whether or for how long Fletcher continued to work for General Electric.

Eroll Goff (1903-1974) of Everett, Massachusetts, was awarded a design patent for the "Tudor" (No. 356) but he received no other design or mechanical patents for clocks or other items.

Robert Goulet of Providence, Rhode Island, was awarded a design patent for the 1939-41 "Advocate" (3H77) and its alarm counterpart the "Guest" (7H89), but received no other design or mechanical patents.

Frank W. Green of Framingham, Massachusetts was awarded two design patents, both of which were assigned to the Warren Telechron Company. He designed the 1936 "Usher" (CF363) and its corresponding alarm versions, the "Constable" and "Sheriff" (CF769), and the 1937 "Butler" (7H79). With slight modification, primarily a new pair of legs, the "Butler" became the "Supervisor" and "Warden" (7H107) and the "Dispatcher" (7H125). The silent versions were the "Domino" (3H73 and CH373) and "Croft" (3H79). Quite a bit of mileage out of two basic designs.

Harriet Heile of Chicago, Illinois, designed the "Daphne" (3F53), her only clock design. Her only other design patent was for a cake box, but she was awarded mechanical patents for a light fixture and a shirt pocket.

Philip Frederick Huy of Framingham Centre was credited with the co-design (with Leo Ivan Bruce) of the "Telechoice" (2H47) and "Motif" (2H49) but has no other design credits.

George Kraber (1912-1983) was awarded design patents for three clocks, all of which were assigned to the Warren Telechron Company. None of his designs appear to have entered production. Kraber, who lived in Newtonville, Massachusetts, at the time his clock designs were patented, held no other design patents. He died in November 1983 in Escondido, California.

Norman F. Lockwood (1911-1987) of Providence, Rhode Island, designed the 1940 Special Campaign Model CH797, but has no other design credits. At the time of death, Lockwood resided in Hyannis, Massachusetts.

George Long of Boston, Massachusetts, was awarded four clock design patents, but only two appear to have reached pro-

Norman F. Lockwood designed the Special Campaign Model CH797. (D122,316, awarded Sept. 3, 1940)

duction—his designs for the 1932-34 "Autolarm" (7B01 & 7B02) and 1930-32 "Nottingham." Appendix 3 shows two other clocks designed by Long that do not appear to have reached production. Long holds no other design or mechanical patents.

John Nickelsen of New York was awarded two clock design patents in 1934, both of which were assigned to the Warren Telechron Company. He designed the slow selling 1934-35 "Commonwealth" (3F01) and the more popular "Squarart" (3F59) and "Squarlarm" (7F59). Although it did not sell very well, the "Commonwealth" is a very attractive design with its stepped base and chrome trim. No other patents were awarded to John Nickelsen although there were a series of automobile-related patents awarded to a John M. Nickelsen of Ann Arbor, Michigan. What relationship, if any, exists between the two John Nickelsens is unknown.

Carl Otto designed the 1951-55 "Tiara" (7H185) and "Enhancer" (7H203) but has no other design credits.

Francis W. Pike of Chicago, Illinois was awarded only one patent, D89790 for the 1932-35 "Petite" (3F52).

Shepard Pond of Winchester, Massachusetts designed the 1931-33 "Bristol" (No. 326) and the 1934-38 "Secretary" (3F58) but holds no other design patents. The two clocks have similar designs.

Harry C. Richardson (1899-1968) was awarded four clock design patents between 1931 and 1932 and another in 1941. His early designs included the "Apollo" and "Diana," which were heavily promoted in the Telechronicle, being pictured with a wide range of film stars. His other design credits include the 1930-32 "Waverly" (No. 605), the "Surrey" (Nos. 528 & 528A), the "Colonist" (4F53), and the "Knickerbocker" (4H99). Little else is known about Richardson's design career, but he resurfaced briefly in 1948 with mechanical patents for bus seats and windows. The patents were assigned to the Troy Sunshade Company of Troy, Ohio. Richardson lived in Troy at the time of his death in 1968.

John G. Wemple was awarded two design patents for combination clock/thermometer/thermostats and one mechanical patent for a safety control device. All three patents were assigned to General Electric.

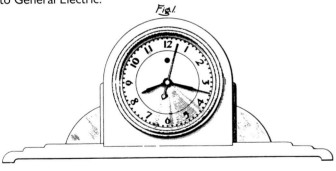

John Nickelsen's design credits include the "Commonwealth" (No. 3F01). (D92,551, awarded June 19, 1934)

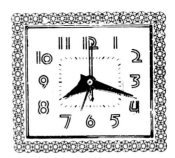

Carl Otto was awarded a design patent for the 1951-55 "Tiara," his only patent. (D164,594, awarded Sept. 18, 1951)

Francis W. Pike designed the elegant "Petite" (No. 3F52). (D89,790, awarded May 2, 1933)

Chapter 6

Deciphering Model Numbers

Although Telechron and General Electric model numbers appear at first glance to be a confusing combination of numbers and letters with no real meaning, they actually tell quite a bit about the clock. Although the following attempts to explain the numbering logic, keep in mind that there are exceptions to every rule, particularly after General Electric assumed control of the company in 1943 and began using model numbers skipped during the 1930s.

Model Numbers on Early Clocks

Early Telechron and General Electric clocks generally had simple three or four digit numeric model numbers. Even these numbers, however, had some meaning. For example, if an "AB" appeared before the model number, then it was a General Electric clock. Many early models were available as both General Electric and Telechron models, particularly around 1931 when the General Electric line was added. A number of clocks that had previously been marketed as Telechron clocks suddenly became General Electric clocks. Although the limited models available in the 1925 catalog were generally numbered sequentially from 101, when a clock was offered in multiple sizes, the last digit would remain the same but the first digit would increase. For example, larger sizes of the Model 101 "Wall Telechron" were numbered 201, 301, and 401.

By 1930, however, the first number had started to take on a new meaning. Models that began with a "3" had a 3 inch dial, those that began with "4" a 4 inch dial, and so on. That worked fine until they got to "7" which designated that the model was an alarm clock.

The other confusion was added by the "R" that appeared before some models. The "R" indicated that the Revere Clock Company made the case and that the clock had a chime movement. Typically, these clocks are General Electric models but Revere marketed some of the same models with Revere dials. All of them should note on the dial that they are "Telechron-motored."

The three digit model numbers are often engraved in the bottom of the wood cases with no further identification.

The Massachusetts Connection

In naming its clocks, Telechron drew heavily from Massachusetts communities and history. In addition to such obvious names as Colonist, Commonwealth, Pilgrim, Puritan, and Minitman, clocks were named after more than 30 Massachusetts towns. These include: Adams, Amherst, Auburn, Belmont, Beverly, Bristol, Burlington, Clinton, Concord, Dorchester, Framingham, Gloucester, Grafton, Hanover, Harwich, Haverhill, Huntington, Manchester, Maynard, Norfolk, Norwood, Oxford, Plymouth, Quincy, Sheffield, Somerset, Sudbury (also the river that flows through Ashland), Wareham, Wellfleet, Winchester, and Winthrop. Although Ashland never received its own clock, several Ashland streets, including Alden, Ballard, Highland, and Waverly, became clock names as did the county in which Ashland is located—

Middlesex. Other clocks with a Massachusetts connection include the Copley, Controlla, Nantucket, Miles Standish, and Hampshire.

The Massachusetts influence carried through to Telechron-motored Revere clocks with models like the Cambridge, Concord, Dawes, Dorchester, Haverhill, Lynn, Middlesex, Plymouth, Puritan, Roxbury, Winthrop, and Worcester, not to mention the name of the company itself.

The 1930s-1950s Numbering Scheme

Model numbers appear to get much more complex around 1933, but they are actually straightforward. Every number and letter in the model number, say AB2F02, has a meaning. If your model number begins with a "C," it is a Special Campaign and Promotional Model that will be discussed later.

Prefixes—AB2H02

If the model number is preceded by the letters "AB," then the dial should identify the clock as a General Electric Telechron. Later in the 1930s and throughout the 1940s, "Telechron" was dropped from the dial, the "AB" dropped from the model number, and the clocks became simply "General Electric." A few models were also sold with the prefix "ABR." These clocks have a "General Electric" dial, a Revere case and chime movement, and a Telechron motor. General Electric tall case clocks were also made by Revere/Herschede Hall but had Telechron movements.

First Number—AB2H02

The first number describes the type of clock
- 1—Commercial models
- 2—Kitchen and other wall clocks
- 3—3 inch dial shelf clock
- 4—4 inch dial shelf clock
- 5—5 inch dial shelf clock
- 6—strike clock
- 7—alarm clock
- 8—cyclometer, day/date, and novelty clocks

Although "6" is generally reserved for strike clocks, there are two exceptions—the No. 6H02 "Alencon" and the No. 6H50 "Jason."

Letter—AB2H02

The letter appearing in the middle of the model number designates the type of rotor used in the clock:
- A—clocks with an auxiliary movement
- F—F rotor
- H—H rotor
- B—B rotor
- S—S rotor

Second Letter—7HA141

When a second letter appears in the model number, it typically designates a slightly restyled model, most likely a new dial. Letters for redesigned dials are assigned sequentially.

General Electric also used an **"X"** in the second position of some models. The meaning of this designation is not clear, but it may refer either to a special campaign model or a model produced to be sold under a store brand such as Montgomery Ward.

Final Numbers—AB2H02

The final two to three digit number is the unique identifier assigned to the clock. For the most part, odd numbers were assigned to Telechron models and even numbers to General Electric models. Similarly, the numbers were normally assigned sequentially as new models were introduced. Model numbers were, however, frequently skipped to keep the two brands in synch. This posed no problem until General Electric began using the skipped numbers for models introduced in the 1950s. For example, they used 7H04 as the model number for the "Repeater" when it was introduced in 1950 even though the low model number suggests it was introduced in the mid 1930s.

There are also instances where a series is divided to differentiate between two types of clocks. For example, cyclometer, day/date, and novelty clocks have model numbers between 01 and 49 while model numbers for timers begin at 50.

Suffix—7H107K

Although most model numbers do not include a suffix, the following should help explain what they mean:

K—Illuminated by a small incandescent light

L—Luminous features

While "K" and "L" are the primary suffixes used, some model numbers may include an abbreviation for the color of the case or type of wood used.

Special Campaign Models

Models that begin with CF or CH are special campaign or promotional models produced for only a short time. Such model numbers are not that different from the normal model numbers except that they begin with "C" and have the rotor designation "F" or "H" placed before rather than after the first number. For example, CF705 is really the same as 7F05 in the ordering of model numbers.

The Telechron Rotors

"B" Rotors were used primarily from 1917 to 1942, but continued to be used in specialty timers and large clocks after World War II. These rotors are easily distinguished from other rotors by their large size and symmetry. They turned clockwise at one RPM. The "B" rotor had to rotate at one revolution per minute because the sweep second hand on virtually all "B" rotor clocks plugged directly into the end of the "B" rotor. A specially geared version of the "B" rotor was the power behind Revere chime clocks.

The **"F" Rotor**, developed in 1932, was a giant step forward for two reasons: First, clocks, especially wall models, could be designed with much thinner cases than with the longer "B" rotor. Second (and more important if you are a clocksmith), an "F" rotor could be changed in as little as five minutes, by removing only four screws. In contrast, taking a "B" rotor out that way results in the second had popping off and falling down between the dial and crystal. The quick motor change with an "F" rotor clock was therefore a real boon. However, the "F" rotor was short-lived as General Electric's engineers saw plenty of room for improvement.

"H" Rotors were exact replacements for the heavy, pot metal "F" rotor, but were made of cheaper, lighter stamped sheet metal (either copper or steel). "H" rotors were the standard power plant for General Electric and Telechron clocks for 20 years from the mid-1930s into the mid-1950s. The "H" rotor, each one hand built, powered a hundred million clocks, clock radios, and appliances.

In 1954, General Electric introduced the **"S" Rotor**, a small, machine-made aluminum rotor. Filled with grease and much lighter than the "H" rotor, they were not nearly as dependable as the "B", "F," and "H" rotors. The development of the "S" rotor was strictly a cost saving measure. Beginning with the "Helper" (No. 2H38S), the first S rotors began to tentatively creep into use. The "S" designation in the model number, which had previously been used to mean that the numerals on the dial were arranged in a square, now referred to the type of rotor used. General Electric was so concerned about the reliability of the new "S" rotor that it instructed repairmen to retrofit the "S" rotor and field coil assembly with one for an "H" rotor in case of motor failure. General Electric clearly ushered in the era of disposable clocks with the "S" rotor. Unlike the "H" rotor that could easily be replaced by removing a couple of screws, the "S" rotor was riveted in place, making repair or replacement extremely difficult. "S" rotors continued to be made in Ashland until 1992, long after the last electric clocks were discontinued.

Chapter 7

Models Introduced Before 1932

Wall Models

Cover to circa 1930 Telechron clock catalog.

Above: Cover to the December 1929 *Telechronicle* featuring Father Time and the new "Electrolarm."

Right: The case for the 1925-28 **Model 103** "Walton," initially known simply as a "Wall Telechron," ($30.00), 5-5/8" x 5-5/8" x 3-1/2", has a statuary bronze finish. The 5 inch dial is etched silver and the movement is the No. 61 Indicator. (876 sold)

The Telechron **Model 457** kitchen wall clock is pictured in this June 11, 1932, *Saturday Evening Post* advertisement. Also pictured is the "Telalarm" (Model 711).

The "Wood Case Telechron," also known simply as the "Wall Telechron," was available in four sizes and three finishes--quartered oak, mahogany, and white enamel.

The **Model 101** ($34.00), 11" x 11" x 4-1/2", has an 8 inch diameter dial; the **Model 201** ($36.00), 16" x 16" x 4-1/2", a 12 inch dial and the **Model 301** ($42.00), 19" x 19" x 4-1/2", a 14 inch dial.

Models 101, 201, and 301 were available with choice of the No. 31 Indicator or No. 71 Auxiliary movement. They were also available with a sweep second hand (Movement No. 21). The largest in the series, the **Model 401** ($50.00), 23" x 23" x 23", has an 18 inch dial and came only with the No. 32 movement.

Introduced in 1918, the Wood Case Telechron was still in production in 1928. Clocks manufactured before 1926 should have a "Warren Clock Co." dial while later versions say merely "Telechron" or have both "Telechron" and "Warren Telechron Co." on the dial. Early versions also have the electrical cord coming out of the top of the case and a screw in connector to fit in a light socket. *Courtesy of Ashland Historical Society.*

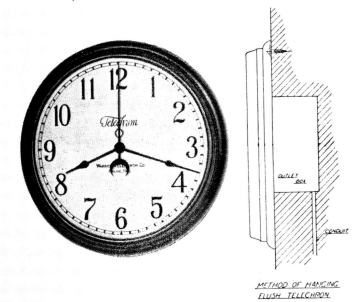

METHOD OF HANGING
FLUSH TELECHRON

The five models comprising the circa 1928 "Semi-Flush Telechron" (**Models 415** (8 inch dial), **416** (12 inch dial), **417** (14 inch dial), **418** (18 inch dial), and **420** (24 inch dial) have a statuary bronze finish and have a case that is recessed into the wall. Prices in 1928 ranged from $34.00 for the 8 inch model to $112.50 for the 24 inch model.

The 15 inch diameter **Model 403** "Wall Telechron" was available with either copper or brass case.

The 1925-30 Telechron **Model 452** "Copley" ($16.00), 6" x 6" x 3-1/4", has a cast bronze case and dial with "Verde antique" finish. It came with the No. 31 Indicator movement. (1,881 sold). *Courtesy of Esther Cooperman.*

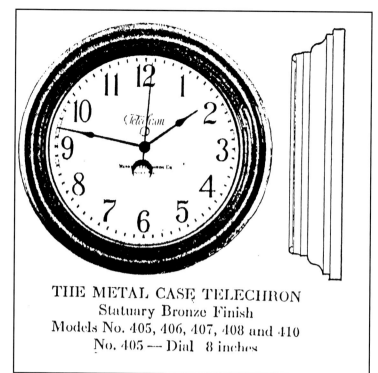

THE METAL CASE TELECHRON
Statuary Bronze Finish
Models No. 405, 406, 407, 408 and 410
No. 405 — Dial 8 inches

The five models of the circa 1928 "Metal Case Telechron" (**Models 405** (8 inch dial), **406** (12 inch dial), **407** (14 inch dial), **408** (18 inch dial), and **410** (24 inch dial)) have a statuary bronze finish case. Retail prices in 1928 ranged from $34.00 to $112.50.

The 1928-31 Telechron **Model 453** "Constance" ($17.00), 8-1/8" x 8-1/8" x 3", has a molded plastic case lacquered in choice of white, ivory, pastel green, or French gray. Selling for $17.00 before the market crash, the price was cut to $10.00 in January 1930. (62,097 sold) Put the "Constance" in an unpainted mottled walnut Bakelite case, and it becomes the 1929-31 **Model 453A** "Denmore" ($17.00). (10,449 sold). *Courtesy of Ashland Historical Society.*

The 1930-32 General Electric Telechron "Hostess" (**Models 454** and **AB454**, $9.75), 7-1/2" x 7-1/2" x 3-3/32", has a Beetle™ case in choice of white, pastel green, ivory, orange, yellow, or black. The sales literature notes that "The case is 'beetle' a processed composition in which the color is moulded, rendering it color-fast and immune to soap and water washings. The case is fireproof and will not warp by the application of water. Beetle is the only processed substance that has been found to date in which a depth of color may be obtained that is as good as marble, onyx, turquoise or other similar natural materials." (109,625 sold)

The "Hostess" was one of a number of Telechron models that were transferred to General Electric around 1932. Another 87,778 of the GE/Telechron variation were sold. Variations of the model, designed by Edgar Bourquin, would remain in the General Electric line for over 20 years. *Courtesy of Jay Kennan.*

The 1932-34 Telechron Special Campaign **Model 457** kitchen clock ($5.50), 7-1/2" x 7-1/2" x 3", has a cast "dura" alloy case finished in light green, light blue, ivory, or white enamel. It has a chrome-plated bezel. The "457" has the same basic case design as Models 257 and 2B01. (23,945 sold)

In this October 1930 advertisement in *Vanity Fair*, the "Hostess" is pictured as Model 452. No evidence was identified to confirm that it was also offered under that model number and it was probably a typographical error. Also pictured in the ad are Models 357 and 557.

Above: The 1932-34 General Electric Telechron **Model AB 458** ($5.50), 7-9/16" diameter, has a "Durametal" case finished in choice of green, blue, ivory, or white enamel. The 4-1/2" dial is cream enamel. (15,704 sold). In 1933-34, a Telechron version (**Model 458**, $3.95), was offered. (4,408 sold)

Right: The 1930-32 Telechron **Model 528A** "Surrey Wall Model" ($33), 15-5/16" x 8-7/16" x 4-3/4". The ad copy reads "Interior decorators suggested the 'Surrey' as an innovation in the clock field. A constant search by decorators has revealed very few things left to put on the walls of new homes and Telechron has really donated a fine piece of wall furniture in this model." (613 sold)

Shelf and Mantel Clocks

Cover to the October 1931 *Telechronicle*, the "Post-Depression Issue!"

The case for the 1923-28 **Model 102** "Executive," initially known simply as a "Mantel Telechron," ($30.00), 5-5/8" x 5-5/8" x 3-1/2", has a statuary bronze finish. "For the desk in office or den, this model of masculinity is particularly designed," reads the 1928 catalog copy. The 5 inch dial is etched silver. It came only with the No. 61 Indicator movement. (775 sold)

Above: The 1926-29 **Model 322** "Vanity," 5-3/4" x 5-3/8" x 4-1/4", was described in the 1926 catalog as a "Desk or Boudoir Telechron." It has a mahogany case and 3-1/2" dial with silver finish. The movement is the No. 31 Indicator. (6,286 sold)

Right: The 1928-30 Telechron **Model 323** "Petite" ($22.00), 6-1/4" x 5-1/2" x 4-1/4", has a wood case finished in choice of ivory, Chinese red, or apple green lacquer. It has a 3 inch silvered dial. (3,693 sold)

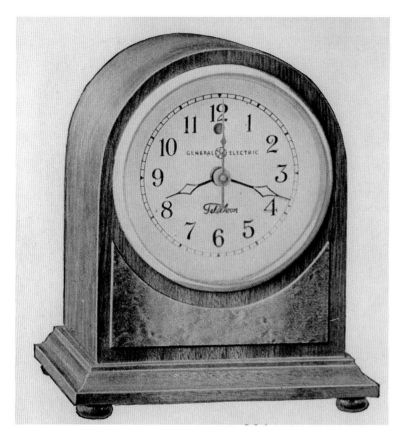

The 1930-32 Telechron **Model 325** "Copley" ($11.00), 6-3/8" x 5-3/4" x 3-3/8", has a wood case with mahogany finish and a 3-1/2" gold finish dial. (6,642 sold)

The 1930-31 General Electric Telechron **Model 324** "Victoria" ($16.00), 6-1/8" x 5-1/2" x 4-1/4", has a two-tone mahogany finish case with Spanish high lighted panel of burl maple. It has a 3 inch silvered dial with Arabic numerals. (1,689 sold). *Courtesy of Esther Cooperman.*

The 1931-35 Telechron **Model 327** "Salisbury" ($9.75), also known as the "Sudbury," 7-1/4" x 5-21/32" x 3-3/16", is a cathedral style clock with a mahogany finish case Spanish highlighted with a Satinwood panel. It has a 3-1/2" gold finish dial. Add an alarm and ivory enamel dial and the "Salisbury" becomes the "Alden" (No. 727, $12.50). (11,016 combined sales). *Courtesy of Esther Cooperman.*

The 1931-33 Telechron **Model 326** "Bristol" ($11.00), also known as the "Bruce," 5-1/2" x 5-1/4" x 3", has a mahogany finish case, Spanish highlighted with four tone inlay border. It has a 3-1/2" gold finish dial. Designed by Shepard Pond. (10,105 sold)

Above: The 1932-33 Telechron Special Campaign **Model 329** "Colony" ($5.95) has a wooden case.

Left: The 1931-33 General Electric Telechron **Model AB328** ($7.50), 7-1/8" X 5-5/8" X 3", has a wood case with decorative inlay and cathedral styling. (10,219 sold). *Courtesy of Jay Kennan.*

The 1926-28 Telechron **Model 331** "Plymouth" ($19.00), 5-1/8" x 13-1/4" x 3-1/8", is a "Tambour Mantel" Telechron with mahogany finished case and 3-1/2" silver finish dial. The movement is the No. 31 Indicator. (8,039 sold). *Courtesy of Jay Kennan.*

The General Electric Telechron **Model AB 330** ($5.95), 5" x 4-3/8" x 3-1/4", has a Colonial-style wood case with Spanish highlighted mahogany-finish, gold finish trimmings, and 3 inch ivory finish dial.

This 1926 catalog photograph of the **Model 331**, then known simply as the "Tambour Model" Telechron, has different hands and a gold sweep second hand.

The 1928-31 Telechron **Model 332** "Duncan" ($22.00), 5-1/4" x 13-1/8" x 4", has a Spanish highlighted, mahogany finished, case with a 3 inch silvered dial. (8,184 sold)

The 1928-31 Telechron **Model 333** "Beverly" ($20.00-$25.00), 5-1/4" x 13-1/8" x 4", has a mahogany finish wood case with two-tone Spanish highlighting. The 3 inch dial is silver. (9,005 sold). *Courtesy of Jay Kennan.*

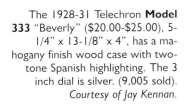

The 1930-33 Telechron **Model 335** and General Electric Telechron **Model AB335** "Englewood" ($12.50), 5-1/4" x 13" x 3-1/4", has a mahogany finish case with Spanish highlighted panels. The 3-1/2" dial has a gold finish. (6,660 sold). *Courtesy of Jay Kennan.*

Above: The 1930-32 Telechron **Model 334** "Jeffrey" ($18.00), 5-7/8" x 10-7/16" x 3-3/16", has a mahogany finish, Spanish highlighted, case with 3-1/2" gold finish dial. (3,409 sold)

Right: The 1930-33 Telechron **Model 336** "Trenton" ($12.50), 5-1/4" x 13" x 3-7/32", has a mahogany finish wood case, Spanish highlighted with Satinwood panels. (5,801 sold)

The 1927-32 Telechron **Model 355** "Cathedral" ($19.00-$25.00), 7-3/16" x 5-5/8" x 3-7/16", has a molded plastic case with mottled brown finish and a 3 inch silvered dial. Originally sold for $25.00, the price dropped to $9.95 after the stock market crash in 1929. (100,074 sold). *Courtesy of Jay Kennan.*

The 1930-33 General Electric/Telechron **Models 357** and **AB357** "Apollo" ($15.00), 7-1/2" x 4-5/8" x 3-5/16", has a black beetle case with chrome plated ornament, bezel, and feet. The 3-1/2" dial is silvered metal with black characters. Introduced in 1930, original sales literature notes that "The 'Apollo' is unique in its field. The design is strictly modern and American in feeling. It has lost the sharp, bizarre lines of the French and German interpretations of modern art and has attained a simplicity which will appeal to the most refined tastes and will adapt itself to most any room in the house." Originally offered only in black, the "Apollo" was later offered in ivory, green, blue, and red beetle cases. These variations are rare and should command significantly higher prices than the more common black case. The "Apollo" was also known as the "Beau." Designed by Harry C. Richardson. (6,588 sold)

The 1930-32 Telechron **Model 356** "Tudor" ($9.75), 6-5/8" x 5-3/8" x 3-5/8", has a moulded "Textolite" plastic case in a mottled walnut finish. The 3" x 3-5/8" dial is lacquered cream. Sales literature notes that "The 'Tudor' design is conventional and is adapted consciously from the English Tudor period. Typical points of its authenticity are shown by the non-pointed arch, which was developed in this era, and the carved ornamentation. A singular feature of the 356 is the fact that the relief carving is deeper than is usually attempted in moulded material." *Courtesy of Jay Kennan.*

In 1931, the Telechron Model 357 "Apollo" was offered with a "LUMITE" illuminated dial as the 1931-33 **Models 358** and **AB358** "Diana" ($18.00). Like the "Apollo," the ivory, green, blue, and red cases are particularly rare and should command significantly higher prices. Designed by Harry C. Richardson. (1,379 sold)

The 1928-32 Telechron **Model 370** "Clinton" ($20.00), 6-1/8" x 5-1/2" x 4-1/4", has a mahogany case with two-tone Spanish highlighted finish. It has a 3-1/2" illuminated gold finish dial. (10,719 sold). Add an etched design to the outer edge of the glass crystal and the "Clinton" becomes the 1929-32 **Model 370A** "Vernon" ($21.00). (14,056 sold). *Courtesy of Jay Kennan.*

The "Vernon" as featured in the May 1930 *House Beautiful*. Also shown is the "Madison" (No. 691).

The 1929-30 Telechron **Model 371** "Auburn" ($23.00), 6-1/8" x 5-1/2" x 4-1/4", has a wood case finished in choice of ivory, Chinese red, or apple green lacquer. A tiny MAZDA bulb illuminates the 3 inch gold finish dial. (2,311 sold)

The 1923-27 Telechron **Model 402** "Mantel Telechron" ($75.00), 6-7/8" x 8" x 4-1/8", has a case finished in choice of (1) a combination of brass and bronze with a Verde antique finish or (2) bronze. The 5 inch dial is etched silver and the movement is the No. 61 Indicator. (140 sold)

The 1928-32 Telechron **Model 431** "Modernique" ($50.00), 7-3/4" x 5-3/4" x 3-3/4", was designed by Paul T. Frankl, best known for his skyscraper furniture designs. The metal case has a brushed silver finish with shaded plane effects, 3-1/2" silvered dial, and highly polished black base. The "Modernique" was also available with a brushed gold finish (**Model 431A**) and a black and purple "Chrome Enameled" finish (**Model 431B**). Although other Telechron designs, most notably the "Electrolarm" (No. 700) have been attributed to Frankl, I found no evidence in either marketing material or US Patent Office records to suggest that Frankl designed any Telechron or General Electric clock other than the "Modernique." (1,570 sold)

Fig.1.

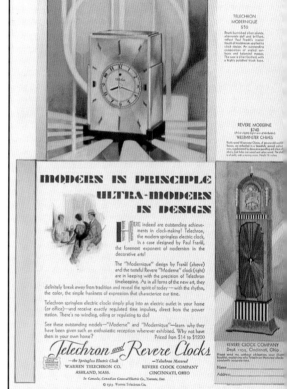

Color drawing of the "Modernique" from a joint Telechron/Revere sales poster.

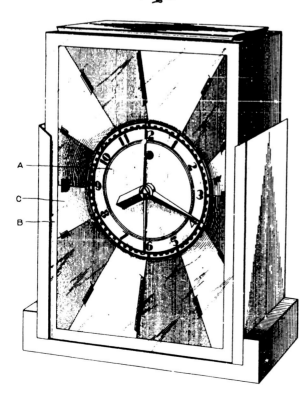

Paul Frankl was awarded the design patent for the "Modernique," his only confirmed clock design. (D82,548, awarded Nov. 18, 1930)

The 1927-30 Telechron **Model 455** "Radio" ($26.00), 7-1/4" x 8" x 4-1/8", has a metal case with "Verde Antique" finish and 5 inch silvered dial. Its design is almost identical to the earlier "Mantel Telechron" (**Model 402**) but has a slightly different base and smaller indicator. (7,670 sold). *Courtesy of Esther Cooperman.*

The "Radio." *Courtesy of Esther Cooperman.*

The circa 1923 **Model 502** "Doric Mantel Telechron" ($50.00), 10-5/8" x 8-1/2" x 5", has an inlaid mahogany case with 5 inch etched silver dial.

The 1923-25 **Model 501** "Gothic Mantel Telechron" ($50.00), 11-3/8" x 8-1/2" x 5-1/2", has an inlaid mahogany case with 5 inch etched silver dial. (40 sold)

The circa 1923 **Model 503** "Gothic Mantel Telechron" ($39.50), 13-1/8" x 8-3/4" x 5", has an imitation mahogany case with 5 inch etched silver dial. *Courtesy of Ashland Historical Society.*

The 1923-27 **Model 504** "Mantel Telechron" ($75.00), 12-1/2" x 8-5/8" x 6", has an inlaid mahogany case and 6 inch etched silver dial. It was available with either the No. 62 Indicator or No. 71 Auxiliary movement. (21 sold)

The 1923-26 **Model 505** "Queen Anne Mantel Telechron" ($75), 9-5/8" x 8-7/8" x 5-3/4", has a mahogany case with Ebony inlay and a 6 inch etched silver dial. (16 sold)

The 1923-26 **Model 508** "Mantel or Desk Telechron" ($65), 13-1/8" x 9-1/4" x 5-1/4", has a mahogany case and a 6 inch etched silver dial. It was available with either a No. 62 Indicator or No. 71 Auxiliary movement. (31 sold)

The 1926-28 Telechron **Model 522** "Salem" ($29), 7" x 7-1/4" x 5", "brings dignity and charm to colonial mantel or library table" according to the 1928 catalog. It has a solid mahogany case with 5 inch etched silver dial and gold sweep second hand. (1,672 sold)

The 1928-30 Telechron **Model 523** "Patricia" ($29.00), 7-7/8" x 7-1/4" x 5-3/4", has a wood case lacquered in ivory, Chinese red, or apple green. It has a 5 inch silvered dial. (2,091 sold)

The 1928-31 Telechron **Model 524** "Oxford" ($25.00), 8-7/16" x 7-3/4" x 4-1/2", has a Spanish highlighted mahogany finish case with 5 inch silvered dial. (7,336 sold)

The 1928-31 Telechron **Model 525** "Windsor" ($32), 8-5/8" x 7-5/16" x 4-7/8", has a Spanish highlighted mahogany finish case with 5 inch silvered dial. (3,911 sold). *Courtesy of Esther Cooperman.*

The "Rejuvenation of Father Time" by M. E. Trimble, district manager of the New York territory. The artwork is by "Jo" Meyer.

The 1928-31 Telechron **Model 526** "Bellevue" ($25), 7-1/4" x 6-7/8" x 5", has a two-tone Spanish highlighted mahogany finish case with burl maple front panel and 5 inch silvered dial. (4,251 sold)

Above: The 1930-32 Telechron **Model 528** "Surrey" ($30.00), 9-13/16" x 7-1/8" x 4-1/8", has a mahogany finish case, 5 inch enameled dial, and brass ornaments. Designed by Harry Richardson. (1,538 sold). *Courtesy of Ashland Historical Society.*

Right: The 1930-32 Telechron **Model 530** "Nottingham" ($30.00), 9-13/16" x 6" x 3-29/32", has a mahogany case with inlay panels. The 4-1/2" dial is silvered with a gold numeral band. The copy reads "The 'Nottingham' faithfully interprets the Sheraton period. Sheraton specialized in inlay and scrollwork, one of his favorite motifs being the claw and ball foot. This latter has been amended somewhat in the feet of the 'Nottingham' by making the feet fluted with the claw and ball suggestion." Both the top ornament and the feet are gold-plated. Designed by George M. Long. (2,261 sold)

Fig. 1.

The design patent for the "Nottingham" was awarded to George M. Long. (D83,627, March 10, 1931)

The 1930-31 Telechron **Model 531** "Lorraine" ($24.00), 8-13/32" x 6-7/8" x 4-13/16", has a two-tone Spanish highlighted mahogany finish case with burl maple front panel and 4-1/2" gold finish dial. The "Lorraine" later became a General Electric model. (1,956 sold)

The 1931-36 Telechron **Model 532** "Standish" ($15.00), 8-27/32" x 6-29/32" x 4-1/2", has a mahogany finish wood case, Spanish highlighted with Lacewood panels. It has a 4-1/2" etched, gold-finished dial. In 1934, the "Standish" was renamed the "Shelburne." (3,976 sold)

The 1931-35 General Electric Telechron **Model AB533**. (3,504 sold). *Courtesy of Esther Cooperman.*

The 1923-28 **Model 551** "Lexington" ($35), 6-7/8" x 17" x 4", initially known simply as the "Tambour Mantel Telechron," has a solid mahogany case, 5 inch etched silver dial, and gold sweep second hand. The movement is the No. 1 Indicator. (3,370 sold)

The 1928-31 Telechron **Model 552** "Adams" ($24.00), 7-1/4" x 17-1/8" x 4-1/2", has a mahogany case with Spanish highlighted finish and a 5 inch silvered dial. (5,865 sold)

The 1928-31 Telechron **Model 553** "Belmont" ($25.00), 7-1/4" x 17-1/8" x 4-1/2", has a Spanish highlighted mahogany finish case with burl maple front panels and 5 inch silvered dial. (7,126 sold)

The 1927-28 Telechron **Model 554** "Miles Standish" ($34.00), 7-1/4" x 18-7/8" x 4", has a solid mahogany case with 5 inch etched silver dial. "Here is a Telechron model of classic beauty and generous size to blend with the most luxurious setting" reads the 1928 catalog. (1,395 sold). *Courtesy of Jay Kennan.*

The 1928-30 Telechron **Model 555** "Burlington" ($35.00), 7-1/4" x 17-1/8" x 4-1/2", has a mahogany case with Spanish highlighted finish and 5 inch silvered dial. (2,063 sold)

The 1928-30 Telechron **Model 556** "Virginian" ($38.00), 7-1/4" x 17-1/8" x 4-1/2", has a mahogany case with two-tone Spanish highlighted finish and a 5 inch silvered dial. (1,488 sold)

The 1930 General Electric Telechron **Model 557** "Lynnwood" ($23.00), 7-7/16" x 16-7/8" x 4-1/2", is a mahogany mantel clock with inlay finish, Spanish highlighted. After 6 months, the model was transferred to GE. (2,126 sold)

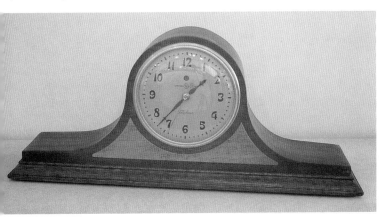

The 1930-31 Telechron "Geneva" (**Models 558 & AB558**, $15.00), 7-3/8" x 17-3/16" x 3-7/8", has a mahogany case with Spanish highlighted finish and burl maple front panel. The 4-1/2" dial has a gold finish. In 1931, the "Geneva" became a GE model. (9,461 shipped) *Courtesy of Orsini & Frost, Inc.*

Advertisement for General Electric clocks featuring the "Lynn-wood." Also shown are the "Hostess" and "Haverhill," a chiming banjo clock manufactured by the Revere Clock Company.

The 1931 Telechron **Model 559** "Durham" ($15.00), 7-3/16" x 17-1/4" x 3-7/8", has a mahogany finish wood case, Spanish highlighted finish with Lacewood panels. The 4-1/2" gold finish dial is etched. The "Durham" was later renamed the "Maynard." It also became **Model 4F01** in 1933. (25,350 sold of the two models, 1931-40)

The General Electric Telechron **Model AB564**, 17" x 7" x 5", was a tambour style clock with mahogany-finished wood case.

The 1931-32 Telechron **Model 560** "Bennington" ($22.50), 7-3/8" x 17-3/16" x 3-15/16", has a mahogany case, Spanish highlighted with Satinwood panels and a carved center ornament. (1,026 sold).
Not Pictured: Sales figures were found for the 1931-35 **Model 562**, but no information was found on case style or composition. (26,813 sold)

The 1931-34 Telechron **Model 563** "Huntington" ($9.95), 7-3/16" x 17-1/4" x 3-7/16", has a mahogany case with Spanish highlighted finish and relief ornaments on the front panel. The 4-1/2" dial is ivory enamel. (6,671 shipped)

The 1926-28 Telechron **Model 601** "Normandy" ($50.00), 11-3/8" x 8-1/2" x 5-1/2", is a "Gothic Mantel" clock with an inlaid mahogany case, 6 inch etched silver dial, and gold sweep second hand. The movement is either the No. 31 Indicator or No. 71 Auxiliary. (775 sold)

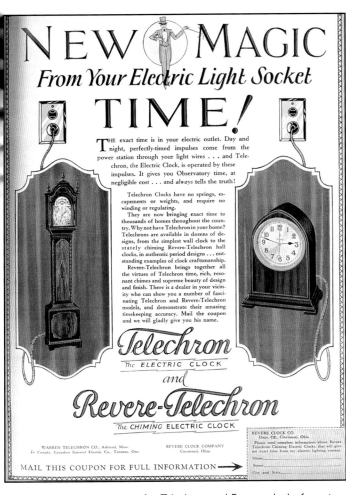

An early joint advertisement for Telechron and Revere clocks featuring the "Normandy" and unidentified Revere tall case clock. (*House & Garden*, June 1928)

The 1928-31 Telechron **Model 602** "Castleton" ($38.00), 11-5/8" x 9-7/8" x 5-1/2", has a mahogany case with Spanish highlighted finish and 6 inch silvered dial. (1,793 sold)

Left: The 1928-31 Telechron **Model 603** "Jefferson" ($38.00-$48.00), 11-9/16" x 9-1/4" x 5-11/16", has a mahogany case with Spanish highlighted finish and 6 inch silvered dial. (1,401 sold)

Above: The 1930-32 General Electric Telechron "Brittany" (**Models AB604 & 604**, $35.00), 11-3/8" x 8-5/8" x 5-3/8", has a mahogany case with carved decorations. Its Spanish highlighted finish has Satinwood panels. The 5-1/2" dial is gold-finished. The "Brittany" appears to be one of the models introduced as a Telechron but later transferred to General Electric. (477 sold)

The 1930-32 Telechron **Model 605** "Waverly" ($40.00), 11-1/2" x 8-3/8" x 6-1/8", has a mahogany case with bronze trim and a 5-1/2" white enamel dial. Designed by Harry Richardson. (676 shipped)

The 1931-33 Telechron **Model 606** "Winchester" ($29.50), 11-1/2" x 8-3/8" x 5-1/16", has a mahogany case, Spanish highlighted with Satinwood panels and carved center ornament. The 5-1/2" dial is etched and gold-finished. The "Winchester" was also known as the "Woodlawn." Introduced at $29.50, the price was later slashed to $12.50 to dispose of remaining stock. (478 shipped)

"Better get a Telechron* Clock, Jim!"

Telechron advertised prolifically in the *National Geographic*. Featured in this ad are the "Apollo" (No. 357), "Geneva" (No. 558), and "Waverly" (No. 605).

The 1927-28 Telechron **Model 654** "Manchester" ($50.00), 8-3/4" x 20" x 5-1/2", has a mahogany case and 6 inch silvered dial. (213 sold)

The 1927-28 Telechron **Model 655** "Versailles" ($60.00), 9" x 21" x 5-1/2", "represents the ultimate in case design and manufacture combined with Telechron accuracy and dependability" reads the 1928 catalog. It has a mahogany case with two-tone finish on the front and a 6 inch silvered dial. (153 sold)

The 1927 Telechron **Model 656** "Aristocrat" ($84), 9" x 20-1/2" x 5-1/2", has a solid mahogany case with rosewood burl inlay and a 6 inch silvered dial. (151 sold)

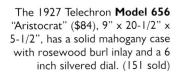

The 1925-30 Telechron **Model 661** "Concord" ($50.00), 8" x 20-3/4" x 4-3/4", has a solid mahogany case with 6 inch etched silver dial. It has a No. 62 Indicator movement. (378 sold)

The 1928 Telechron **Model 662** "Magnolia" ($56.00), 8-1/2" x 19-3/4" x 5-1/2", has a Spanish highlighted mahogany finish with burl redwood panels. The 6 inch dial is silvered. (1,146 sold)

The 1928-30 Telechron **Model 663** "Pilgrim" ($50), 8-1/2" x 19-3/4" x 5-1/2", has a Spanish highlighted mahogany finish with a 6 inch silvered dial. (486 sold). *Courtesy of Ashland Historical Society.*

The 1930-31 Telechron **Model 664** "Dorchester" ($33.00), 8-5/8" x 19-9/16" x 5-1/2", has a Satin-wood case with inlay finish and Spanish highlighting. The 5-1/2" dial has a gold finish. This model was transferred to General Electric in 1931. (577 sold)

The 1931-33 Telechron **Model 666** "Norwich" ($29.50), 8-11/16" x 20" x 5", has a mahogany case, Spanish highlighted, and carved base. The "Norwich" later became the "Norwood" (Model 5F01). (1,433 sold)

Alarm Clocks

T-E-L-E-C-H-R-O-N

T—stands for time
Correct to the dot.
Telechron gives it
As others cannot.

E—means Electric
The time without ticks
It never runs down
Nor calls you to fix.

L—is the Light Socket
Standing close by
The Telechron motor's
One source of supply.

E—means exact
Or efficiency plus
No clock springs to oil
No winding or fuss.

C—stands for Current
Consumed in a year
A dollar and ten
Is not very dear.

H—suggests Handsome
which Telechrons are
The finest collection
Of models by far.

R—stands for Running
continuously.
The benefits therefrom
Are easy to see.

O—means "on Time"
to your dates from now on
The right time is given
By your Telechron.

N—is for Need
for a perfect timepiece
Buy Telechrons now
And your clock troubles cease.

S. D. Woodward in the April 1929 *Telechronicle*.

The illuminated 1929-31 Telechron **Model 700** "Electrolarm" ($25.00), 7-5/8" x 6" x 3-5/8", has a molded plastic case in walnut, green, or white and a 3 inch gold dial. The fluted brass trim is often missing from this clock. Design of the "Electrolarm" is commonly attributed to Paul Frankl, but I was able to find no documentation in either Telechron sales and marketing materials or in patent records to support the attribution. Telechron prominently advertised Frankl's design of the "Modernique" and it appears doubtful that they would have missed the opportunity to similarly promote the "Electrolarm" had Frankl designed it. In addition, the book that cites Frankl as the designer of the "Electrolarm" incorrectly cites Rockwell Kent and Russel Wright as the designers of two other pictured models. (27,013 sold (brown case); 4,012 sold (ivory or green case).

Telechron The "Electrolarm" in green. The missing trim decreases the value of this example, but even in rough shape, the "Electrolarm" is one of the most valuable Telechron's. *Courtesy of Ashland Historical Society.*

THE VINYLITE HOUSE

Cover to a circa 1929 Carbide and Carbon Chemicals Corporation brochure *The Vinylite House* extolling the virtues and potential uses for its newly developed plastic "Vinylite." The entire interior and exterior of the house were made from Vinylite.

A page from *The Vinylite House* showing the Electrolarm in red, black, and marbleized green cases. None of these cases appear to have entered production. The prototypes shown in the picture would probably sell for more than $1,000 at auction.

Circa 1930 advertisement for General Electric clocks. Shown are the "Hanover" tall case clock, "Geneva" mantel clock, "R-130" chime clock, and the "Electrolarm." What is interesting about the "Electrolarm" is that it is pictured in charcoal gray with silver color trim. The ad copy, however, indicates that it was available only in walnut, green, and ivory.

The 1931-36 Telechron **Model 711** "Telalarm" ($9.95), 5" x 4-1/4" x 3", has a case of "Dura-silver-alloy" and a base of black Bakelite. The dial has a satin finish and is illuminated through diffusing glass by a tiny Mazda lamp. The Telalarm was later made available in green, ivory, orchid, and blue enamel case for $8.95. Designed by George Graff. (105,977 sold)

The 1931-36 General Electric Telechron "Alarm Lite" (**Models AB712** & **AB712A**), 5" x 4" x 3-1/4", has a dura-metal case with brushed silver finish. It has a recessed dial and Arabic numerals. The illuminated dial has a switch to control intensity or turn the light off altogether. The base is black moulded plastic. Designed by George Graff.

The cover to the August 1931 *Telechronicle*, announcing the "Telalarm." Note that the same issue announces the Revere "Loyal," the lowest priced Westminster chime clock.

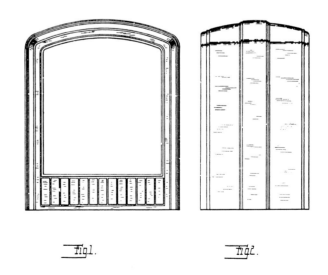

George Graff was awarded a design patent for the case to the "Telalarm." Unlike most clock design patents, which include the dial, this patent covers only the case design. In addition, it was awarded to the Dura Corporation rather than to the Warren Telechron Company, indicating that Dura probably manufactured the cases for Telechron and GE. (D85,094, Awarded Sept. 15, 1931)

Between 1931-32, the Telechron "Telalarm" was offered without the illuminated dial (**Model 715**, $8.50). The dial of the Model 715 was gold finished. Designed by George Graff. (38,646 sold). *Courtesy of Jay Kennan.*

Like the "Telalarm," the General Electric Telechron "Alarm Lite" was available without the illuminated dial under a separate model number (**Model AB716**). Designed by George Graff. *Courtesy of Jay Kennan.*

The 1931-1935 Telechron **Model 727** "Alden" ($12.50), 7-1/4" x 5-21/32" x 3-3/16", has a case similar to the "Salisbury" (No. 327), but has a 3-1/2" ivory dial and alarm movement with alarm hand. (11,016 combined sales). *Courtesy of Ashland Historical Society.*

The Telechron **Model 728**, 7-1/8" X 5-5/8" X 3". *Courtesy of Jay Kennan.*

Special Campaign Models

The 1931-33 Telechron Special Campaign **Model AA**, 7-3/16" x 17-1/4" x 3-7/16", has a wood case with brown mahogany finish and a 4-1/2" ivory enamel dial with brown numerals and dial. It was advertised as "…a $24 value for a limited time only… $9.95." (55,360 sold). *Courtesy of Ashland Historical Society.*

The 1931-32 Telechron Special Campaign **Model BB** ($9.95), 7-1/8" x 17-1/4" x 3-1/8", has a mahogany case with relief ornamentation. The 4-1/2" gold-finished dial has two-tone etched ornamentation and black numerals. (8,288 sold)

You can call me "AL." The Telechron Special Campaign **Model "AL"** alarm ($4.95), 4-7/16" x 4-7/16" x 3-1/4", has a molded catalin case in choice of black or ivory and gold color finish "goldine" base and bezel. The 3-1/2" metal dial has an ivory lacquer finish with black Arabic numerals. Announced on May 13, 1933, the "AL" was discontinued only 5 months later, on October 26, 1933. (20,560 sold)

Kitchen Timers

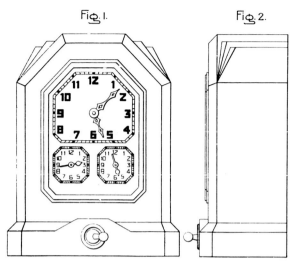

Fig. 1.   Fig. 2.

Raymond E. Patten designed the Edison General Electric Appliance Company's "Hotpoint Range Timer" (**Catalog No. TM-2**), the only clock I found in the General Electric catalog that did not have a movement made by the Warren Telechron Company. The Lux Clock Manufacturing Company of Waterbury, Connecticut made it. (D81,068, awarded April 30, 1930)

The General Electric Hotpoint Electric Clock Range Timer (**Catalog No. TM-19, Model No. 3T20**), 5-3/8" x 4-5/8" x 2-1/2", has a black Bakelite case with stepped side motif and base. The ivory dial is marked "Hotpoint" and "Telechron Movement." The back of the case notes that the clock is manufactured by General Electric for the Edison General Electric Appliance Company, Chicago, Illinois. Rather than a sweep second hand, the timer has a revolving disk showing seconds.

Left: The 1930 General Electric "Hotpoint Telechron Electric Clock and Automatic Range Timer" (**Catalog No. TM-8**), 7-1/2" x 8-1/2" x 4-1/2". It has a chrome-plated case with black Bakelite base. The case is a streamline moderne interpretation of the Gothic arch. Designed by Raymond E. Patten.

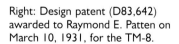

Right: Design patent (D83,642) awarded to Raymond E. Patten on March 10, 1931, for the TM-8.

Above: This 60 minute Hotpoint Timer (**TM-24**), 4-1/2" x 3-1/4" x 2-1/4", has a black Bakelite case. Although made by the Edison General Electric Appliance Company, it is a manual not electric timer.

Banjo Clocks

The 1928-32 Telechron **Model 691** "Madison" ($65.00), 32-1/2" h, has mahogany panels and a colored glass scene of Mt. Vernon. The 6 inch dial is silvered. (Author's note: It is not clear why the "Madison" has a scene of Mt. Vernon rather than Montpelier, Madison's home.) (3,051 sold)

Above: The "Madison" is featured in this April 1930 advertisement in *House Beautiful*. Also pictured are the "Modernique" (No. 431) and "Vernon" (No. 370A).

Left: The General Electric Telechron "Washington Bi-Centennial" banjo-style clock ($50) was issued to commemorate the 200th Anniversary of George Washington's birth (February 21, 1732). The dial features Roman numerals. The wood case has brass ornamentation and is decorated with a Mount Vernon scene and a portrait of George Washington.

The General Electric/Telechron **Model AB692** "Bullfinch," 20-1/2" high, is a half-size banjo clock in a mahogany finish case. The glass panel features a reverse painted scene of Paul Revere's ride from the Old North Church.

Closeup of the Model 692 "Bullfinch."

The 1931-36 Telechron **Model 694** "Bullfinch" ($19.75), 20-1/4" h, is a half size banjo clock in a mahogany case with colored glass panels. It features an Early American clipper ship scene and a brass eagle ornament on top. The 3-1/2" dial is enameled. (6,669 sold)
Not Pictured: The 1927 Telechron Model 1258 "Banjo" ($100.00), 40-1/2" h, has a wood case with brass ornamentation. It appears to be decorated with a Mount Vernon scene. The dial is 8 inches.

Closeup of the Model 692 "Bullfinch."

Chapter 8

Kitchen, Banjo, and Other Wall Clocks

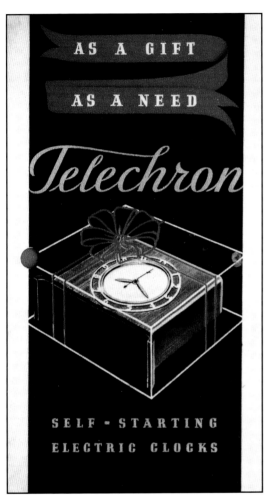

Cover to a mid-1930s Telechron sales brochure.

The 1932 Telechron **Model 2B01** "Priscilla" ($6.75), 7-1/8" x 7-1/8" x 3", has a cast Dura-alloy case finished in choice of green, blue, ivory, white, or black enamel. The base and front are chrome plated. The 4-1/2 inch dial is enameled. The 2B01 has the same basic case design as the earlier models 257 and 457. (6,589 sold)

The 1932-39 Telechron **Model 2F01** "Consort" ($4.95), 5-3/4" x 5-3/4" x 2-3/8", has a chrome-plated metal case with "Beetle" molded bezel in green, ivory, white, black, blue, or red. The 4-1/2" dial is lacquered metal. Designed by Edgar Bourquin. (285,693 sold) *Courtesy of Jay Kennan.*

Edgar Bourquin was awarded the design patent (D89,236) for the "Consort" on February 7, 1933.

The 1932-34 General Electric Telechron **Model AB2B02** ($6.75) was available in choice of green, ivory, white, blue, or black case. (4,202 sold)

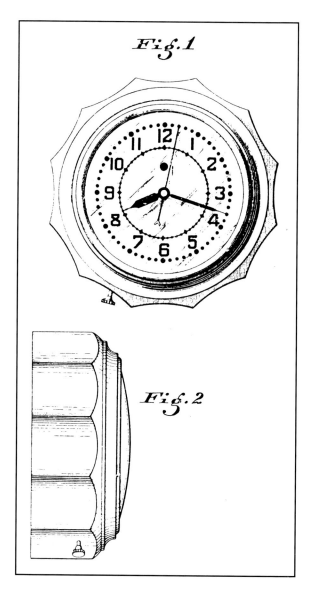

The 1934-41 General Electric "New Hostess" (**Models AB2FO2 & 2F02**, 7-1/2" x 7-1/2" x 2-13/16", $4.95) has a molded plastic case in choice of ivory, black, green, or red; all with a 5" ivory lacquer dial. Both the back of the case and bezel ring are "Nicral." This basic case design by Edgar Bourquin had the longest run of any GE clock, having originally been introduced in 1930 as the **Model AB454** "Hostess." It was again reintroduced in 1947 (**Model 2H02**, $6.95) and continued in production until 1952. *Courtesy of Jay Kennan.*

Right: Edgar Bourquin was awarded the design patent (D83,789) for the original "Hostess" (No. 454) on March 31, 1931.

Right: Although the "Hostess" and "New Hostess" have the same basic case design, the case for the "New Hostess" is thinner because of the development of the "F" and "H" rotors. *Courtesy of Jay Kennan.*

The 1935-40 Telechron **Model 2F03** "Kitchenguide" ($4.95), 6-1/4" x 7-3/4" x 2-1/4", has a molded plastic case in choice of green, antique ivory, white, or black, all with a buffed Nicral bezel. Designed by Eugene J. Lux. (166,738 sold)

The "Kitchenguide" shown on the cover of a circa 1935 Telechron sales brochure.

The "Kitchenguide" model was reintroduced in December 1940 as the Special Campaign **Model CH203** ($3.95) with a redesigned dial. The case was available in choice of ivory, white, or red plastic. Another 33,133 were sold before the campaign ended in 1941. Designed by Eugene J. Lux.

Eugene J. Lux was awarded the design patent (D97,775) for the "Kitchenguide" on December 10, 1935.

The 1934-41 General Electric **Model 2F04** "Chef" ($4.95), 6-7/8" x 6-7/8" x 1-7/8", has a metal case finished in choice of green with ivory stripes, ivory with red stripes, or black with white stripes. It has a chrome bezel ring and 5" light ivory dial with black Arabic numerals. (197,830 sold).

The "New Chef" (**Models 2HX12** and **2HX16**) were special campaign and promotional models of the "Chef" that had a wide band of chrome trim on the sides in place of the three stripes. Designed by Raymond E. Patten.

Cover to a circa 1934-35 Telechron sales brochure.

The 1936 Telechron Special Campaign **Model CF205** "Matron" ($4.50), 5-1/2" x 6-1/2" x 2", has a metal case finished in choice of ivory, green, black, or red lacquer. The light cream dial, surrounded by a chrome bezel, has black numerals. (38,853 sold)

The 1936-46 General Electric **Model 2F06** "Kitchen Hostess" ($4.50), 7" x 7" x 2-1/8", has a round metal case available in bronze, chrome, black, gold, green, ivory, blue, red, or white finish. Also known as the "Kitchen King," it features a white dial with black numerals, "storm blue" hour and minute hands, and chrome-plated bezel and second hand. Designed by Raymond E. Patten. (135,597 sold)

The 1937-53 Telechron **Model 2H07** "Buffet" ($3.80), 6-5/8" x 6-7/16" x 2-1/4", has a molded plastic case in ivory, green, white, or red with a lacquered metal bezel, dark blue hands that are no longer moderne in style, and black numerals on a 5 inch cream white dial. Put the "Buffet" in a conservative brown plastic case and it becomes a living room wall clock with a dignified new name—"Administrator" (**Model 2H07-Br**, $3.95). The 1937-40 "Administrator" also features a brass bezel, moderne style brass hands, and a 5 inch metal dial with medium brown numerals on a light cream background and tan center. A special campaign version of the "Buffet" (**Model 2HC07**) was offered from 1950-53 in choice of white or red case. Designed by Leo Ivan Bruce. (1,708,130 combined sales.). *Courtesy of Esther Cooperman.*

Saturday Evening Post, circa 1939.

Catalog listing for the "Garcon" showing the available colors.

The 1937-48 General Electric **Model 2H08** "Garcon" ($3.50), 7-1/4" x 7-1/4" x 2-1/4", is a square metal kitchen clock available in bronze, chrome, black, gold, green, ivory, blue, red, or white finish. The dial features black characters on a cream white background, storm blue minute and hour hands, and vermilion sweep second hand. The dial on the pictured example is not standard and contains the title "Lotus" as well as "General Electric." Designed by John P. Rainbault. (1,440,839 sold). *Courtesy of Jay Kennan.*

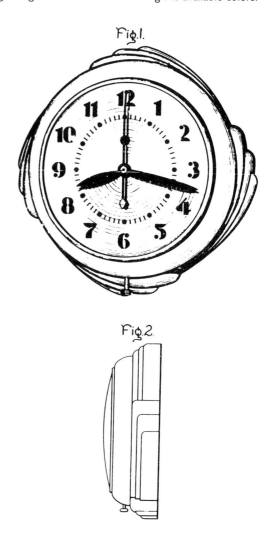

The 1939-42 Telechron **Model 2H09** "Stewardess" ($4.95), 7-5/8" x 7-5/8" x 2-5/16", was available in choice of all chrome-plated case or combinations of chrome and ivory, green, black, or red lacquer. It has a 5 inch metal dial with black numerals, red dots, and a cream and white background. The hands are blue lacquer. (149,485 sold.). In 1940-42, a variation was offered with a tan and gold case (**Model 2H09A**, $5.95) and marketed as a living room wall clock. Designed by Findley Williams. (6,496 sold)

Findley Williams was awarded the design patent (D117,916) for the "Stewardess" on December 5, 1939.

The 1940-42 General Electric **Model 2H10** "Domestic" ($4.95), 6-7/8" x 6-7/8" x 2-1/4", is a square-cased kitchen clock with five decorative lines at the center of the top, bottom, and sides. It was available in green, ivory, red, and white. Designed by John P. Rainbault. (101,354 sold)

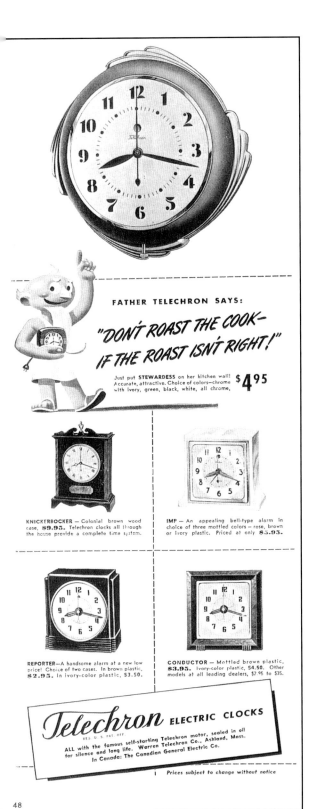

48

Father Telechron says "Don't Roast the Cook— If the Roast Isn't Right."

The 1940-51 Telechron **Model 2H11** "Café" ($4.95), 6-15/16" x 6-15/16" x 2-1/4", has a molded plastic case available in ivory, green, white, blue, yellow, and red, all with chrome trim and bezel. It has black hands and numerals against a cream-white and gray finish dial. (772,807 sold). *Courtesy of Esther Cooperman.*

The "Café" in ivory.

The 1940-41 General Electric **Model 2HX12** "New Chef" (7" x 7" x 2-1/2") was a 1940-41 Special Campaign Model of the "Chef" that has a wide chrome band with engraved parallel line motif in place of the parallel stripes of the "Chef." It was available in choice of green, ivory, red, or white case. (25,929 sold)

The 1941-45 Telechron **Model 2H13** "Patron" ($2.95), 6-5/8" x 6-5/8" x 2-5/16", has a metal case finished in ivory, green, red, or white lacquer. The 4-1/2" square dial has a white center with a light ivory numeral band and black characters. The hands are blue lacquered metal. Designed by Leo Ivan Bruce. (200,578 sold)

The 1941-42 General Electric **Model 2H14** "Pantry" ($2.95) was available in choice of green, ivory, red, or white case. (150,143 sold)

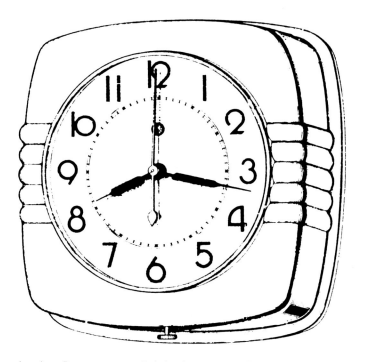

Leo Ivan Bruce was awarded the design patent for the "Patron." (D131,801, awarded March 31, 1941.) Although no design patent was awarded for the companion GE "Pantry," it has the same decorative motif and was likely designed by Bruce.

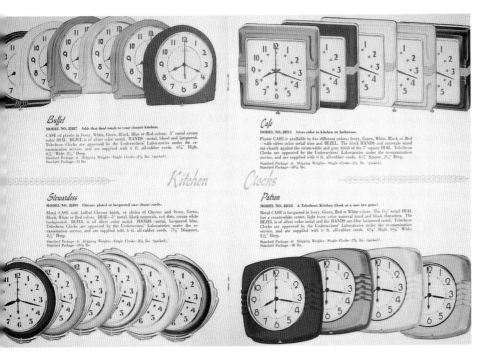

Pages from the Telechron catalog showing the color choices for the "Buffet," "Café," "Stewardess," and "Patron."

The 1946-50 Telechron "Kitchenguide" (**Models 2H15 & 2H15S**, $4.95), 7" x 7" x 2-1/2", has a molded plastic case in choice of ivory, green, red, yellow, light blue, or white. The 5 inch metal dial has a cream-white center, light gray numeral band, and black numerals. The bezel is buffed aluminum and the hands blue lacquered metal. On the 2H15S, the numerals are arranged on a square whereas they are on a circular numeral band on the 2H15. (67,791 sold). *Courtesy of Esther Cooperman.*

The 1941-42 General Electric Special Campaign **Model 2HX16** "New Chef" differed from the prior year's 2HX12 "New Chef" only in the back of the case and was available in the same colors. (7,439 sold)

The 1946-51 Telechron **Model 2H17** "Minitmaster" ($7.95), 7" x 7-1/4" x 2-1/2", is a combination kitchen wall clock and 60 minute timer. It was available in a choice of green, red, white, or ivory molded plastic case. The 4-1/2 inch dial has black hour characters and red timer characters on a cream-white background. The bezel is buffed aluminum; the hands, dark blue. (232,511 sold)

The 1946-48 General Electric **Model 2H18** "Chef" ($6.95), 5-7/8 x 5-7/8 x 2-13/16", was billed as "the first combination kitchen clock and timer." It featured a plastic case in choice of white, ivory, Chinese red, or Nile green. The ivory dial is set in an opalescent gray frame. (234,786 sold)

The 1949-53 Telechron **Model 2H19** "Prudence" ($4.50), 5-3/4" x 6-3/8" x 2-1/2", was the lowest priced Telechron kitchen clock available in 1949. It featured a "clear vision dial" and plastic case in choice of red or white. The dial features black numerals on a white background. (692,462 sold)

The 1948-53 General Electric **Model 2H20** "Epicure" ($5.95), 7-1/4" x 7-1/4" x 2-1/2", is described in the 1950 catalog as "America's most popular kitchen clock." The molded plastic case was available in red, green, ivory, and white. The cream white dial has mahogany-colored numerals and hands. The second hand is vermilion, the bezel is aluminum. (562,386 sold)

The 1948-53 Telechron **Model 2H21** "Decorator" ($6.95), 7-1/8" x 7-1/8" x 2-3/4", has a pierced white plastic numeral band with colored dials. The dial was available in choice of black, yellow, red, blue, gray, tan, or aqua blue, with choices varying by year. The "Decorator" is designed so that it can be hung in the traditional manner or recessed so that the numeral band is flush with the wall. Designed by Leo Ivan Bruce. (1,184,513 sold)

The 1948-53 General Electric **Model 2H22** "Pantry" ($4.50), 6-1/4" x 7" x 2-9/16", is described in the catalog as "neat and natty." The plastic case came in choice of red, yellow, ivory, or white. The dark mahogany-colored hands and numerals contrast sharply with the white face. "Molded, one-piece-plastic case is easy to keep clean. No metal to polish—no dingy tarnish…" reads the ad copy. In other words, this is one cheap clock!

The 1949-51 General Electric **Model 2H24** "Dinette" ($6.95), 6-7/8" x 8-7/16" x 2-3/4", was available in choice of red, ivory, blue, or white plastic case. It has a glass crystal and Masonite back.

The 1949-53 Telechron **Model 2H25** "Stewardess" ($5.75), 7-3/16" x 6-5/8" x 2-3/8", was available in choice of white, ivory, red, or blue plastic case. The ad copy notes that the "Stewardess" was "Gay as a Lark." Its large, square face is "plainly visible from anywhere in the room." It has a glass crystal. (352,946 sold)

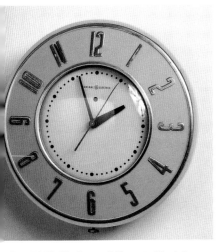

The 1950-52 General Electric **Model 2H26** "Gourmet" ($5.95), 7-1/4" x 7-1/4" x 2-1/4", was "voted America's finest kitchen clock." It has a plastic case and crystal and a raised numeral bezel. The "Gourmet" was available in four color schemes—red with white numerals, green with white numerals, white with red numerals, and yellow with white numerals.

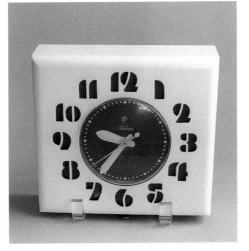

The 1949-55 Telechron **Model 2H27** "Advisor" ($5.95), 6-1/4" x 6-3/4" x 2-5/16", has a white plastic case with pierced numerals and matching dial in choice of red, black, blue, or yellow. In 1950, a mint green dial was added. The "Advisor" was also available in "duo-tone" blue, yellow, and green. The crystal is clear plastic. (942,645 sold). *Courtesy of Esther Cooperman.*

Drawing of the 1950-52 **Model 2H28** "Grille" ($4.98) from a General Electric parts manual. It has a plastic case and crystal. The hour and minute hands are mahogany; the sweep second hand is red.

Above: The 1950-53 Telechron **Model 2H29** "Pageant" ($6.95), 5-5/8" x 9-1/2" x 2-3/4", was available in choice of red, yellow, green, or blue plastic case. (70,531 sold). *Courtesy of Jay Kennan.*

Right: The 1952-53 General Electric **Model 2H30** "Clansman" ($5.75), 6-3/4" x 7-1/4" x 2-1/2", has a plastic case with a scotch tartan design in red, green, or blue on the 6-1/4" x 7" dial. The contrasting numerals are on the snap in plastic crystal. The hands are white; the sweep second hand is chrome. Also featured in this advertisement from the April 1952 *Woman's Day* is the 1952-53 **Model 2H32** "Domestic" ($6.95-$7.95), 7" x 7-5/16" x 2-5/8". It has a plastic case in choice of red, green, blue, or yellow and "snap in" plastic crystal. The dial features raised silver-colored numerals. The hands are mahogany; the sweep second hand is red.

The 1950-55 General Electric/Telechron "Jubilee" (**Models 2H31 & 2HA31**, $4.95), 5-1/16" x 8-1/4" x 2-13/16", has a plastic case in choice of red, yellow, ivory, or white. It features a "snap in" wide-angle vision crystal. The hands are black; the sweep second hand is red. (703,692 sold)

Excerpt from a Telechron catalog showing the "Ivy," "Prudence," and "Jubilee."

Above: The 1951-53 Telechron **Model 2H33** "Ivy" ($7.95), 6-1/16" x 8-1/2" x 2-5/8", has a plastic case in choice of red, green, gray, or yellow and a glass crystal. The side containers lift out for planting and watering. Designed by Leo Ivan Bruce. (161,505 sold)

CONTOUR — MODEL 2H-34

The 1952-54 General Electric **Model 2H34** "Contour" ($6.95), 7-3/8" x 7-3/4" x 2-3/8", has a plastic case and "snap in" numeraled crystal. Available in white case with red numerals or "decorator" red or green case with white numerals. The hands are mahogany; the sweep second hand is red.

The 1952-55 General Electric Telechron **Model 2H38** "Helper" ($4.95), 5-1/4" x 6-3/4" x 2-1/4", has a plastic case in choice of red, white, yellow, or pink and "snap in" crystal. The dial is white; the hands black. (706,259 sold)

Above: The 1952-56 Telechron **Model 2H39** "Originality" ($8.95), 8-1/2" x 8-1/2" x 2-1/2", has a clear plastic ring joining the numeral ring to the case. Available in red, yellow, aqua, and white. Design of this clock has been incorrectly attributed to Russel Wright. It was designed by Leo Ivan Bruce (D172,266, awarded May 25, 1954). (410,486 sold)

Left: The 1953-58 Telechron "Butler" (**Models 2H41** & **2HA41**, $7.95), 6-1/8" x 7-3/8" x 2-5/8", has a plastic case and 6" x 6-1/2" snap in crystal. The dial, which features "three dimensional" numerals, was available in red, yellow, white, and blue. (311,593 sold)

Drawing of the 1953-54 General Electric **Model 2H40** "Carousel" ($6.95), 7-1/4" x 7-1/4" x 2-7/8", from a General Electric parts manual. It features a plastic case in choice of red, yellow, or white and a 3-1/2" plastic crystal. A wide numeral band features raised numerals. The hands are gray; the sweep second hand is either white or red.

Even in the mid 1950s, Telechron continued to plug "modern electric time." Featured in this advertisement are the "Butler" (No. 2H41), "Gracewood" (7H209), and "Perspective" (7H213).

The 1953-57 General Electric **Model 2H42** "Jackstraw" ($6.95), 6-3/4" x 7-1/4" x 2-1/2", has a white plastic case with dial in three (red, blue, green) or four (red, blue, green, gray) color background. The "Jackstraw" was "designed to match the outstandingly popular floor covering design." It has a numeraled snap on crystal. (8,753 sold)

The 1953-63 General Electric Telechron **Model 2H44** "Topper" ($3.98), 6" x 6" x 2", was available in choice of pink, cherry red, azure blue, golden yellow, or dove gray plastic case. The dial and hands are housed under the clear plastic crystal. In 1963, the "Topper" was offered in a special white and black case. (1,443,585 sold). In 1960-61, a variation of the "Topper" (**Model 2H44-C**, $4.98) was added in choice of chrome and aqua, chrome and yellow, or copper and white case. (158,131 sold)

The 1954-55 Telechron **Model 2H43** "Telemaid" ($6.95), 6-5/8" x 7-3/16" x 2-3/8", has ribbed "chrome color" side panels contrasting with the red, white, or yellow plastic case. (144,632 sold)

The 1953-60 Telechron **Model 2H45** "Swirl" ($3.98), 6-1/2" diameter, has a plastic case in choice of red, blue, yellow, or gray. Cut out numerals create a "three dimensional effect." (784,068 sold). The "Swirl" (**Model 2H45C**, $4.98) was also available with chrome color numerals and outer bezel and pink or red case (1955-58) and copper color numerals and outer bezel with white case (1956-58). The "Swirl" included a device for storing the excess cord in the back of the case. (545,534 sold) **Not Pictured**: The 1954-55 General Electric **Model 2H46** "Gay Wall" ($5.98), 6-1/4" x 7-1/2" x 2-1/2", has a plastic case and 3-1/2" snap on plastic crystal. The dial was available in choice of red, blue, green, or yellow overlaid with a "net pattern in harmonizing colors." The hands and hours dots are white.

The 1954-56 General Electric Telechron **Model 2H48** "Ceramic" ($8.98), 7-3/4" x 7-3/4" x 2-3/4", has a ceramic case finished in choice of golden spice, meadow green, coral sand, or charcoal. The dial features raised numerals and the case is molded as one unit. The case should be signed "Russel Wright" on the back. Early versions of this clock were designed to hang on the wall, but the case was later redesigned to allow the clock to be used as a shelf clock. (115,370 sold)

The 1954-57 General Electric Telechron **Model 2H47** "Telechoice" ($5.98), 4-3/4" x 8" x 6-3/4", has a plastic case and crystal with "chrome color" ornamentation. The "Telechoice" was available in choice of white, red, or yellow for use in kitchens and bathrooms and brown with "brass color" trim for use in other rooms. It was designed to hang on the wall or stand on a shelf. The "Telechoice" was also available without the ornaments as **Models 2HC47** and 2**HC47S**. (349,853 sold)

The 1954-56 Telechron "Motif" (**Models 2H49 & 2HA49**, $7.98), 9-1/4" x 6-3/4" x 2-1/4", has a plastic case in choice of black, cherry red, teal blue, or olive green and plastic crystal. Described as a "Beautiful Tole wall clock—an early American Motif," it is not one of Ivan Bruce's better design efforts. (100,304 sold)

The 1939-41 General Electric **Model 2H50** "Dinette" ($5.95), 6-3/4" x 6-3/4" x 2-5/8", was available in choice of dark walnut or antique maple with a decorative center panel of tan facsimile leather. Both have an ivory and gold-colored dial with blue-black hour and minute hands and gold color sweep second hand. (13,334 sold)

The 1938-40 Telechron **Model 2H51** "Shield" ($6.75), 9" x 9" x 2-5/8", is a wall clock of solid black walnut with beveled ends. The inner bezel is polished brass, while the outer bezel is "gold bronze lacquered metal." The dial is metal with a light cream background, golden tan dots, and brown moderne numerals. Designed by Leo Ivan Bruce. (8,276 sold). *Courtesy of Jay Kennan.* **Not Pictured:** The 1940-42 General Electric **Model 2H52** "Sunburst." **Not Pictured:** The General Electric **Model 2H54** "Bordeaux."

The 1955-57 General Electric Telechron **Model 2H55** "Colonist" ($14.95), 14" x 11" x 2-1/2", has scrolled numerals set against a jet black, colonial red, or gold color case. "Scalloped edge frames this clock in beauty." In my opinion, one of the homeliest clocks GE/Telechron produced. (87,626 sold) **Not Pictured:** The 1940-41 General Electric **Model 2H56** "Marseille"($30.00) was classified as a 4-1/2" Louis XVI wall clock. Only 145 were sold. Unfortunately, no photograph is available and I was able to find no information about the appearance or size of the model.

The 1955-63 General Electric Telechron "Inheritance" (**Models 2S57 & 2SB57**, $29.95), 13-3/8" x 13-3/8" x 2-5/8", has a Fruitwood finish wood case and base-relief solid brass dial. The dial rotates on the Model 2SB57 so that the clock can be hung as a diamond. *Courtesy of Ashland Historical Society.*

The 1956-59 General Electric/Telechron **Model 2H59** "Wallwood" ($9.98), was available in combinations of black, brass, and chrome; black and brass; and birch and black. (146,672 sold). Also available in a combination of gold and "ginger spice" wood as the **Model 2H59G** ($12.95). (24,087 sold)

Among the clocks advertised in the December 1937 *House & Garden* was the "Swarthmore." Also shown are the "Seville," "Olympic," and "Sportsman."

The circa 1937-41 Telechron **Model 2F81** "Swarthmore" ($14.95), 24-1/2" x 7" x 2-13/16", is a smaller, updated version of the "Madison" (Model 691). It has a brown wood case, colored glass panels with Mt. Vernon scene, and brass bezel, eagle, and side ornaments. The dial has black Roman numerals on a cream background. (11,917 sold)

The 1954-57 General Electric **Model 2H100** "Gossamer" ($6.98), 6-3/4" x 7-3/8" x 2-3/4", has a clear plastic numeral band with white numerals and snap on shatterproof crystal. The dial and trim accents were available in brass, chrome, or copper color. The hands are white; the sweep second hand is red. A small foot can be attached to make the "Gossamer" a shelf or desk clock. (86,011 sold)

The 1954-57 Telechron **Model 2H101** "Diameter" ($14.95), 9-3/4" diameter, was available in copper, brass, or chrome color brushed finish metal case with three dimensional numerals and white dial. In 1956, a black finish was added. (132,043 sold)

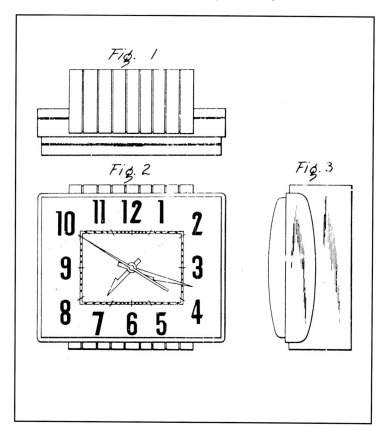

The circa 1955-56 General Electric Telechron **Model 2H105** "Illusion" (6-7/8" x 8-1/2" x 2-1/2") features a "smart, clear, easy to read dial" that "floats" against the textured backdrop of the red, green, yellow, or white plastic case.

Leo Ivan Bruce designed (D174,615, awarded May 3, 1955) the 1955-57 General Electric Telechron **Model 2H103** "Cupboard" ($2.98), 5-1/4" x 8-1/4" x 2-3/4". It has a white, yellow, or red plastic case with white dial or brown plastic case with wood-grained dial. (711,734 sold)

"3" Series

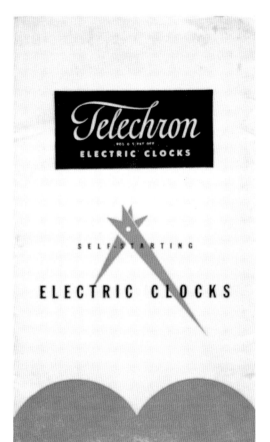

Cover to a circa 1935 Telechron sales brochure.

The 1934-35 Telechron **Model 3F01** "Commonwealth" (4-5/16" x 12" x 3-1/4") has a mahogany case with stepped base and chrome plated side ornaments. The ivory lacquer dial has black characters on a gray numeral band. Buffed Nicral bezel. Designed by John Nickelsen. (4,827 sold) **Not Pictured:** The circa 1932-35 **Model 3A01** featured an auxiliary movement. I found reference to the model number and sales figures, but no further details about case composition and design. (612 sold)

The 1933-37 General Electric Telechron **Model AB3F02** "Puritan" ($6.50), 12-1/4" w, was available in choice of mahogany veneer or hand-rubbed maple. Designed by John P. Rainbault. Sales totaled 18,665.

The 1935-37 Telechron **Model 3F03** "Esquire" ($6.95), 5-5/8" x 8-5/8" x 3", has a veneered walnut case with a polished brass center band and bezel. The 3-1/2" metal dial is finished with black numerals on a cream background. Designed by Eugene J. Lux. (16,462 sold)

The 1936-38 General Electric **Model 3F04** "Vivienne" ($7.95), 5-3/8" x 9-1/8" x 2-1/4", was described in 1936 sales literature as "modern in design, yet harmonizing with furniture of any period." It has a case of striped mahogany with a base of zebrawood; a brass telescope-type bezel, and an ivory dial with black numerals and hands. (5,254 sold)

The 1947-48 General Electric **Model 3H06** "Pristine" ($12.50), 4-5/8" x 12-5/16" x 2-1/4", was a small mantel clock with a traditional tambour-style mahogany case. It features etched black numerals on a satin-white dial and a wide brass bezel. (84,530 sold). *Courtesy of Jay Kennan.*

The circa 1932 General Electric Telechron **Model 3A05** ($14.95) has a mahogany case with brass bezel, ornament, and feet. It features a spring-wound auxiliary movement to keep the clock operating in case of a power failure.

The 1945-48 Telechron **Model 3H07** "Gracewood," 5-5/8" x 10-1/2" x 2-1/8". (54,008 sold). *Courtesy of Jay Kennan.*

The circa 1934-35 Telechron **Model 3A51** "Renault" ($16.00), 6" x 4-7/8" x 3-3/8", has a "Directoire" style mahogany case with Spanish highlighted, lacquer finish with inlaid border. The dial is gold finished with a convexly raised numeral band. Take away the auxiliary movement and the "Renault" becomes the 1935 Special Campaign **Model CF351** "Minaret" ($5.95). *Courtesy of Jay Kennan.*

The 1932-36 Telechron **Model 3F51** "Duke" ($4.50), 4-3/8" x 4" x 2-1/4", has a black composition plastic case with gold-finished bezel, base outline, and feet. The 3" dial is lacquered metal. One piece of trim is missing in the example photographed, decreasing its value. Designed by Kurt Rettich. (51,027 sold). *Courtesy of Esther Cooperman.*

The 1932-35 General Electric **Model AB3F52** "Petite" ($3.95), 4-3/4" x 3-7/8" x 2", has a black molded plastic case with chrome plated feet, bezel ring, and trim. It has a 3" light ivory dial with black moderne Roman numerals. The "Petite" was also available in ivory with brass trimmings and Chinese red with chrome trimmings. Designed by Francis W. Pike. (35,271 sold)

Left: The 1933-36 Telechron **Model 3F53** "Daphne" ($4.50), 3-5/8" x 4-3/16" x 2-3/16", has a hexagonal catalin case in choice of green, ivory, black, red, or rose quartz. The paint peeling off the dial of the pictured clock reduces its value slightly. (30,535 sold). *Courtesy of Jay Kennan.*

The "Daphne" was also offered in a case of "moulded transparent clear catalin" (**Model 3F53-T**, $4.95). The movement was nickel-plated and polished and the coils and leads are aluminum lacquered. The dial features a silver finish with black numerals. Because of its rarity, the clear case "Daphne" commands a significantly higher price.

Rear view of the clear case "Daphne."

The circa 1933-35 General Electric **Model AB3F54** "Little Hostess" ($3.95), 5-1/2" x 5" x 2", is a small table model of the "Hostess" kitchen wall clock. It has an ivory beetleware case with brass bezel ring, decorative edge, and feet. The 3-1/2" cream enamel dial has black Arabic numerals. Introduced in 1933, the "Little Hostess" was also available with a green or black beetleware case with chrome trimmings. Designed by John P. Rainbault. (32,839 sold)

The 1933-36 Telechron **Model 3F55** "Newberry" ($6.95), 6-1/2" x 6" x 2-3/4", offers colonial design in choice of mahogany or maple finish, both with relief ornamentation. It features a lacquered dial and brass telescoping bezel. Designed by Harriet Heile. (14,794 sold). *Courtesy of Jay Kennan.*

Interior of a mid-1930s Telechron sales brochure.

Raymond E. Patten was awarded a design patent (D94,560, Feb. 12, 1935) for the "Vogue."

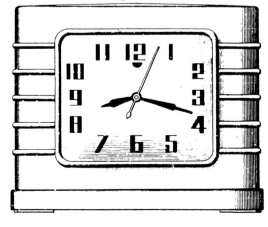

The 1934-37 General Electric **Model AB3F56** "Vogue" ($5.95), 5" x 5-7/8" x 1-7/8", was described in 1934 sales literature as a "striking combination of copper and black." It has a copper case with a black base and bezel ring. The dial is light cream with black Arabic numerals. It has 4 raised parallel lines on the sides. Designed by Raymond E. Patten. (17,387 sold)

The "Squarart" in black and chrome. *Courtesy of Jay Kennan.*

The 1934-36 Telechron **Model 3F59** "Squarart" (4-7/8" x 4-7/8" x 2-1/4") has a metal case finished in choice of black, ivory, or green. Designed by John Nickelsen. (50,499 sold). *Courtesy of Esther Cooperman.*

The 1934-38 General Electric **Model AB3F58** "Secretary" ($7.50), 5-5/8" x 5-5/8" x 3", has a mahogany case with contrasting inlaid wood trim. The 3-1/2" light ivory dial has black Arabic numerals. Designed by Shepard Pond. (5,563 sold)

The 1934-36 General Electric **Model AB 3F60** "Fleet" ($3.95), 5" sq., is an easel-type clock with a molded plastic case in green, ivory, or black, chrome bezel, and light ivory dial with Roman numerals. (45,654 sold)

The 1935-37 Telechron **Model 3F61** "Tempo" (4-1/4" x 4-5/8" x 2-3/4") has a molded plastic case in choice of black with ivory lacquered outer bezel ($3.95) or antique ivory with black lacquered outer bezel ($4.50). The inner bezel on both is brass. The dial features a light cream background with black and gray numerals with gray centers. Designed by Jacques Bars. (38,241 sold). *Courtesy of Jay Kennan.* **Not Pictured:** The 1935-36 General Electric **Model 3F62**. (1,398 sold)

The 1936-37 Telechron **Model CF363** "Usher" ($4.25 (Iv) & $3.75 (Bk)), 4" x 4-3/4" x 2-9/16", has a molded black plastic case with antique white lacquered front plate and gold finished bezel. The metal dial has a light cream enamel background with black characters on a light gray numeral band. The "Usher" was also available with an antique ivory plastic case with dark gunmetal lacquered front plate. Designed by Frank W. Green. (45,825 sold). *Courtesy of Jay Kennan.*

The 1936-42 Telechron **Model 3F65** "Iris" ($5.95), 5" x 5" x 2-1/2", has a blue glass case with mirror finish. The 3" dial has a satin gold center with gold-color numerals on blue numeral band. The bezel and hands are brass. (67,714 combined sales). *Courtesy of Esther Cooperman.*

The 1935-38 General Electric **Model 3F64** "Wellfleet" or "New Fleet" ($3.95), 5" x 5" x 1-7/8", has a black molded plastic case. A rectangular chrome bezel sets off a light ivory dial with ivory numerals on a black circular background. (17,273 sold)

The "Iris" was also available in rose glass with mirror finish. The dial features black numerals on a dark ivory numeral band. *Courtesy of Esther Cooperman.*

The 1936-38 General Electric **Model 3F66** "Concord" ($4.95), 4-3/4" x 8" x 2-1/8", has a case finished in a combination of striped mahogany and rosewood. A brass telescope-type bezel surrounds the ivory dial with Arabic numerals and black hands. "The Concord is, without question, one of the most handsome clocks on the market today" reads the 1936 sales literature. Designed by John P. Rainbault. (8,287 sold)

The 1936-38 General Electric **Model 3F68** "Longwood" ($7.95) as shown in the design patent awarded to John P. Rainbault on September 22, 1936. (9,126 sold)

The 1937-41 Telechron **Model 3F67** "Pageant" ($3.95), 4-9/16" x 4-5/16" x 3", has a molded black plastic case with brass bezel, hands, and ornaments on the side. The 3-1/4" metal dial has black characters on a dark ivory numeral band and satin gold center. The "Pageant" also comes with a brown (No. 3F67-Br, $3.95) or ivory (No. 3F67-I, $4.95) case, with the same trimmings. Designed by Jacques Bars. (32,469 sold). *Courtesy of Jay Kennan.*

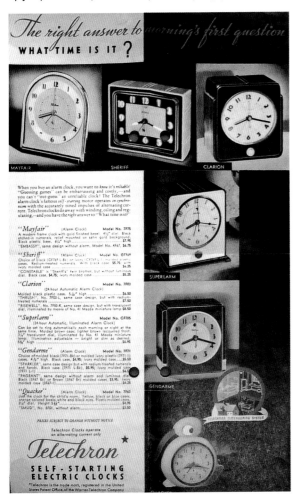

Interior of a mid-1930s Telechron sales brochure.

The 1937-39 Telechron **Model 3F69** "Nassau" ($6.95), 5-3/4" x 5-1/16" x 2-7/8", has a wood case of modern design with brown walnut front and sides and Burma Padouk back and rolls. It has a wood ball footrest and white dial with black outline numerals and cream center and band. Designed by Leo Ivan Bruce. (12,728 sold). *Courtesy of Esther Cooperman.*

The 1936-39 General Electric **Model 3F70** "Park Avenue" ($8.50). Designed by John P. Rainbault. (9,797 sold)

The 1937-40 Telechron **Model 3F71** "Coronado" ($6.75), 4-3/8" x 7-3/4" x 2-7/8", has a brown mahogany case with contrasting light vertical side flutings. The hands and bezel are polished brass; the metal dial has a white background with black outline numerals and a cream center and band. Designed by Leo Ivan Bruce. (27,966 sold)

The Telechron Special Campaign **Model 3H73** Domino has a redesigned dial.

The sales literature for the 1937-38 General Electric **Model 3F72** "Brevet" ($7.95), 6-5/8" x 6-5/8" x 3", describes it as "masculine in treatment" with a striped mahogany case that "makes it most suitab[le] for use in practically any room in the house…" (5,211 sold)

The 1937-39 Telechron **Model 3H73** "Domino" ($2.95), 4-1/2" x 4-1/4" x 2-1/2", has a molded plastic case in black or mottled brown, buffed Nicral bezel, satin gold dial with cream color center, and numerals with black outlines. The "Domino" was also offered as the Special Campaign **Model CH373**. Designed by Frank W. Green. The alarm version is the "Butler" (**Model 7H79**). (47,902 sold)

The 1937-41 General Electric **Model 3F74** "Duncan" ($3.95), 5-1/8" x 4-3/4" x 2-1/8", was available in a choice of black or navy blue Fiberlon case. Both variations featured an ivory dial with black numerals and hands, and brass bezel, second hand, and ball feet. (30,209 sold)

The 1937-39 General Electric **Model 3H76** "Ithaca" ($2.95), 5" x 4-1/2" x 2", has a black or walnut brown molded plastic case, a Nicral or chrome bezel, a cream and silver dial, black numeral band and hands, and a chrome sweep second hand. (45,339 sold)

The 1939-41 Telechron **Model 3H77** "Advocate" ($5.95), 5-1/4" x 5-5/8" x 2-3/4", has a wood case covered in black "Textileather" striped with bold bronze lines. The bezel and hands are polished brass. The dial has a light cream background with black lithographed numerals. Designed by Robert W. Goulet. (13,546 sold)

The 1937-39 General Electric **Model 3H78** "Basque" ($4.95), 4-1/4" x 5" x 2-1/4", has a fluted black or ivory color "Fiberlon" case, brass bezel, ivory and buff gold dial, and black hands and Roman numerals. (20,355 sold)

The 1939-40 Telechron **Model 3H79** "Croft" ($3.25), 4-1/2" x 4-9/16" x 2-1/2", has a mottled brown plastic case, brass bezel, and blue-lacquered metal hands. The 3-1/4" metal dial has black lithographed characters on a light cream background with gold bronze color center. (14,441 sold). Alarm versions were the "Supervisor" (**7H107**) and "Warden" (**7H107-K**).

The 1937-39 General Electric **Model 3H80** "Morgan" ($5.95), 6" x 5" x 2-1/4", has a mahogany case with black base and feet, a brass bezel and gold dial with black numerals and hands. It featured a new "Enameloid cloisonné" dial in brocade effect. Although not really an art deco design, it blends well with many crossover styles, such as Regency modern. (10,312 sold)

The 1939-42 Telechron **Model 3H81** "Virginian" ($5.95), 5-1/4" x 4-5/8" x 3", has a walnut finished case with fluted lower section finished in dark brown. The 3-1/2" metal dial has a light cream background with black characters on a cream white numeral band. (11,885 sold)

"There are Telechron Electric Clocks to Delight Every Bride" according to this advertisement in *House Beautiful Guide for the Bride* (Fall/Winter 1940).

The 1937-39 General Electric **Model 3H82** "New Lotus" ($8.50), 6-1/4" h, has a flower shaped mahogany case with decorative inlay. The ivory dial has black numerals. (5,350 sold)

The 1939-42 Telechron **Model 3H83** "Melbourne" ($7.95), 5-5/16" x 6" x 2-7/8", has a green "marblette" case with brass bezel and hands. The 3-1/2" dial has a light cream background with gold bronze numerals on a black band. (7,007 sold)

The 1937-38 General Electric **Model 3H84** "Monmouth" ($9.95), 6-1/2" x 8-1/8" x 2-1/2", has a mahogany case with top ornament and base plated in gold. The bezel and dial have a gold finish with black numerals and hands. (5,136 sold)

The 1940-42 Telechron **Model 3H85** "Resolute" ($5.95), 6-3/4" x 7-1/2" x 3", is a ship's wheel clock with a polished brass case and spokes. The cream dial has blue-starred numerals matching the color of the lacquered hands. "A ship's wheel clock that effects the correct decorative note for the deep water sailor ashore!" (40,245 sold). *Courtesy of Esther Cooperman.*

The front, top, and back of the 1938-40 General Electric **Model 3H86** "New Brevet" ($6.95), 6-3/8" x 7-1/8" x 3-1/8", are covered with a grained, mahogany-toned facsimile of Italian leather. The sides and base are mahogany, the oblong dial features Roman numerals on a gilt center. (6,673 sold)

The 1940-41 Telechron **Model CH387** "Somerset" ($5.95), 5-5/8"
x 6-1/8" x 2-7/8", has a brown mahogany color case, dark brown
base, brass bezel and fluted ornament, blued metal hands, and tan
and cream finished dial. Designed by Leo Ivan Bruce. (5,248 sold)

The 1940-42 Telechron **Model 3H89** "Bancroft" ($6.95), 5-1/4" x 5-
1/2" x 3", has a square dark wood case with light wood decorative
side flutings and brass feet, bezel, and hands. The 3-1/2" dial is light
cream. Designed by Leo Ivan Bruce. (12,053 sold)

The 1939-41 General Electric **Model 3H88** "Farragut" or "World's
Fair" ($3.50), 5" x 4-5/8" x 2-1/2", has a brown plastic case, brass
bezel, gold and buff dial with black numerals, and brass sweep second
hand. (9,862 sold)

The 1939-41 General Electric **Model 3H90** "Norfolk" ($7.50), 5-3/8"
x 6-1/4" x 2-7/8", has a walnut case with contrasting stripes of maple
inlay. The gold bezel and dial have black Arabic numerals and hands
with a gold-finish second hand. (4,993 sold)

The 1940-42 Telechron **Model 3H91** "Glamour" ($9.95), 5-1/4" x 5-1/4" x 3-1/4", has a square onyx case with brass bezel and hands. The dial is cream with a light brown numeral band. (7,024 sold). *Courtesy of Esther Cooperman.*

Above: The 1939-40 General Electric **Model 3H92** "New Lorraine" ($5.95), 4-3/4" x 5" x 3", has a solid wood case with dark walnut finish cradled in an oblong base finished in black. The ivory and gold-colored dial has black numerals. (8,986 sold)

Right: December 9, 1940, Telechron advertisement in *Life* featuring the "Glamour." Other models are the "Stewardess," "Bancroft," "Satellite," and "Imp."

GLAMOUR is a simple, effective design in onyx, suitable for almost any room in the home. A model that enhances any setting, it is priced at only **$9.95.** An ideal clock for a Christmas gift.

GIFT TIME

Appropriate gifts present no problems to the person who is familiar with the attractive array of Telechron electric clocks. Among these excellent time-keepers there is a gift for every one. And you give not only a handsome design, but time-proved accuracy and reliability as well! Telechron clocks, priced from $2.95 to $17.50, are sold by leading dealers throughout the country.

STEWARDESS adds a smart touch to a kitchen or bathroom wall! The metal case is available in a variety of colors: chrome with ivory, green, black, white, red or all chrome. Priced at **$4.95.**

BANCROFT, a new design in brown wood with horizontal flutings of lighter wood, is **$6.95.** Telechron clocks are powered by the self-starting Telechron motor, sealed in oil for quietness and long life.

SATELLITE is an effective design in glass and gold-colored metal. The numerals are etched on the plate glass dial with mirror center. Perfect for a modern setting, it is priced at **$9.95.**

IMP is a handsome new alarm clock in plastic, available in rose, ivory or brown colors. Modestly priced at **$5.95.** Telechron is the most famous name in the electric clock field.

Telechron
Reg. U. S. Pat. Off.

SELF-STARTING ELECTRIC CLOCKS

WARREN TELECHRON CO.
Ashland · Massachusetts
IN CANADA:
THE CANADIAN GENERAL ELECTRIC CO.

A Telechron clock in every room provides a complete synchronised timekeeping system — like the Telechron systems that keep time so efficiently for schools, hotels, hospitals and public buildings.

The circa 1940-42 Telechron **Model 3H93** "Investor" ($3.50), 4-1/4" x 5-1/2" x 3", has a mottled brown plastic case with vertical flutings. The 3-1/2" metal dial has a cream center, light cream background, and brown characters. Both the hands and bezel are brass. Add an alarm, and the "Investor" becomes the "Secretary" (No. 7H91). This basic Ivan Bruce design was used in a series of models well into the 1950s. (17,549 sold)

Above: The 1939-42 General Electric **Model 3H94** "Conway" ($5.95), 4-3/4" x 5-1/8" x 2-7/8", is "a perfect reflection of good taste" according to sales literature, with its blue mirror glass case, brass bezel and hands, and tan and ivory dial with brown numerals. It was also available in rose-colored mirror glass with a golden tint. The alarm version is the Ashby (**Model 7H102**). (32,893 sold)

Right: The April 5, 1941, *Saturday Evening Post* ran this Telechron advertisement for the "Investor," "Supervisor," "Buffet," and "Vagabond."

The 1941-42 Telechron **Model 3H95** "Snug" ($4.95), 4-11/16" x 5-1/8" x 2-3/4", has a brown wood case with vertical flutings below the dial. The 3 inch dial has a tan center, light cream numeral band, and tan numerals. Both the bezel and hands are brass. (18,744 sold). *Courtesy of Jay Kennan.*

The catalog photograph shows the original color of the "Dartmouth."

The 1939-40 General Electric **Model 3H96** "Dartmouth" ($7.50), 5-1/2" x 5-1/2" x 2-7/8", has a green, facsimile onyx, Bakelite case, a two-toned dial in ivory and gold, black moderne numerals, and gold-color hands. Over the years, the green "onyx" has turned into a yellowish-green. (6,055 sold)

The 1941-42 Telechron **Model 3H97** "Vassal" ($5.95), 5-9/16" x 5-3/4" x 3-1/2", has a square brown wood case with metal ball feet and movement cover. The dial has a light cream background, gold color stripe, and black characters. Designed by Eugene J. Lux. (12,308 sold)

The 1940 General Electric **Model 3H98** "Navigator" ($5.95), 6-5/8" x 6-5/8" x 3-1/8", has a light brown plastic case with gold-colored spokes, star decoration, bezel, and motor housing. It has a light ivory dial with gold-colored numerals and nautical motif. The hands are also gold-colored. Also available with mahogany brown plastic case. Between 1940 and 1948, almost 239,000 were shipped. Production continued into the early 1950s.

A new version, the **Model 3HA98** "New Navigator" ($8.95) with a dark dial and Roman numerals was offered from 1954-56. Sales of the new version totaled 22,234.

The Telechron Special Campaign **Model CH399** ($4.95), announced June 26, 1942. Based on Norman F. Lockwood's 1940 design of **Model CH797**. (4,684 sold)

MODEL 3HX-150

The 1946-50 Telechron **Model 3H99** "Yachtsman" ($5.85), 6" x 7" x 2-1/2", is a brass ship's wheel clock with ivory plastic movement cover. The 3-1/2" ivory dial is surrounded by a brass numeral band with engraved numerals. The hands are blued metal. (141,645 sold).
Courtesy of Ashland Historical Society.

The 1940-41 General Electric Special Campaign **Model 3HX150** "Briarcliff" ($5.95), 5-5/8" x 5-3/8" x 2-3/8", has a mahogany-finished wood case with gold-colored bezel, hands, and feet. The white dial has brown and gold numerals. (3,067 sold)

The 1946-50 Telechron **Model 3H151** "Pharaoh" ($9.95), 5-1/2" x 6-1/4" x 3-3/4", has a "pyramid" design with a brown mahogany finish and satin bronze bezel and hands. The 3" square dial has a satin gold center and numerals on a black numeral band. (103,033 sold). *Courtesy of Jay Kennan.*

SHERWOOD—MODEL 3H-152

A skillful blending of old and new is this wood-cased occasional model with its richly grained mahogany-finished case of simplified modern design. Light cream dial. Gold-colored square bezel. Gold-colored hour, minute and sweep second hands. Width, 5⅜ inches. Height, 5½ inches. Depth, 3 inches. Price, $6.95.

The 1940-42 General Electric **Model 3H152** "Sherwood" ($6.95), 5-1/2" x 5-3/8" x 3", has a mahogany-finished wood case of "simplified modern design." It has a brass bezel and hands and a light cream dial with tobacco brown numerals. (5,346 sold)

The 1940-41 General Electric **Model 3H154** "Saddle" ($5.95), 4-7/8" x 4-7/8" x 2-3/4", has a case covered in pigskin-grained facsimile leather cradled between base strips of figured walnut. It has a tan and ivory dial and brass bezel and hands. (3,986 sold)

The 1947-48 Telechron **Model 3H155** "Glamour" ($4.95), 5-1/8" x 5-1/8" x 3", has a square black plastic case, a 3-1/2" black lithographed dial with golden tan numerals, and brass bezel and hands. (80,885 sold). *Courtesy of Jay Kennan.*

The 1940-42 General Electric **Model 3H156** "Narcissus" ($9.95), 5-1/4" x 5-1/4" x 3-1/4", has a white onyx case with brass bezel, hands, and motor housing. The light ivory dial has gold-colored center portion and black numerals. (5,329 sold)

Circa 1950 advertisement featuring the "Yachtsman" and "Airlux."

The 1949-50 Telechron **Model 3H157** "Yachtsman" ($7.95), 6-1/8" x 7" x 2-1/2", is a polished brass clock that is "shipshape and right" for office or den. (31,418 sold)

The 1940-42 General Electric **Model 3H158** "Gay" ($3.50), 4" x 5" x 3", has a walnut brown plastic case with brass bezel and hands. The light cream dial has a golden tan decorative outer panel with tobacco-brown numerals. (17,788 sold)

The 1950-53 Telechron **Model 3H159** "Suave" ($21.00), 5-1/2" x 5-1/2" x 4", has a "jewel-like" case that is a bubble of crystal glass, a white cowled dial, and gold numerals and hands. (16,854 sold)

Side view of the "Suave."

The 1940-42 General Electric **Model 3H160** "Rapture" ($9.95), 6-1/8" x 7-3/4" x 2-5/8", features twin discs of transparent plastic set on a metal base. It was available with disks of sapphire blue with chrome base and trimmings or rose pink with brass base and trimmings. Both featured a light cream dial with black and gold numerals. (10,124 sold)

The "Rapture" with rose pink disks.

The 1950-53 Telechron **Model 3H161** "Somerset" ($22.50), 10-1/8" x 7-5/8" x 3-1/8", features "authentic colonial design" in a hand polished mahogany case and decorated glass panel. (14,804 sold)

The 1941-42 General Electric **Model 3H162** "Thrill." (3,904 sold)

The 1941-42 General Electric **Model 3H164** "Bounty" has a brown wood case, brass bezel, and light cream dial with outline numerals. (14,239 sold)

The 1951-53 Telechron **Model 3H163** "Swarthmore" ($22.50), 9-1/4" x 6-1/2" x 3-1/16", has a traditional mahogany color case on a jet black base. The dial features Roman numerals and fleur-de-lis decoration. (9,862 sold). *Courtesy of Ashland Historical Society.*

The 1941-42 General Electric **Model 3H166** "Nimbus" ($5.95), 4-5/8" x 6-7/8" x 2-1/4", (4,314 sold).

The 1945-47 General Electric **Model 3H168** "Debutante" ($6.95), 4-5/8" x 6-7/8" x 2-1/4", is a wood case clock with matching end panels in lighter wood. The dial features a pale ivory background with green numerals. The bezel and hands are brass. (53,424 sold). *Courtesy of Jay Kennan.* **Not Pictured:** The Telechron **Model 3H169**. Reference to this model was found, but no additional details of case design or composition were identified.

The 1946-48 General Electric **Model 3H172GL** "Candlelight" (5-1/2" x 6-1/2" x 2-1/2") has a polished black glass case with brass bezel and hands. Gold numerals and finely lined gold dots are etched into the satin-silver face. The "Candlelight" was also available in "velvety, glowing, brown East India lambskin or pigskin bordered by white saddle stitching (**Model 3H172LR**). (86,324 combined sales)

The 1947-51 General Electric **Model 3H176** "Geneva" ($12.95), 4-5/8" x 7-1/4" x 2-1/4", was available in choice of polished mahogany, birch, or blond wood case, all with fluted brass feet, bezel, and hands. The dial features bronze color numerals on a light cream background. (53,270 sold)

The 1949-50 General Electric **Model 3H178** "Candidate" ($9.95) has a brown plastic case.

The 1949-51 General Electric **Model 3H180** "Voyageur" ($11.95), 5-7/32" x 5-7/8" x 3", has a brown plastic case with wide polished brass bezel. The hands are brown.

The circa 1950-52 General Electric **Model 3H182** "Designer" ($10.95), 4" x 5-1/2" x 2-3/4", has a polished mahogany case, wide polished brass bezel, and embossed ivory dial with raised gold numerals.

The 1951-55 General Electric **Model 3H184** "Concord" ($19.95), 8" x 5-7/8" x 3-3/8", has a polished mahogany case with colonial styling. The top ornament is brass. Distinctive numerals and hands contrast with the scrolled dial. *Courtesy of Ashland Historical Society.*

"Evolutime"

Old Adam and his little Moll
Could never tell the time,
Except by gazing up at Sol
When he came out to shine.

As time passed on and man increased,
Improving as a class,
A great invention was released—
It was the hour-glass.

The sands of time went trick'ling down,
The world commenced to talk
When someone won himself renown
By giving it the clock.

The clock told time and nearly right,
It was a clever thing,
But often in the day or night
'Twould stop or bust a spring.

Then Mr. Warren came along
And slowly shook his head
He thought the principle was wrong
And this is what he said:

"Take out the tick, take out the tock
And hitch a motor on":
His 'lectric clock is now in stock,
Behold the Telechron!

Gladys Knowlton
Telechron Field Manager's Office

"4" Series

The 1932-40 Telechron **Model 4A01** "Bishop" ($20.00), 6-7/8" x 17" x 3-3/4", has a Sheraton-style mahogany case, Spanish high-lighted lacquer finish, and inlaid border and carved overlay ornaments. The 4-1/2" dial is gold-finished with convexly raised numeral band. (976 sold). The "Bishop" was offered without the auxiliary movement as the 1935 Special Campaign **Model CF401** ($8.50). (1,055 sold)

The 1931-40 Telechron **Model 4F01** "Maynard" ($9.95), 7-5/16" x 17-1/4" x 3-7/8", has a mahogany case with Spanish highlighted finish and Lacewood front panels. The 4-1/2" dial is gold finished and etched. The "Maynard" was originally sold as the "Durham" (No. 559). (28,210 sold).
Not Pictured: Reference to a Telechron **Model 4A02** was found but no details about case design or composition were identified.

The General Electric **Model 4F02** is a tambour-style mantel clock with traditional design.

The 1935-39 Telechron **Model 4F03** "Perry" ($7.95), 8-1/8" x 18-13/16" x 3-7/8", has a brown mahogany case with polished lacquer finish and relief ornament. It has a gold-finished bezel and metal dial with gold-bronze numerals on satin finish background. (11,313 sold)

The 1936-37 General Electric **Model 4F04** "Lynnwood" ($9.95), 7-5/8" x 18-1/2" x 3", is a mantel clock with traditional design. It has a striped mahogany case with decorative front panels in light finished mahogany, ivory dial, black numerals and hands, and brass bezel. (5,309 sold)

Above: The Telechron **Model 4A05** or General Electric Telechron **Model AB4A05**.

Right: The 1936-37 Telechron **Model 4F05** "Gracewood" mantel clock ($8.85), 5-7/8" x 14-3/16" x 3-1/8", has a brown mahogany case with cherry base. The 4-1/2" metal dial has a moderne brass "skeleton" numeral bezel. Designed by Jacques Bars. (13,130 sold) *Courtesy of Jay Kennan.* **Not Pictured**: The 1936-39 General Electric **Model 4F06** "Londonderry" ($9.95) is a mantel clock with traditional tambour design, inlay panels, and decorative relief ornamentation above the dial. The specifications sheet for the "Londonderry" identifies the designer as John P. Rainbault. (17,996 sold)

The 1940-42 Telechron **Model 4B07** "Harwich" ($35.00), 5-7/8" x 10" x 3", has a case of grained white onyx with contrasting brown onyx base. A gold color numeral band and hands set off the 3-1/2" blank dial. Designed by Leo Ivan Bruce. (506 sold)

The 1937-42 General Electric **Model 4H08** "New Geneva" ($6.50), 6-3/8" x 12" x 3", has a solid wood case finished in brown walnut, gold-colored dial with black numerals on a light cream background, and gold-colored hands. (64,200 sold).
Not Pictured: The 1939-41 General Electric **Model 4H10** "Amherst" ($9.95), 7-3/4" x 17-5/8" x 4", is a silent tambour clock in a richly grained brown mahogany case with dark brown base and distinctive stripes of maple-finished inlay. The dial is cream with black and gold numerals. (4,138 sold)

The 1940-42 General Electric **Model 4H12** "Candlelight" ($9.95), 7-5/8" x 15-1/8" x 4-1/4", is a tambour clock with case finished in mahogany veneer. The hands and bezel are brass. With a gong strike, it was offered as the "Hearth" (**Model 6B10**). (8,095 sold)

The 1933-34 Telechron **Model 4F51** "Telart" ($5.95), 5-1/2" x 6-1/2" x 3", was available in choice of polished brass (pictured) or chrome frame and supports on a glossy black plastic base. The 4-1/2" dial has moderne black numerals. Add an alarm and the "Telart" becomes the "Signalette" (**Model 7F55**). (23,296 sold). *Courtesy of Esther Cooperman.*

The 1932-40 Telechron **Model 4A51** "Pemberton" ($20.00), 8-1/4" x 6-1/4" x 3-5/8", has a colonial-style mahogany case with an inlaid panel. (655 sold). The 1935-36 **Model CF451** "Wedgewood" ($8.50), was a Special Campaign Model with the same case design as the "Pemberton," but without the auxiliary movement. (781 sold)

The "Telart" in chrome. *Courtesy of Esther Cooperman.*

This 1933 variation of the "Telart" (**Model 4F51A**) has brass supports that curve into the frame and a plain black base. I was able to date this variation from a 1933 magazine ad, but found no production data.

The 1933-38 General Electric **Model 4F52** "Debutante" ($6.75), 5-1/8" x 5-1/4" x 2-1/2", has a chrome case with a matching 4-1/2" numeral band set in a jet black background. The "Debutante" was also available with a brass case and numeral band. Designed by John P. Rainbault. (84,969 sold)

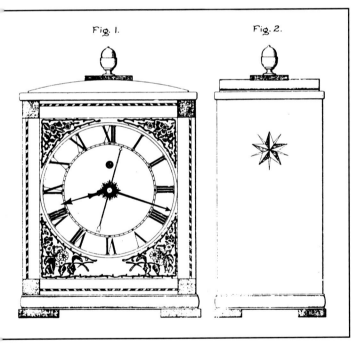

The 1934-36 Telechron **Model 4F53** "Colonist" ($19.75), 9-1/4" x 6-3/16" x 3-3/16", as shown in the design patent awarded to Harry C. Richardson on March 8, 1932. It features "year 1820 period design" in choice of walnut with white holly case and Ebony finish marquetry border and star ornament or maple case with ebony finish and white holly marquetry border. Both feature a white enamel dial with gold border design and black numerals. (791 sold)

The General Electric **Model 4F54** "Stanwood" ($7.50), 6-3/8" x 6-3/8" x 1-7/8", came in three variations: a Zebra wood frame with gold finish dial and bezel, a Harewood frame with chrome trimming, and Ebony with chrome trimmings. All featured black Arabic numerals. (25,996 sold)

The 1934-40 Telechron **Model 4F55** "Airlux" ($12.50), 5-1/4" x 5-1/4" x 2-5/8", has a white African onyx case, polished brass numeral band with etched-in white Roman numerals, cream white dial, and brass hands. Also available in green San Raphael onyx (**Model 4F55G**). (19,295 sold). Add an alarm and the "Airlux" becomes the "Sportsman" (**Model 7F57**). Change the onyx case to wood and the "Airlux" becomes the 1934-37 "Airman." The "Airman" came in walnut with a chrome bezel and etched-in black numerals and black dial (**Model 4F55-W**, $6.75) and maple finish with brass bezel and etched in white Roman numerals and cream white dial (**Model 4F55-MP**). (29,151 sold). After the wood case version was discontinued, the onyx "Airlux" was renamed the "Airman." The alarm version of the wood-cased "Airman" was the "Airlarm" (**Model 7F57**). The original "Airlux" design was reintroduced in October 1946 as the "Statesman" (**Model 4H55**, $14.00) with white plastic replacing the onyx case. (43,951 sold). The "Sportsman" (**Model 7H57**) was also reintroduced in 1947 with a plastic case. In August 1948, however, the case again became genuine onyx. Designed by Simon de Vaulchier. *Courtesy of Jay Kennan.*

The 1934-36 Telechron **Model 4F57** "Starman" ($6.75), 5-1/4" x 5-1/4" x 2-5/8", is yet another variation of the "Airman." It was available in choice of (1) walnut case with chrome bezel and dial finished in black lacquer and silver stars or (2) maple case with brass bezel and gold stars. Designed by Simon de Vaulchier. (7,396 sold)

The "Airman" is shown in this advertisement from the June 8, 1935, *Saturday Evening Post*. Other models pictured are the "Pharaoh," and "Attaché."

Not Pictured: The 1935 General Electric **Model 4F56** ($8.50) has a colonial-style wood case with brass top handle, feet, and bezel. The dial features Roman numerals on a light background. (515 sold)

The 1935-36 General Electric **Model 4F58** "Lotus" ($9.95), 6" x 6-1/2" x 3", has a chrome plated metal case in the shape of a lotus leaf set on a molded black plastic base. The dial is heavy plate glass mirror with a "black Lyco" finish. The numerals and center are etched in cream enamel by a special photographic process. A base lamp lights the clock through the bottom edge. Designed by Raymond E. Patten. (10,295 sold)

Raymond E. Patten was awarded a design patent (D97,782) for the "Lotus."

The 1934-36 Telechron **Model 4F59** "Attaché" ($6.75), 5-1/8" x 5" x 2-3/4", is the non-alarm version of the "Vedette" (**Model 7F61**). It came in choice of (A) "gold finish" bezel and base with gold bronze lacquered back or (B) chrome with silver lacquered metal back. Unlike the dial on the "Vedette" (pictured), the "Attaché" featured polished gold characters on a glossy black background and etched satin silver center. (7,504 sold)

The 1935-38 General Electric **Model 4F60** "Dictator" ($5.50), 5" x 5-1/2" x 3", is an easel clock with combination black mirror and chrome frame dial. The numerals are etched on a circular polished chrome band formed in the shape of a cup. The exposed hands are buffed nickel silver. The clock was sold as the "Rex" under the same model number with a dark blue rather than black mirror. Designed by Raymond E. Patten. (12,802 combined sales)

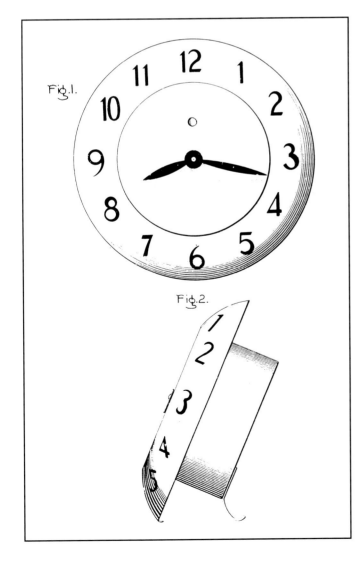

Above: The 1934-42 Telechron **Model 4F61** "Pharaoh" ($9.95), 6-3/4" x 7-5/8" x 4-11/16", has a mahogany case with a "pyramid" design and vertical side inlays. The metal dial has a satin gold center and polished gold numerals on a black numeral band. Designed by Jacques Bars. (61,915 sold). *Courtesy of Jay Kennan.*

Left: Raymond E. Patten was awarded the design patent (D97,780, Dec. 10, 1935) for the "Dictator."

The "Pharaoh" with dark mahogany finish.

The 1936-38 General Electric **Model 4F62** "Blue Night" ($5.95), 5-3/4" x 5-3/4" x 2", is an occasional clock with a circular faceted blue mirror glass dial. This variation features black numerals etched into a dull silver numeral band. The exposed hands are polished chrome. Based on design by John P. Rainbault. "Night" is sometimes spelled "Nite" in promotional literature. (7,308 sold)

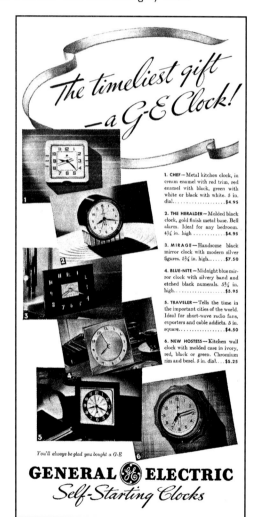

General Electric clock advertisement appearing in the December 7, 1936, *Time*. Featured models are the "Chef," "The Heralder," "Mirage," "Blue-Nite," "Traveler," and "New Hostess."

The 1935-36 Telechron **Model 4F63** "Aztec" ($7.95), 5-5/8" x 5-1/2" x 2-7/8", has an onyx base with choice of (A) polished brass bezel with gold bronze lacquered back or (B) polished chrome bezel with silver lacquered back. Both featured a 4-1/2" dial with polished gold characters on glossy black background and satin silver center. Add an alarm movement and the "Aztec" becomes the "Carillon" (No. 7F67). (6,164 sold)

The 1936-38 General Electric **Model 4F64** "Blue Night" ($5.95), 5-3/4" x 5-3/4" x 2", has a square faceted blue mirror dial and black numerals etched into a dull silver numeral band. Designed by John P. Rainbault. (10,410 sold)

Above: The 1936-38 General Electric **Model 4F66** ($5.95), 5-3/4" x 5-3/4" x 2", also named the "Blue Night" is the same as the Model 4F62 except that the blue mirror dial/case is arched rather than circular. Designed by John P. Rainbault. (10,083 sold)

Right: The 1936-42 Telechron **Model 4F67** "Embassy" ($6.75), 6-1/4" x 5-1/4" x 3-3/8", has a polished brass frame; satin gold colored dial, 4-1/2" diameter satin brass numeral band with black filled etched numerals, and black plastic base. Add an alarm to the "Embassy" and it becomes the "Mayfair" (**Model 7F75**) or, with luminous hands and dial, the "Nocturne" (**Model 7F75L**). (51,241 sold)

The 1935-39 Telechron **Model 4F65** "Luxor" ($9.95), 6-1/4" x 7-3/8" x 2-9/16", has a blue glass case with mirror finish, polished chrome base and hands, light blue imitation cloisonné dial, and silver finished bezel with black etched-in Roman numerals. Introduced in 1935, two variations were added in 1936: (1) clear mirror glass case (No. 4F65-Wh), silver imitation cloisonné dial, and black hands and (2) amethyst mirror glass (No. 4F65-Am). The white and amethyst models were discontinued after 1 year, but the blue glass version continued in production until December 1939. Designed by Jacques Bars. (46,102 sold, blue; 43,613 sold, amethyst and white)

TO GRACE YOUR HOME

4 OF MANY ACCURATE, ATTRACTIVE

Telechron CLOCKS

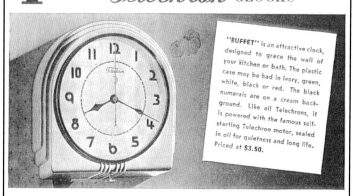

"BUFFET" is an attractive clock, designed to grace the wall of your kitchen or bath. The plastic case may be had in ivory, green, white, black or red. The black numerals are on a cream background. Like all Telechrons, it is powered with the famous self-starting Telechron motor, sealed in oil for quietness and long life. Priced at $3.50.

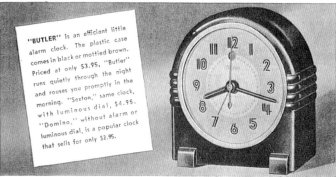

"BUTLER" is an efficient little alarm clock. The plastic case comes in black or mottled brown. Priced at only $3.95, "Butler" runs quietly through the night and rouses you promptly in the morning. "Sexton," same clock, with luminous dial, $4.95. "Domino," without alarm or luminous dial, is a popular clock that sells for only $2.95.

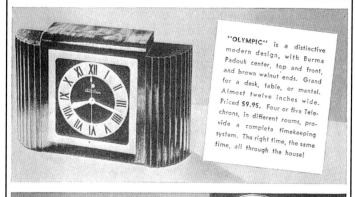

"OLYMPIC" is a distinctive modern design, with Burma Padouk center, top and front, and brown walnut ends. Grand for a desk, table, or mantel. Almost twelve inches wide. Priced $9.95. Four or five Telechrons, in different rooms, provide a complete timekeeping system. The right time, the same time, all through the house!

"EMBASSY" has a graceful case of gold-colored metal. The numerals are etched in black on a silvered band. Price $6.75. "Mayfair," same design with alarm, $7.95. "Nocturne," with alarm, luminous hands and numerals, $8.95. Telechrons, priced as low as $2.95, are sold by good jewelry, electric, gift and department stores.

WARREN TELECHRON COMPANY • ASHLAND, MASSACHUSETTS
(In Canada, the Canadian General Electric Co.)

Schools, hotels, hospitals and office buildings are synchronizing their time with efficient Telechron commercial systems

Telechron
(Reg. U. S. Pat. Off. by Warren Telechron Co.)

SELF-STARTING ELECTRIC CLOCKS

Pictured in this April 9, 1938, advertisement in the *Saturday Evening Post* are the "Buffet," "Butler," "Olympic," and "Embassy."

The 1937-39 General Electric **Model 4H68** "Tuileries" ($6.95), 6-1/4" h, is a round glass clock in choice of blue with white hands or rose gold with cream hands. It is mounted on a glass base. (10,296 sold)

The 1936-37 Telechron **Model 4F69** "Traymore" ($8.50), 6-1/4" x 7-5/8" x 2-3/4", features a brown mahogany case with black, molded plastic base. The 4-1/2" dial features modern skeleton Arabic numerals on a polished brass outer bezel. The hands are also polished brass. Designed by Eugene J. Lux. (11,618 sold)

The 1936-37 Telechron **Model 4F71** "Casino" ($7.95), 6-7/8" x 7-5/8" x 2-3/4", has a mirrored blue glass case, antique ivory plastic base, light blue imitation cloisonné dial, and polished brass skeleton numeral band/bezel and hands. The back of the case is lacquered gold bronze. The "Casino" was also available in mirrored amber glass (No. 4F71 Am) with lavender imitation cloisonné dial. (18,255 sold). *Courtesy of Esther Cooperman.*

Although available literature describes the "Casino" as being available only in blue and amber mirror glass, the variation shown here looks more like charcoal gray than amber. *Courtesy of Esther Cooperman.*

The 1937-39 General Electric **Model 4H72** "Breton" ($8.95), 7" h, is an edge-illuminated clock of white glass with 2 degrees of illumination through the bottom edge. It features a stepped chrome base. Although the "Breton" design was not patented, the numerals and central motif are variations of designs patented by John P. Rainbault. (9,515 sold)

This example of the "Breton" has a solid back, photo-style corner treatment and edges with hammered aluminum appearance, and no lamp. Although the clock still looks good, Jay Kennan was able to identify the Sessions™ hands, indicating that the clock has been repaired. The repairs significantly lower the value.

The 1937-39 Telechron **Model 4F73** "Smartset" ($8.95), 6-5/8" x 7-7/8" x 3", has "Prima Vera" wood on the center, top, and back and dark, simulated rosewood on the sides and base. The 4-1/2" square dial has a satin gold center and polished gold numerals on a black numeral band. Hands and bezel are polished brass. Designed by Leo Ivan Bruce. (11,151 sold). *Courtesy of Ashland Historical Society.*

The 1937-39 Telechron **Model 4F75** "Lido" ($6.95), 5-1/2" x 5-1/2" x 2-3/8", has a blue mirror glass case, silver opalescent lacquered back, blue simulated cloisonné dial, buffed and lacquered silver finish bezel with etched in black Roman numerals, and buffed silver color hands. *Courtesy of Jay Kennan.*

The 1937-39 General Electric **Model 4H74** "Chantilly" ($4.95), 5" x 5" x 2", has a brass, easeltype frame with burgundy red Enameloid cloisonné dial. It has black numerals on a gold numeral band and brass hands. (20,311 sold)

The **Model 4F75** "Lido" was also available with black Carrara glass case, black lacquer dial, polished brass numeral band and hands with etched in white Roman numerals. (15,593 combined sales). *Courtesy of Jay Kennan.*

The 1939-41 General Electric **Model 4H76** "Samson" ($5.95), 7-3/8" x 7-7/8" x 3-3/4", is the non-strike version of the "Grafton" (**Model 6B04**). It has a molded plastic case with walnut brown finish. Unlike the dial on the "Grafton" (pictured), the dial on the "Samson" has a light cream center, cream white numeral band, and rich brown Arabic numerals. (11,462 sold)

The 1937-39 Telechron **Model 4H77** "Deauville" ($7.95), 7" x 6" x 3-1/2", has a blue mirror glass case, gold bronze lacquered back, polished brass base, light blue dial, and polished brass bezel with skeleton Arabic numerals. The "Deauville" was also available with black Carrara glass and black lacquered back and dial. (12,331 sold) *Courtesy of Esther Cooperman.*

The "Deauville" in black Carrara glass. *Courtesy of Esther Cooperman.*

The 1939-41 General Electric **Model 4H78** "Ballard" ($6.95), 5-1/8" x 5-1/2" x 3", has a brass frame, a cream white dial with black outer band, and gold-colored numerals and hands. The sales copy reads "Breathtaking in its beauty, this new metal-framed occasional clock gloriously radiates the color and charm of natural gold." Designed by Jacques Martial. (7,858 sold)

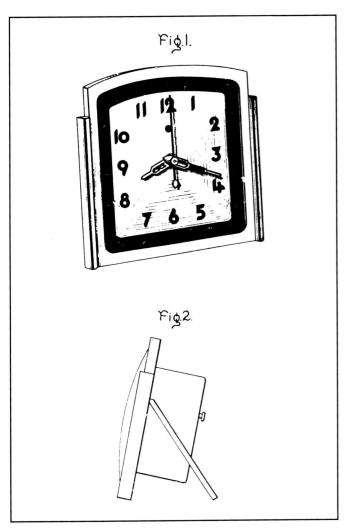

Fig.1.

Fig.2.

Jacques Martial was awarded a design patent (D120,012, awarded April 16, 1940) for the Ballard. With a redesigned dial, it became the "New Ballard" in 1941.

The 1937-40 Telechron **Model 4B79** "Olympic" ($9.95), 6-7/8" x 11-9/32" x 3-1/4", has a wooden case executed in "Burma Padouk" in the center and brown walnut on the rounded and fluted ends. The dial has a gloss black background with black numerals on a satin gold numeral band. Both the hands and bezel are brass. Designed by Jacques Bars. (15,952 shipped). *Courtesy of Esther Cooperman.*

Above: The 1939-41 General Electric **Model 4H80** "Tuscan" ($9.95), 6-1/2" x 8-1/4" x 3-1/4", has a central section of dark walnut supported on the sides by grained panels of zebrawood. It has an ivory and gold-colored dial, black numerals, and brass bezel and hands. (7,475 sold). *Drawing by Robert M. Merchant.*

Left: The 1937-42 Telechron **Model 4H81** "Statesman" ($12.50), 6-1/2" x 6" x 3-1/4", features the same basic case design as the "Deauville" (Model 4H77) but has a white Pedrara onyx case, a cream white dial, and no base. In 1940, an alarm variation of the "Statesman," the "Legislator" (**Model 7H105**) was introduced. Unlike the "Legislator" (pictured) the skeleton bezel on the "Statesman" has no background and the dial has no alarm features. (11,700 sold). *Courtesy of Esther Cooperman.*

The 1939-41 General Electric **Model 4H82** "Quincy" ($9.95), 6-3/8" x 7-7/8" x 3", has a case finished in genuine wine-colored, morocco-grained leather and ebony-finished wood. It has a white and cream dial, brown numerals, and brass bezel and hands. The "Quincy" was also available in blue leather with mahogany side panels and base. (7,294 sold)

The 1938-39 Telechron **Model 4H83** "Naples" ($5.95), 5-3/4" x 6-3/16" x 2-7/8", has a walnut-finished wood panel with rounded sides, tan dial and skeleton numeral band with polished brass inner bezel and hands. Add an alarm and the "Naples" becomes the "Mentor" (**Model 7H87**). (4,083 sold)

Advertisement appearing in the October 1938 House & Garden. Shown are the "Jubilee" (No. 6B01), "Organizer" (No. 8B53), "Statesman" (No. 4H81), and "Pharaoh" (No. 4F61).

The 1939-41 General Electric **Model 4H84** "Athens" ($7.95), 7-3/8" x 6-9/16" x 3", has a dark brown walnut case, light cream dial with black and gold numerals, and brass bezel and hands. It is described as "…a trim bent wood mantel clock of modern classic design." *Courtesy of Ashland Historical Society.*

The 1938-40 Telechron **Model 4B85** "Cordova" ($12.50), 7-1/2" x 7-3/4" x 3-1/4", has a wood case covered in maroon color Morocco leather, striped with gold leaf on the top and front. The dial features burgundy numerals on a light cream background, with satin gold center and bands. The bezel and hands are brass. Designed by Leo Ivan Bruce. (5,183 sold)

The 1939-42 General Electric **Model 4H86** "Nantucket" ($9.95), 7-1/8 x 7-1/4" x 4-1/4", has a mahogany-finished case, lacquered brass spokes and numeral plate, etched numerals filled with blue enamel, and ivory dial. Designed by Leo Ivan Bruce. (22,779 sold)

The 1939-42 Telechron **Model 4H87** "Kirkwood" ($6.50), 6-7/16" x 10-1/2" x 3-1/16", has a solid walnut-finished wood case with vertical graining, 4-1/2" dial with medium brown numerals on a gray numeral band and light cream center, and polished brass bezel and hands. Designed by Leo Ivan Bruce. (28,446 sold). *Courtesy of Esther Cooperman.*

The 1939-42 General Electric **Model 4H88** "Wareham" ($12.50), 5-3/4" x 5-3/8" x 2-7/8", features a gold colored numeral plate mounted on a genuine white onyx base. The etched numerals are filled with white enamel. The dial and sweep second hand are gold-colored, the hour and minute hands, white. (3,918 sold). *Courtesy of Ashland Historical Society.*

The 1939-42 Telechron **Model 4H89** "Vagabond" ($9.95), 7-1/2" x 6-5/8" x 3-1/4", has a brown mahogany panel, dark mahogany base, pedestal, and wheel, brass spokes and hands, satin silver dial, and brass numeral band with etched in vermilion Roman numerals. Designed by Leo Ivan Bruce. (21,478 sold)

Above: The 1940-42 General Electric **Model 4H90** "Ridgefield" ($9.95), 12" x 7-5/8" x 4-1/8", features a colonial design in a mahogany finished wood case with a decorative print in the lower panel opening. The white dial features black numerals and a colorful floral wreath design. (8,996 sold). *Courtesy of Jay Kennan.*

Right: Cover to the 1939-40 General Electric clock catalog.

142

The 1939-42 Telechron **Model 4H91** "Finesse" ($9.95), 6-1/2" x 8-1/4" x 3-1/4", has a wood case covered with genuine leather (choice of blue or brown) and brown mahogany base, top, and side trim. The dial features brown numerals on a tan numeral band and light cream center. Bezels and hands are polished brass. The poor condition of the case seriously detracts from the value. Designed by Leo Ivan Bruce. (10,339 sold). *Courtesy of Esther Cooperman.*

The 1941-42 General Electric **Model 4H92** "New Ballard" ($6.95), 5-1/8" x 5-1/2" x 3", has the same brass case as the original "Ballard" (4H78) but has a redesigned dial. Designed by Jacques Martial. (5,011 sold)

The April 1939 *American Home* contained this advertisement featuring the "Finesse." Other models pictured were the "Pharaoh," "Consort," "Explorer," and "Luxor."

The 1939-41 Telechron **Model 4H93** "Highland" ($5.95), 6-7/8" x 7-1/8" x 3-3/4", has a mottled brown Bakelite case, cream white dial with medium brown numerals on a light ivory colored numeral band, and polished brass bezel and hands. Add a strike to the "Highland" and it becomes the "Angelus" (No. 6B11, $9.95). The dial was also changed to feature a cream-white center with light cream numerals on a medium brown numeral band. Designed by Leo Ivan Bruce. (7,635 sold). *Courtesy of Esther Cooperman.*

The 1941-42 General Electric **Model 4H94** "Ulysses" ($9.95). (3,968 sold)

The 1939-41 Telechron **Model 4H95** "Kendall" ($7.95), 7-3/8" x 7-1/8" x 3", has a wood case with dark walnut finish, cream white dial with medium brown numerals on a light ivory numeral band, and polished brass bezel and hands. Designed by Findlay Williams. *Courtesy of Esther Cooperman.*

The 1940-42 Telechron **Model 4H97** "Forum" ($9.95), 7-3/8" x 7-7/8" x 3-1/8", has a brown wood case with rounded, fluted edges, four bronze ball feet, polished brass bezel and hands, and light cream dial with gold center and black numerals. Designed by Leo Ivan Bruce. (14,821 sold)

The 1940-50 Telechron **Model 4H99** "Knickerbocker" ($19.95), 11-3/4" x 7-3/4" x 3-3/4", has an inlaid mahogany case in an Early American style. It has a brass bezel and ornament. The later versions of the "Knickerbocker," such as the one pictured, have a redesigned case that eliminates the vertical fluting on the edges. Designed by Harry C. Richardson. (20,436 sold). *Courtesy of Esther Cooperman.*

The 1940-42 Telechron **Model 4B151** "Shoreham" ($22.50), 6-1/16" x 7-1/2" x 3", has a white onyx case with brown onyx lateral inlays. The brass bezel incorporates the numerals on an ivory background. The dial is silver, the hands brass. Designed by Leo Ivan Bruce. (810 sold)

The 1940-42 Telechron **Model 4B153** "Barclay" ($27.50), 6-5/16" x 10-3/16" x 3", has a white onyx case with brown grained onyx feet and vertical inserts, brass hands and bezel. The dial has a gold center, brown numerals, and light cream background. Designed by Leo Ivan Bruce. (707 sold)

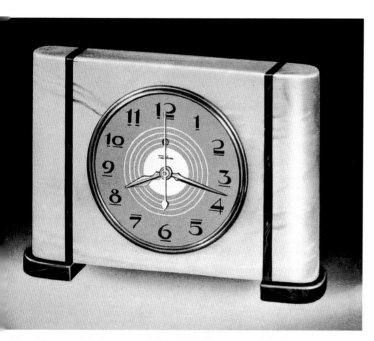

The 1940-42 Telechron **Model 4B155** "Hampshire" ($30.00), 6-5/8" x 9-1/4" x 3", has a white onyx case with brown onyx feet and vertical inlay. The dial has a gold center, light cream background, and brown numerals. Both hands and bezel are brass. Designed by Leo Ivan Bruce. (737 sold)

The 1941-42 Telechron **Model 4H157** "Banker" ($8.95), 6-1/16" x 7-3/4" x 3-3/16", has a brown wood case with a fluted dark brown base section and black vertical lines, brass hands and bezel, and dial with black numerals on tan background and light cream center. (11,248 sold). *Courtesy of Jay Kennan.*

The 1951-52 Telechron **Model 4H167** "Wickford" ($24.00), 9-3/16" x 7-3/4" x 4-5/8", is the non-chime version of the **Model 6B15**. It has a brown wood case with light wood inlays. The 4-1/2" metal dial has a white background with black Roman numerals. The bezel and decorative handle are brass. (1,741 sold)

The 1951-52 Telechron **Model 4H169** "Resolute" ($24.00), 8" x 16-1/2" x 5", is a mahogany-finished, modified tambour-style mantel clock. It is the non-chime version of the **Model 6B17**. The white dial has black Roman numerals. The bezel is brass; the hands deep blue. (2,689 sold)

The 1953-55 Telechron **Model 4H173** "Woodmont" ($29.95), 13" x 7-3/8" x 2-3/4", has a mahogany-finish case with light wood inlay and gold color ornaments. (4,925 sold). *Courtesy of Ashland Historical Society.*

You Can't Date a Clock by its Mechanical Patents

Many appraisers, dealers, and collectors attempt to date the manufacture of clocks and other items by determining the year in which the latest patent was issued. Although this approach can give an earliest possible date of manufacture, it is often off by 10 years or more when used to determine the actual date of manufacture. This is because the patents appearing on clocks are almost always mechanical patents to protect the movement and other production techniques. That is why most Telechron and General Electric clocks have the same patent numbers—they have the same movements. The highest mechanical patent number can be used to determine when the last significant change in the mechanics of the clock were made. Such changes, however, may have been invented 20 years or more before the case was designed. Frequently, the last patent number listed on a Telechron or General Electric clock is from 1927, leading appraisers and dealers to incorrectly conclude that the clock dates from that period. Only design patents (6 digit numbers preceded by a "D") should be used to determine when a model was introduced. Design patents, however, are seldom included on the clock case.

Even the use of design patents, however, is not foolproof. For example, Edgar Bourquin received a design patent for the Model 454 "Hostess" in 1931. The clock remained in production with the same basic case design into the 1950s as the "New Hostess" (No. 2F02 and No. 2H02). Here, the model number and type of rotor can help date the clock. "F" rotors were used for a short period in the early 1930s whereas the "H" rotor was used from 1935 well into the 1950s.

"5" Series

The 1931-40 Telechron **Model 5A01** "Danforth" ($25.50), 8-3/4" x 19-7/8" x 4-5/8", has a Chippendale-style mahogany case, Spanish highlighted lacquer finish and molding, and light mahogany overlay panels. (355 sold)

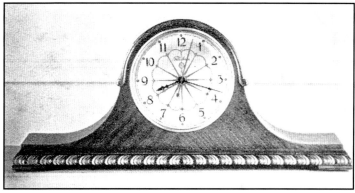

The 1931-34 Telechron **Model 5F01** "Norwood" ($17.50), 8-11/16" x 20" x 5", was billed as "Telechron's finest and largest tambour model." It has a mahogany case with Spanish highlighted finish and carved base. The 5-1/2" dial is gold finished and etched. (1,433 sold)

The circa 1932 General Electric Telechron **Model AB5A02** is a tambour-style mantel clock with a mahogany finish case. It has an auxiliary movement to keep the clock operating in case of a power failure.

The circa 1938 General Electric **Model 5F02** "Tampa" ($14.95), 20-1/2" l, is a silent tambour mantel clock with mahogany case, ivory dial, and black numerals.

The 1940-42 Telechron **Model 5B07** "Barrington" ($9.95), 7-3/4" x 18-3/8" x 4-1/8", has a brown wood case with brass bezel and hands. The light cream dial features gold numerals on a black band. Add a strike movement and the "Barrington" becomes the "Minstrel" (**Model 6B07**). (7,303 sold)

The 1935-36 Telechron **Model 5F03** "Brandon" ($12.50), 7-15/16" x 15" x 3-11/16", has the same basic case design and dial as the "Doric" (Model 5F51), but is suspended between two arched supports. Designed by Belle Kogan. (2,644 sold). *Courtesy of Orsini & Frost, Inc.*

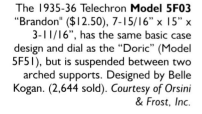

The General Electric **Model 5F50** "Mirage" (5-3/4" x 7-1/2" x 2") has moderne characters and central motif deeply cut into the back of the mirrored glass dial. It comes in black glass with silver characters and white glass with gold characters. Designed by John P. Rainbault.

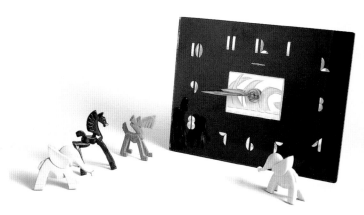

The "Mirage" in black with silver numerals.

The 1935-36 Telechron **Model 5F51** "Doric" ($9.95), 7-9/16" x 6-9/16" x 3-11/16", has a combination mahogany and maple case, an arched brass bezel, a satin silver dial, and gold Roman numerals with black outlines. Based on a design by Belle Kogan, it is basically the "Brandon" without the side mounts. (6,091 sold). *Courtesy of Esther Cooperman.*

Above: Telechron also advertised in *Time*, this advertisement appearing in the November 25, 1935 issue. It features the "Doric" and "Controlla."

Right: The circa 1938 General Electric **Model 5F52** "Mirage" ($7.50), 6" x 6" x 2", has moderne characters and quatrefoil motif cut deeply into the back of the round mirror glass. It was available in white glass with gold characters and black glass with silver characters. Designed by John P. Rainbault.

The 1937-39 Telechron **Model 5B53** "Sheffield" ($12.50), 8-1/2" x 11-7/8" x 5-1/8", is the non-strike version of the "Picardy" (**Model 6B05**). It has a quartered grain Padouk front with brown mahogany sides, top, and back. Designed by Jacques Bars. (2,784 sold)

The General Electric **Model 5F54** "Salon" has moderne Roman numerals and center design cut deep into the back of the round mirror glass. Designed by John P. Rainbault.

John Rainbault chose to use the longer "IIII" rather than the abbreviated "IV" commonly used today, but used the abbreviated "IX" rather than the equally acceptable "VIIII." *Photograph by Stephen Kruft. Courtesy of Stephen Kruft.*

The 1937-39 Telechron **Model 5B55** "Congress" ($12.50), 8-3/8" x 11-1/8" x 4-5/8", has a ripple grain walnut case with white holly inlay and dark walnut base, top, and back. The 5-1/2" metal dial has a light tan background and brown lithographed numerals with gold stripe. Both hands and bezel are brass. Designed by Leo Ivan Bruce. (1,926 sold). Add an hour strike and the Congress becomes the "Seville" (**Model 6B03**).

Promotional photograph of the General Electric **Model 5F56** "Soiree." The "Soiree" has the moderne Arabic numerals found on the "Mirage" (Model 5F50) and a center design based on the "Salon" (**Model 5F54**). The numerals are cut into the back of the square mirror glass. Although this specific clock design was not patented, other design patents held by John P. Rainbault cover both the numerals and center design.

It's easy to see why the "Soiree" is one of the most collectible General Electric clocks. *Photograph courtesy of John and Judy McLain.*

The 1939-41 Telechron **Model 5H57** "Suave" ($5.95), 6-7/16" x 5-3/16" x 3-1/4", features a 5-1/2" metal dial with tan background and gold bronze numerals set on a brown numeral band, brass bezel and hands, and brown plastic base. Designed by Leo Ivan Bruce. (12,217 sold)

The circa 1937-38 General Electric **Model 5F58** "Ecstasy" ($5.95), 5-3/4" x 5-3/4" x 2", is a round mirror glass clock with modern white "stick" numerals and hands. Available in choice of "shimmering" blue or gunmetal gray mirror glass.

The 1940-42 Telechron **Model 5H59** "Satellite"($9.95), 6-7/8" x 5-13/16" x 3-15/16", features a transparent glass dial with cream-white etched numerals and a mirror center. The case consists of a brass case ring, base, and back cover and ivory plastic standard. The exposed hands are brass. The damage to the mirror in the photographed example detracts from its value. (23,144 sold)

The 1941-42 Telechron **Model 5H61** "Fort" ($5.95), 6-5/8" x 5-13/16" x 3-3/16", has a brass case ring supported on an ivory plastic base. The center and outer ring of the dial are of "silver color, raised, pattern plate." The numeral band is satin silver with relief numerals lacquered maroon. Designed by Belle Kogan. (7,903 sold). *Courtesy of Esther Cooperman.*

The circa 1938 General Electric **Model 5F60** "Ecstasy" ($5.95), 5-3/4" x 5-3/4" x 2", has a midnight blue glass case with white stick numerals and hands. The "Ecstasy" was also available in gunmetal mirror glass.

The General Electric **Model 5H64** "Lorraine" ($6.95), 5-3/4" h, has a square blue mirror frame with white stars, chrome bezel, silver Enameloid cloisonné dial, and blue numerals. It was also available with a rose mirror frame, brass bezel, gold Enameloid cloisonné dial, and black numerals.

The 1954-55 Telechron **Model 5H65** "Outline" ($36.00), 14" x 6-5/8" x 4", has a maple case floating in a see-through black metal frame. Introduced in June 1954 as part of a new designer line, it was not a popular style and was discontinued in October 1955. More than 800 of the 1,127 sales were made after the price was slashed to $15.50 to dispose of remaining stock.

Fig. I.

Fig. 2.

John P. Rainbault was awarded the design patent (D118,834, Feb. 6, 1940) for the "Overseer."

The circa 1940 General Electric **Model 5H66** "Overseer" ($5.95), 6-3/4" x 5-3/4" x 3", has a round brass case and brass base. It has a cream and gold color dial with brown numerals. Designed by John P. Rainbault.

The 1954-55 Telechron **Model 5H67** "Showpiece" ($100.00), 13-5/8" x 6-1/4" x 3-5/16", another in the designer series introduced in June 1954, has a frame of silver plated metal and solid brass. It was discontinued in October 1955 and the price dropped to $35.00 to dispose of stock. Only 853 were sold, over 660 at the clearance price.

The "Showpiece" and other designer line clocks from 1954-55 are the most collectible Telechron clocks from the 1950s. *Photograph courtesy of Alicia Petrainas.*

The General Electric **Model 5H68** "Caprice."

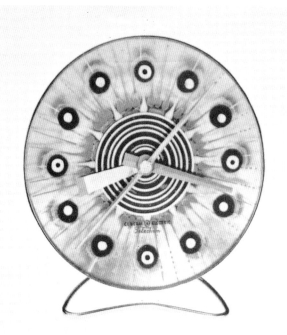

Above: The 1954-55 Telechron **Model 5H69** "Illumitime" ($40.00), 7-3/4" x 11" x 3-1/4", is an illuminated clock meant to be used either as a table or wall clock. It was manufactured both with and without a sweep second hand. The sales literature notes that "Its soft diffused glow silhouettes hands and numerals and highlights its location in any room." Another of the poorly received designer line introduced in June 1954 and discontinued in October 1955, the "Illumitime" was the best seller, with 1,340 sales. Like the other models in the series, however, most of the sales occurred after the price was slashed to $17.00.

Left: The 1954-56 General Electric **Model 5H70** "Higgins Glass" ($34.95), 8-7/16" x 7-1/4" x 3-1/8", features a distinctive hand-crafted glass dial against "the soft brilliance of brushed brass." The 1955 advertising copy notes that "vermilion adds dash on uniquely designed hands." The brass stand detaches to allow use as either a shelf or wall clock. This clock commands a high price because it is a crossover collectible appealing to both clock and Higgins Glass collectors. One recently sold on eBay™ for over $1,000. (3,259 sold)

The 1954-55 Telechron **Model 5H71** "Panorama" ($45.00), 6-3/8" x 14-1/8" x 3-7/8", was "inspired by modern architecture." Hand-rubbed walnut is accentuated by golden brass. "Sparkling translucent curtain makes a perfect setting for the handsome dial." The final member of the ill-fated designer line, there were only 1,137 sold. Like the other designer line models, most sales occurred after the model was discontinued in October 1955 and the price was slashed to $19.00.

"6" Series

The General Electric **Model 6H02** "Alencon" ($12.95), 7-5/8" x 16-1/2" x 4", is a glass mantel clock with blue glass that is partly mirrored and has white numerals and hands and central motif. Design of this clock is often inappropriately attributed to Walter Dorwin Teague, Russel Wright, or Rockwell Kent. Although I found no design patent for the case, patents awarded to John P. Rainbault for the Mirage and other models cover the numerals and central motif. The "Alencon" was also available with rose glass partly mirrored in gold with cream numerals and hands. Metal ball feet.

The 1938 General Electric **Model 6H50** "Jason" ($12.00), 5-3/4" x 8-1/4 x 3", is "an unutterably smart and interesting model, done completely in shades of gold, which inspired the name, being reminiscent of the Golden Fleece." The rectangular gold-plated frame and base envelops a gold Enameloid cloisonné dial featuring horizontal stripes, black outline numerals, and black hands.

155

Chapter 10

Strike and Chime Clocks

The Warren Telechron Company produced a number of strike clocks in the "6" series but never produced chime clocks. The Revere Clock Company, however, produced Telechron-motored chime clocks that sold both under its own trademark and under the General Electric and, to a limited extent, the Telechron trademarks. Telechron and Revere had a joint sales force and, in Canada, both were sold as General Electric clocks by the Canadian General Electric Company.

Early Revere-cased Chime Clocks

The following models feature Revere cases and chime movements, Telechron movements, and General Electric Telechron dials.

The following three models were included in the catalog "Gift Suggestions, 1930-31" issued by the General Electric Supply Corporation of Chicago. They were identified as Telechron clocks. The Revere Clock Company, a subsidiary of the Herschede Hall Clock Company of Cincinnati, Ohio, probably made cases and chimes for these clocks.

Cover to the Edison General Electric Supply Company's 1930-31 catalog. The catalog includes a wide range of clocks, including both Telechron and General Electric models. The General Electric models include chime and tall case clocks made by Revere.

The General Electric Telechron **Model ABR 130** ($74.00) is a mahogany cased cathedral clock. An auxiliary movement could be added for an additional $5.

The General Electric **Model R-150** ($75.00) is a Sheraton Colonial-style chime mantel clock with mahogany case. Also pictured in this circa 1930 advertisement are the R-632, another Revere-cased General Electric clock, the "Tudor," and the "Copley." Like other clocks manufactured by Revere, the dials of the General Electric versions of the R-150 and R-632 are marked "Telechron motored." By contrast, the "Tudor" and "Copley" have "General Electric Telechron" dials.

The General Electric Telechron **Model ABR 407** ($80.00) is a tambour-style chime clock. An auxiliary movement was available for $5 extra.

Three General Electric Telechron chime models from the 1930-31 General Electric Supply Corporation Catalog. From top to bottom: The **Model R632** "Early American" ($68.00), 18" x 9-3/4" x 6-1/2", has a Honduras mahogany case, decorated glass door, Spanish highlighted lacquer finish, and Westminster chimes. Revere sold this clock under the same model number.

The "**Haverhill**" ($90.00), 40" x 10-1/2" x 5-1/4", has a Honduras mahogany case with crotch mahogany front, brass eagle decoration, etched numeral band, and Westminster chimes.

The **Model R622** ($60.00), 11-1/2" x 8-1/2" x 6-1/2", has a Honduras mahogany case with burl overlay, a Spanish highlighted lacquered finish, and Westminster chimes.

General Electric Telechrons

R634

Honduras Mahogany
Westminster Chimes
Silver Dial with Etched Black Numerals
Height 11½ Inches, Width 8½ Inches
Depth 6¼ Inches

Price, Each $47.00

R636

Honduras Mahogany
Westminster Chimes
Silver Dial with Etched Black Numerals
Height 8⅝ Inches, Width 17¾ Inches
Depth 5½ Inches

Price, Each $49.00

R624
Gothic

Honduras Mahogany
Lacquer Finish
Height 12¾ Inches, Width 8½ Inches
Depth 6¾ Inches
Etched Numeral Dial
Westminster Chimes

Price, Each $64.00

R602
Colonial

Honduras Mahogany
Lacquer Finish
Height 8½ Inches, Width 20½ Inches
Depth 6 Inches
Etched Numeral Dial
Westminster Chimes

Price, Each $57.00

Four General Electric Telechron chime models from the 1930-31 General Electric Supply Corporation Catalog. Top to bottom: The **Model R634** ($47.00), 11-1/2" x 8-1/2" x 6-1/4", has a Honduras mahogany case and a silver dial with etched black Arabic numerals. Westminster chimes.
The **Model R636** ($ 49.00), 8-5/8" x 17-3/4" x 5-1/2", has a Honduras mahogany case, silver dial, etched black numerals, and Westminster chimes.
The **Model R624** "Gothic" ($64.00), 12-3/4" x 8-1/2" x 6-3/4", has a Honduras mahogany case with a lacquer finish, an etched numeral dial, and Westminster chimes.
The **Model R602** "Colonial" ($57.00), 8-1/2" x 20-1/2" x 6", has a Honduras mahogany case with lacquer finish, etched numeral dial, and Westminster chimes.

Both the R632 and R634 were offered with Revere as well as General Electric dials as shown in this October 1930 *House Beautiful* advertisement. Even the prices were the same. Although Revere also made GE tall case clocks, the "Midland" pictured has not been found in GE catalogs.

The General Electric Telechron **Model ABR 638** ($39.00) is a wood-cased tambour-style mantel clock. It was available with an auxiliary movement for $5 extra.

The General Electric Telechron **Model ABR 855** ($42.00) is a wood-cased tombstone-style chime clock. It was available with an auxiliary movement for $5 extra.

The General Electric Telechron **Model ABR 865** ($29.00) is a tombstone-style chime clock. It was available with an auxiliary movement for $5 extra.

The General Electric Telechron **Model ABR 857** ($45.00) is a wood-cased tambour-style chime clock. It was available with an auxiliary movement for $5 extra.

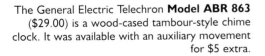

The General Electric Telechron **Model ABR 863** ($29.00) is a wood-cased tambour-style chime clock. It was available with an auxiliary movement for $5 extra.

The General Electric Telechron **Model ABR 867** ($35) is a tambour-style chime clock. It was available with an auxiliary movement for $5 extra.

The General Electric Telechron **Model ABR 869** ($48.00) is a steeple-style chime clock. It was available with an auxiliary movement for $5.00 extra.

The General Electric Telechron **Model ABR 981** ($19.50) is a cathedral-style strike clock with wood case.

The General Electric Telechron **Model ABR 983** ($19.50) is a tambour-style chime clock with wood case.

The General Electric Telechron **Model ABR 985** ($24.50).

Circa 1931 General Electric advertisement featuring the "Lynnwood," "Hostess," and "Haverhill."

Four of the Telechron models shown in the 1930-31 General Electric Supply Corporation Catalog. From top to bottom: The **Model 524** "Oxford" is not a chime clock. (See chapter 7). The **"Louis XVI"** ($110.00), 11-1/2" X 22-1/2" X 6-1/2", has a Honduras mahogany case with Redwood burl face. The carvings and turnings are maple with a lacquer finish. The dial features raised numerals. The "Louis XVI" came with both Westminster and Canterbury chimes. The **"Chippendale"** ($125.00), 19-1/8" x 17-1/2" x 7-3/8", has a Honduras mahogany case with Redwood burl face. It includes both Westminster and Canterbury chimes. The **"Louis XIV"** ($110.00), 12-7/8" x 22-1/8" x 7-3/4", has a hand carved East India Rosewood face and raised numeral dial. It includes both Westminster and Canterbury chimes.

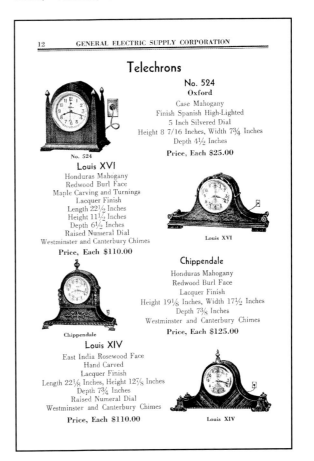

12   GENERAL ELECTRIC SUPPLY CORPORATION

Telechrons

No. 524
Oxford
Case Mahogany
Finish Spanish High-Lighted
5 Inch Silvered Dial
Height 8 7/16 Inches, Width 7¾ Inches
Depth 4½ Inches
Price, Each $25.00

No. 524

Louis XVI
Honduras Mahogany
Redwood Burl Face
Maple Carving and Turnings
Lacquer Finish
Length 22½ Inches
Height 11½ Inches
Depth 6½ Inches
Raised Numeral Dial
Westminster and Canterbury Chimes
Price, Each $110.00

Louis XVI

Chippendale
Honduras Mahogany
Redwood Burl Face
Lacquer Finish
Height 19⅛ Inches, Width 17½ Inches
Depth 7⅜ Inches
Westminster and Canterbury Chimes
Price, Each $125.00

Chippendale

Louis XIV
East India Rosewood Face
Hand Carved
Lacquer Finish
Length 22⅛ Inches, Height 12⅞ Inches
Depth 7¾ Inches
Raised Numeral Dial
Westminster and Canterbury Chimes
Price, Each $110.00

Louis XIV

This 1929 Revere Clock Company advertisement shows the "Louis XIV" without identifying it as a Revere or Telechron model. Also featured is the "Vernon," a Telechron model, and the "Prescott," a tall case clock, believed to be a Revere model.

"6" Series Strike Clocks

The 1937-40 Telechron **Model 6B01** "Jubilee" ($14.95), 8-1/2" x 10-7/8" x 4-5/8", features an hour strike movement in a brown mahogany case with white holly inlay and dark mahogany base, top, and back. The 5-1/2" dial has a light tan background and brown lithographed numerals with gold stripes. The hands and bezel are gold finished. (5,433 sold)

The 1937-42 Telechron **Model 6B03** "Seville" ($17.50), 8-5/16" x 11-1/8" x 4-5/8", is the strike version of the "Congress" (**Model 5B55**). It strikes on the hour and half hour on a "rich tone spiral silvertoned rod." The 5-1/2" dial has a light tan background and brown lithographed numerals with gold stripes. Designed by Leo Ivan Bruce. (4,600 sold) **Not Pictured:** The 1933-39 General Electric **Model 6B04** "Grafton" ($9.95), 7-3/8" x 7-7/8" x 4-1/8", is a bell strike clock with a molded walnut brown plastic case and brass bezel and hands. Introduced in 1933 and discontinued in 1939, the "Grafton" has a cream white dial with a brown numeral band and light cream Roman numerals. Just as the "Grafton" was being discontinued, the "Samson" (**Model 4H76**) was introduced with the same case design but no strike movement.

162

Telechron Time WILL TELL!

SEVILLE, a handsome clock, is cased in ripple-grain walnut, inlaid with white holly. Strikes hour and half-hour with a melodious silver tone. Priced at **$17.50. Congress,** same design without strike feature . . . only **$12.50.** Good jewelry, electric, gift and department stores everywhere sell Telechron clocks for as low as $2.95.

BUFFET, a smart new wall clock for kitchen or bathroom. Choice of ivory, green, white, black or red in molded case. Modestly priced at **$3.50.** Other kitchen or bathroom models at $4.95. All Telechron clocks are powered by the famous self-starting Telechron electric motor, sealed in oil for quietness and long life.

SMARTSET, of modern, distinctive design, has center, top and back of Prima Vera wood, and sides and base of simulated rosewood. Suitable for many settings, Smartset is moderately priced at **$8.95.** Four or five Telechron clocks in different rooms in your home provide a complete timekeeping system for the whole family.

CORDOVA, elegant in its maroon Morocco grain leather, is of distinctive design. The square, cream-colored dial has contrasting numerals in Burgundy. This clock is new and refreshing in appearance and priced at only **$12.50.** There is a Telechron clock designed by an expert for every room background in your home.

WARREN TELECHRON COMPANY   •   ASHLAND, MASSACHUSETTS
(In Canada, the Canadian General Electric Co.)
Schools, hotels, hospitals and office buildings are synchronizing their time with efficient Telechron commercial systems.

SELF-STARTING ELECTRIC CLOCKS

Above: November 1938 advertisement in *House & Garden* featuring the "Seville," "Buffet," "Smartset," and "Cordova."

Right: The 1938-42 Telechron **Model 6B07** "Minstrel" ($14.95), 7-3/4" x 18-3/8" x 4-1/4", has a plain brown mahogany case, metal dial with brown and tan characters on a light cream background, and gold color hands and bezel. (10,622 sold). Courtesy of *Orsini & Frost, Inc.*

The 1937-40 Telechron **Model 6B05** "Picardy" ($17.50), 8-1/2" x 11-7/8" x 5-1/8", features an hour strike movement in a case composed of quartered grain Padouk front, brown mahogany sides, top, and back, and black ebony finished ornaments. The 5-1/2" metal dial has a light tan background with brown lithographed numerals with gold stripe. Designed by Jacques Bars. (2,949 sold). Take away the strike feature and the "Picardy" becomes the "Sheffield" (**Model 5B53**).

The circa 1939 General Electric **Model 6B06** "Gloucester" ($18.95), 7-7/8" x 17-3/4" x 4-5/8", is a ship's bell strike clock with a mahogany-finished case and brass bezel, spokes, and hands. It has a cream and gold colored dial with black numerals. *Courtesy of Jay Kennan.*

The circa 1939 General Electric **Model 6B08** "Maestro" ($14.95), 7-3/4" x 17-5/8" x 4-1/4", has a mahogany finish case with dark brown base and contrasting stripes of maple-finished inlay. The dial is tan and ivory with "rich brown" numerals. Both bezel and hands are brass.

The General Electric **Model 6B10** "Hearth" ($14.95), 7-5/8" x 15-1/8" x 4-1/4", is the strike version of the "Candlelight" (**Model 4H12**). It strikes the hour and half hour on a deep toned spiral gong. The dial on the "Hearth" is light cream with gold numeral band and brown numerals. *Courtesy of Orsini & Frost, Inc.*

The 1938-42 Telechron **Model 6B09** "Yachtsman" ($17.50), 8-1/8" x 18-3/8" x 4-5/8", "brings the tang of the ocean to your den or mantel." The brown mahogany, tambour style case has an integral mahogany dial ring having eight ship's wheel spokes of lacquered bronze. The dial has tan and brown characters on a satin gold background. (12,361 sold). *Courtesy of Esther Cooperman.*

The 1939-42 Telechron **Model 6B11** "Angelus" ($9.95), 6-7/8" x 7-1/8" x 3-3/4", is the strike version of the "Highland" (**Model 4H93**). It has a mottled brown plastic case, cream white dial with medium brown numeral band, and light cream numerals. Designed by Leo Ivan Bruce. (9,402 sold). *Courtesy of Esther Cooperman.*

The General Electric **Model 6B12** "Philosopher."

The 1941-42 Telechron **Model 6B13** "Magnolia" ($12.50), 7-1/2" x 8-15/16" x 4-13/16", features a strike movement in a brown wood case with darker brown base. The 4-1/2" diameter metal dial has a cream-white center and brown numerals on a light cream numeral band. Hands and bezel are brass. (6,105 sold). *Courtesy of Esther Cooperman.*

The General Electric **Model 6B14** "Winthrop."

Cover to a Telechron sales brochure.

The 1941-50 Telechron **Model 6B15** "Wickford" ($17.50), 10-1/2" x 7-3/4" x 4-5/8", has an Early American design case of hand-rubbed mahogany with blond mahogany inlay and brass ornamentation. It strikes the hour and half-hour. (18,214 sold). *Courtesy of the Ashland Historical Society.*

The 1947-50 Telechron **Model 6B17** "Resolute" ($37.00), 8" x 16-1/8" x 5", has a solid mahogany case with ship's wheel design. The "carved rope" design trim and polished brass wheel spokes "give a nautical air." The "Resolute" has a "silver-toned ship's bell strike." (10,855 sold)

The 1949-51 General Electric **Model 6B20** "Ridgefield" ($32.00), 9-1/2" x 7-1/4" x 3-3/4", has a polished mahogany case and 4-1/2" round crystal. It strikes each half hour on a deep-toned gong.

The 1948-51 General Electric **Model 6B18** "Nantucket" ($37.00), 6-1/2" x 15-3/4" x 5", has a mahogany case with polished brass ship's wheel spokes. It features a real ship's bell strike. *Courtesy of Orsini & Frost, Inc.*

Numbered General Electric Chime Clocks

General Electric catalogs from the mid-1930s through the early 1950s included chime and tall case clocks with 3 digit model numbers. The cases and chime movements for the following clocks were probably made by Revere and the clocks assembled by Revere. All are Telechron motored.

The circa 1933-34 General Electric **Model 201** "Melody," 9-1/4" x 20-1/2" x 6", has a Honduras mahogany case, Spanish highlighted with burl maple panels and décor. The 5-1/2" silver dial features black Arabic numerals. The "Melody" has full Westminster chimes.

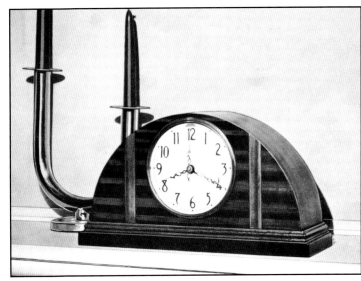

The circa 1935 General Electric **Model 350** "Rhapsody" ($24.75), 7-1/4" x 13-1/2" x 4", has a mahogany case with contrasting mahogany flutings, a 5 inch silver-finished dial with raised cast bronze numerals, brass bezel, and blued steel hands. It features full Westminster chimes.

The circa 1933-34 General Electric **Model 203** "Harmony," 11-1/2" x 21 " x 7-1/4", has a Honduras mahogany case, Spanish highlighted with burl maple panels and décor. It features Westminster chimes. The brass bezel is hinged to permit resetting from the front.
Not Pictured: The **Model 310** (not named) has a mahogany-finish tambour-style case with decorative inlay along the base. The dial features Arabic numerals. The blued steel hands are like those on the Model 350.

The 1936 General Electric **Model 352** "Concerto" ($24.75), 8" x 14-1/4" x 4", is a semi-upright chime clock with mahogany case and base. The front is finished in herringbone mahogany. Full Westminster chimes with chord strike.

The circa 1937 General Electric **Model 356** "Full Dress" ($32.00), 14-1/2" w, is a modern variation of the traditional tambour style clock. It has a striped mahogany case and Westminster chimes.
Not Pictured: The **Model 358** "Campanila," a tambour-style mantel clock with mahogany finish case, Spanish highlighted with inlay panels. The dial features Arabic numerals and blued steels hands like those on the Model 350. **Not Pictured:** The **Model 362** "Orpheus," a tambour-style mantel clock with mahogany finish case, Spanish highlighted with inlay panels. The "Orpheus" has an oval dial with Arabic numerals.

The circa 1937 General Electric **Model 364** "Abbe" ($39.50), 20-1/4" w, is a traditional tambour, Westminster chime clock in a striped mahogany case with large contrasting panels.

Sales copy for the circa 1937-40 General Electric **Model 366** "Haverhill" ($29.50), 8" x 15" x 3-3/4", notes that "the oval dial and unusual numerals add a pleasing note of modernism" to this modified tambour design in striped mahogany with a decorative panel of light tone burl maple. The oval dial is ivory with black hands. Westminster chimes. *Courtesy of Orsini & Frost, Inc.*

The circa 1937-40 General Electric **Model 368** "Lafayette" ($40.00), 7-3/4" x 22" x 4", has a mahogany case with oval gold-plated bezel, ivory dial and black hands, and full Westminster chimes. The sales literature notes that the "Lafayette" is a "new and very sleek chime clock of almost streamline design, for the lover of up-to-date decoration."

The circa 1937-40 General Electric **Model 370** "Dorchester" ($35.00), 8-1/4" x 16" x 4-1/4", has a Victorian style mahogany case with gold bezel, ivory dial, raised bronze numerals, and black hands. Westminster chimes. The "Dorchester" is, the catalog notes "styled for the conservative minded."

The sales literature for the circa 1937-40 General Electric **Model 372** "Hanover" ($45.00), 8-1/4" x 15-1/2" x 4", notes that "in its stark simplicity, the "Hanover" is an almost daring departure from the conventional tambour chime clock." The case is mahogany-finished. A brass bezel encloses a dial in two tones of silver with black numerals and modern styled brass hands. Catalog copy states that the "Hanover" "strikes an almost daring note in Westminster chime clock design."

The circa 1939 General Electric **Model 374** "New Philharmonic" ($32.00), 8-1/8" x 20-1/4" x 4-1/8", is a tambour Westminster-chime clock in a striped mahogany case faced with matched panels grained diagonally for contrast. The silver colored dial is fitted with raised numerals and gold-colored hands.

The circa 1940 General Electric **Model 378** "New Concerto" ($24.50), 8" x 18" x 4-1/4", has a mahogany-finished case with diagonally grained front panels. The silver-colored dial has a satin finish and black numerals. It features full Westminster chimes.

The circa 1939-40 General Electric **Model 376** "New Rhapsody" ($29.50), 8" x 18-3/4" x 4-1/4", is a "modern, modified tambour chime clock …that will appeal to the most discriminating." It features a silver and black colored oval dial with gold-colored hands. The mahogany finish case conceals full West-minster chimes.

The circa 1940 General Electric **Model 400** "Festival" ($19.95), 6-7/8" x 14-1/8" x 4", is a walnut-finished tambour chime clock with full Westminster chimes. The silver color dial features black numerals and brass hour and minute hands.

The 1940 General Electric **Model 402** "Serenade" ($19.95), 6-1/4" x 14" x4", is a walnut-finished tambour chime clock of "modified modern design." The oval, silver-colored dial features black numerals and storm-blue hour and minute hands.

The General Electric **Model 412** "Prelude" has a walnut finished case, silver dial, and brass bezel and hands. *Courtesy of Ashland Historical Society.*

Among the models shown in this General Electric advertisement from the Saturday Evening Post is the **Model 404** "Joy" ($19.95), 6-3/4" high. It is walnut finished contrasted with a darker base strip.
Not Pictured: The **Model 406** "Overture" has a gently curving case with large oval dial and Arabic numerals.
Not Pictured: The **Model 408** "New Maestro," is a tambour-style mantel clock with a round dial and Arabic numerals.
Not Pictured: The **Model 410** "Chorus" has a low, gently sloping case and oval dial.

The circa 1951 General Electric **Model 418** "Concerto," 8" x 19" x 5-1/2", has a grained mahogany case with "a hint of moulding at each end." It features full Westminster chimes.

The circa 1951 General Electric **Model 420** "Overture," 7-3/8" x 18-5/8" x 4-1/2", is a tambour chime clock in rich Honduras mahogany. It features full Westminster chimes.

The 1954-56 General Electric **Model 416** "Maestro" ($60.00), 6-3/8" x 17-1/8" x 4-1/2", has a mahogany case with scalloped border and scrolled base. A polished brass bezel surrounds a glass crystal. Features full Westminster chimes. (1,242 sold). *Courtesy of Orsini & Frost, Inc.*

Four circa 1955 General Electric mantel chime clocks. Top to Bottom: The **Model 428** "New Overture" ($60.00), 7-3/4" x 15-3/4" x 4-1/4", has a hand-rubbed mahogany case on a dark brown mahogany base. The silver color dial has black numerals and serpentine scroll hands.

The **Model 414** "Rhapsody." The **Model 416** "Maestro." The **Model 430** "New Concerto" (No. 430, $65.00), 7-3/4" x 15-3/4" x 4-1/4", has a hand-rubbed blond mahogany case with black base. The silver color dial features black Roman numerals and serpentine scroll hands. Full Westminster chimes.

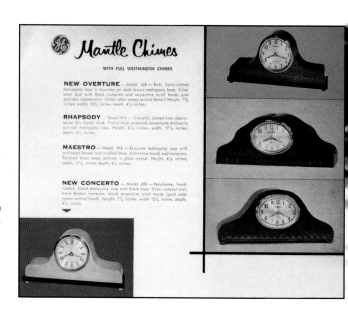

Above: The 1933 General Electric **Model 701S** "Symphony" ($34.50), 9" x 20-1/2" x 5-7/8", has a case of Honduras mahogany, Spanish highlighted, with burl maple décor panels. It features Westminster chimes.

Left: Four General Electric chime clocks. Left to right: The **Model 426** "Chorus," 9-3/4" x 8-3/16" x 4-3/4", has "modern Gothic" styling with richly grained mahogany case. It has a satin silver dial and full Westminster chimes.

The **Model 416** "Maestro." The **Model 422** "Prelude," 8-1/8" x 18-1/4" x 5-1/2", has a mahogany finish case, raised numeral dial, scrolled hands, and full Westminster chimes.

The 1951-55 **Model 414** "Rhapsody" ($72.00), 6-3/8" x 17-1/8" x 4-1/2", has a rich, diagonally grained mahogany case with distinctive fluted base. It features full Westminster chimes.

Not Pictured: The General Electric **Model 424** "Philharmonic," 8-1/4" x 18" x 5-1/4", has a diagonally-grained mahogany case, brushed silver dial, raised numerals, scrolled hands, and Westminster chimes.

Tall Case Clocks

The following tall case clocks were marketed as General Electric models. The case and chimes were made by Revere and the clock movement by Telechron. In many cases, they are identical to Revere models with the exception of the substitution of a General Electric dial.

General Electric Telechrons

Plymouth

Case Honduras Mahogany
Lacquer Finish
Height 68½ Inches, Width 13½ Inches
Depth 8¼ Inches
Louis XVI
Westminster Chimes on Symphony
Chimetone Rods

Price, Each $125.00

Plymouth

Winthrop

Honduras Mahogany
Bird's Eye Maple Panel at Top and Bottom
Lacquer Finish
Height 67 Inches, Width 14 Inches
Depth 8¾ Inches
Westminster Chimes on Symphony
Chimetone Rods

Price, Each $150.00

Winthrop

Two General Electric Telechron tall case clocks from the 1930-31 General Electric Supply Corporation catalog. Left: The **"Rosemary"** ($190.00), 72" x 11-1/2" x 7-1/2", has a colonial-style case of Honduras mahogany with a lacquer finish. It features Westminster and Canterbury chimes on Symphony Cleartone rods. Right: The **"Cambridge"** ($195.00), 68-1/2" x 15-1/2" x 9", has a Honduras mahogany case with Charles II styling. It features Westminster chimes on four tubular bells. Both models were available as Revere clocks under the same names.

The General Electric Telechron **"Hanover"** ($340), 87-1/4" x 18-1/4" x 11-1/4", has a Honduras mahogany case with colonial styling. Westminster chimes are played on five tubular bells. The pierced gold dial has a moving moon. An auxiliary movement was standard. Revere also offered the "Hanover" with silver dial, raised gold numerals, and four tubular bells ($365.00). It is not clear whether this variation was available with a GE dial.

The General Electric Telechron **"Dawes"** ($520) included an auxiliary movement.

The General Electric/Telechron **"Devonshire"** ($440) included a standard auxiliary movement.

Left: This 1929 Telechron advertisement also features the Revere "Hanover" along with the Telechron "Oxford" (No. 524).

Bottom left: The General Electric Telechron **"Mayfair"** ($99 with chime, $67 without chime), 72" x 16-1/2" x 8", was a corner clock with Honduras mahogany case in the Georgian style. Revere also sold this clock with the same name and pricing. Offered with an auxiliary movement for $5 extra.

Bottom center: The General Electric Telechron **"Middlesex"** ($360) included a standard auxiliary movement.

Bottom right: The General Electric Telechron "Roxbury" ($225), 72-1/2" x 17-1/4" x 12", has a Honduras mahogany case with Colonial styling. It has a silver dial with raised gold numerals and Westminster chimes on four tubular bells. An auxiliary movement was standard.

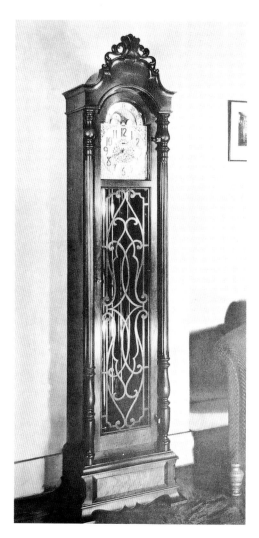

This advertisement from the May 1929 *National Geographic* shows the "Hanover" as a Revere Clock Company model. Also shown is the Telechron "Windsor."

Two General Electric/Telechron tall case clocks from the 1930-31 General Electric Supply Corporation catalog. Top: The **"Plymouth"** ($95-$125), 68-1/2" x 13-1/2" x 8-1/4", has a Honduras mahogany case with Louis XVI styling. The Plymouth featured Westminster chimes on Symphony Chimetone Rods. An auxiliary movement was available for $5 extra. Bottom: The **"Winthrop"** ($150.00), 67" x 14" x 8-3/4", has a Honduras mahogany case with bird's eye maple panels at the top and bottom. It features Westminster chimes on Symphony Chimetone Rods. Both were offered as Revere models under the same names.

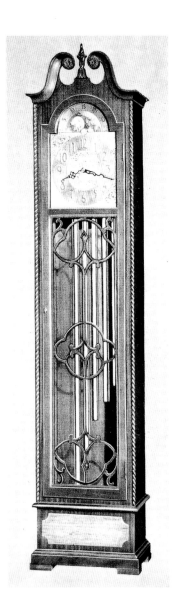

The General Electric **Model 301** "Concord" ($150.00), 72-7/8" x 16-1/8" x 9", is somewhat smaller than a true grandfather clock. It has a mahogany case with maple base panel. Four tubular bells sound the Westminster chimes every quarter hour. The dial is silver color with raised numerals.

The General Electric **Model 303** "Sussex," 80" x 18-1/4" x 12-3/8", features a moving moon dial that indicates the phases of the moon. Five tubular bells sound the Westminster chimes every quarter hour. The "Sussex" has a mahogany case and gold dial with raised numerals and decoration.

The General Electric **Model 305** "Winthrop," 79-1/4" x 22-3/8" x 14", has a mahogany case and colorful moon dial. Five tubular bells sound the Westminster chimes each quarter hour. The gold dial features raised numerals and decoration.

The circa 1939 General Electric **Model 307** "Middlesex" ($325.00), 79-1/2" x 22-3/8" x 14", has a mahogany case in period design, moon dial, and five tubular bells that sound the Westminster chimes each quarter hour. The gold-colored dial has raised numerals.

Top left: The "Middlesex" as it appeared in a Revere advertisement in *House Beautiful*, June 1930.

Top left: The "Adams" makes an appearance in the *Saturday Evening Post*, circa 1951. Also featured are the "Ridgefield" (6B20), "Rhapsody" (414), Candlelight (3H172), "Morning Glory" (7H166), "Gay Hour" (7H162), and "Heralder" (7H160).

Right: The 1939-51 General Electric **Model 309** "Adams" ($375), 79-1/4" x 20-1/4" x 13-3/4", is an electrically operated reproduction of an 18th century grandfather clock. It has a mahogany case, gold-colored dial, and raised numerals and decoration. The Moon dial records the phases of the moon. Westminster chimes sound each quarter hour on five tubular bells.

Far right: The circa 1951-55 General Electric **Model 313** "New Virginian" ($635.00), 76-3/4" x 17-3/4" x 11", features colonial styling in a carved mahogany case. It has brushed brass weights and swinging pendulum. Full Westminster chimes play on five tubular bells.

Not pictured: The **Model 380** "Puritan" ($49.50), 6' tall, is a grandmother clock with a striped mahogany case and mahogany trim.

Not pictured: The **Model 382** "Puritan" ($49.50), 6' tall, has the same design as the No. 380, but has Zebrawood trim.

Not pictured: The **Model 384** "Dowager" ($69.50) 72" x 14" x 9", has a mahogany case and decorative moon dial. The ivory dial features black numerals and hands.

Right: The General Electric **Model 386** "Dearborn" ($89.50), 72" x 15" x 9-1/4", has a mahogany case, decorative moon dial in full color, and ivory dial with raised bronze numerals. It strikes Westminster chimes every quarter hour and has a chime hour strike.

Far right: The circa 1951 General Electric Telechron **Model 388** "Winthrop" (70" x 14-1/2" x 8-1/2") has a polished brown mahogany case, etched, two-tone dial in scrolled, brushed gold color finish, and Westminster chimes.

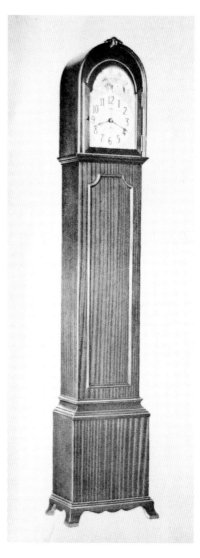

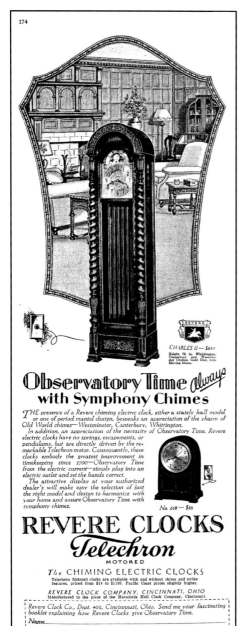

Above: Not all Revere models were also offered with General Electric dials. This advertisement in the April 1929 House & Garden features the "Charles II" tall case clock and Model 618 mantel clock, neither of which appear to have been offered as GE models.

Right: Another Revere tall case model not found in General Electric catalogs is the "Lynn," featured in this 1929 Telechron advertisement. The close relationship between Telechron, Revere, and General Electric is demonstrated by this advertisement. It notes that, in Canada, both Telechron and Revere clocks are sold as Canadian General Electric Company clocks.

Chapter 11

Alarm Clocks

Cover to a 1935 Telechron clock catalog.

The 1932-34 Telechron **Model 7B01** "Autolarm" ($12.50), 6-1/8" x 4-3/4" x 3-1/2", has a 24 hour movement that "when set to give alarm at 7 A.M.—it doesn't ring at 7 P.M.!" It has a walnut color moulded plastic case with gold-finished handle and feet. The 3" white enamel dial is illuminated with a miniature Mazda bulb. **Model AB7B02** appears to differ from the "Autolarm" only in its dial which identifies it as a General Electric Telechron model. Designed by George Long. (3,448 sold)

The 1935-36 Telechron **Model 7F01** "Announcer" ($8.50), 5-5/16" x 5" x 3-1/2", is an illuminated alarm clock in a black molded plastic case with metal front lacquered antique white. The dial has a translucent cream background with black and gray numerals. It is illuminated by means of No. 41 Mazda miniature lamp. The poor condition of the photographed example significantly reduces its value. (10,512 sold). *Courtesy of Jay Kennan.*

The 1936-37 Telechron **Model 7F03** "Clarion" self-starting alarm clock ($6.50), 5-1/16" x 4-7/16" x 3-1/2", has a molded black plastic case with black lacquered metal front and buffed Nicral bezel. The dial has black characters on a cream background; the hands are blued metal. (13,569 sold). Add radium treated hands and numerals on a black numeral band and the "Clarion" becomes the **Model 7F03L** "Thrush" ($7.50). (8,350 sold). With a translucent dial illuminated with a Mazda bulb, the "Clarion" becomes the **Model 7F03K** "Risewell" ($8.50). Designed by Walter Dorwin Teague. (4,611 sold). *Courtesy of Jay Kennan.*

The 1950-52 General Electric **Model 7H04** "Repeater" ($9.95), 4" x 5-1/2" x 2-5/8", has a mahogany case. It was touted in the 1950 catalog as a GE first at a popular price—the "Repeater" resets itself and wakes the user at the same time every morning.

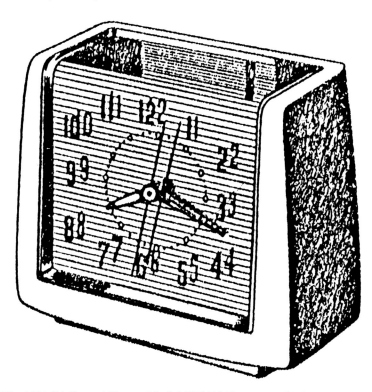

The 1951-54 General Electric **Model 7H06LI** "Drummer ($7.95), 4" x 5" x 2-5/8", has an ivory plastic case and plastic crystal. It features an automatic 24 hour alarm. The numerals are on the crystal "that rolls graciously over the top of clock," rather than the gold-finish dial. It has luminous features.

The Telechron Special Campaign **Model CF705** has the same case design as the No. 7F01 "Announcer" (pictured). It was introduced in September 1936 and discontinued in October 1937. (10,033 sold)

The 1950-53 Telechron **Model 7H07LI** "Everset" ($8.85), 3-3/4" x 4-7/8" x 3", features an alarm that you "set and forget" until you change your getting up time. It has luminous features. The case and crystal are genuine plastic. (122,874 sold)

The 1951-55 Telechron **Model 7H09L** "Nocturne" ($7.95), 4-1/2" x 4-7/8" x 3", has a 24 hour automatic alarm. Brown or ivory plastic case. Luminous features. The case design is the same as the No. 7H159L "Nocturne." Designed by Leo Ivan Bruce.

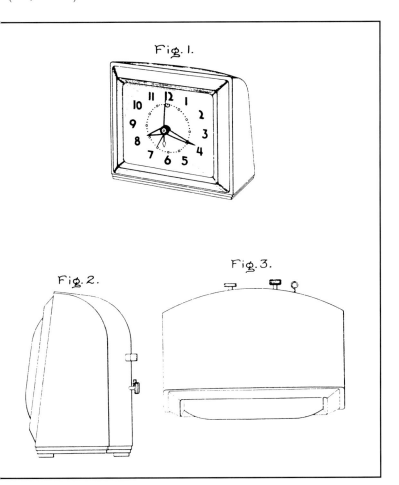

Leo Ivan Bruce was awarded a design patent (D163,930, July 17, 1951) for the "Nocturne."

The General Electric **Model AB 7F52** "Morning Star" ($6.95), 5" x 4-5/8" x 3", has a molded plastic case in choice of black, ivory, or robin's egg blue, all with gold-color trimmings, or French gray with chrome trim. The dial features black, spade-shaped, hands and Arabic numerals. With luminous features, the "Morning Star" becomes **Model 7F52L**. Designed by John P. Rainbault. *Courtesy of Jay Kennan.*

181

The 1933-36 Telechron **Model 7F53** "Telebell," initially known as the "Telecall," ($5.95), 4-3/4" x 4-1/2" x 3", comes in choice of (**A**) brass case with black or ivory molded plastic base and (**B**) chrome with green, black, or red plastic base. Both cases have a "butler" (satin) finish. The 3-1/2" dial has an ivory finish with black characters. A variation of the "Telebell" was introduced in 1934 with a black molded plastic case on an ivory base (**Model 7F53BK-I**, $6.50). Designed by Irwin W. Kokins. (33,744 sold)

The General Electric/Telechron **Model AB7F54** "Deb Alarm" ($8.95), 5" x 5" x 3", is a square, easel-type alarm clock available in choice of chrome or brass case with matching dial and hands. Arabic numerals are etched on a brilliant black enamel ring on a silver or gold-finished background. The "Deb Alarm" was also offered with a radium dial and hands (**Model 7F54L**, $8.95). The "Luminous Deb" has a black numeral band. Designed by John P. Rainbault.

Irwin Kokins was awarded a design patent (D92,007, April 17, 1934) for the "Telebell." Kokins became President of the Warren Telechron Company upon Henry Warren's retirement in 1943.

The 1933-34 Telechron **Model 7F55** "Signalette" ($9.95), 5-1/2" x 6-1/2" x 3", is the alarm version of the "Telart" (**Model 4F51**). It was available in choice of brass or chrome frame and support on a glossy black plastic base. (8,697 sold)

House & Garden, June 1934.

The circa 1935 General Electric **Model 7F56** "Vedette," 5" x 4-1/2" x 3-1/4", has a black molded plastic case with side band of fluted chrome. The dial has black Arabic numerals on a cream background; the hands are blued steel. Also available in ivory plastic with gold-color trimmings. The "Radium Vedette" (**Model 7F56L**, $5.95) features the same choice in cases but has a dial with luminous characters against a black band background. The hands are also luminous. A "Vedette" is a mounted sentinel. The "Utility Timer" (**Model 7F64**, $4.95 (black), $5.50, (ivory)) features the same case design in a kitchen timer. The "Utility Timer" came with an oven chart that provided ready reference to the time required for most roasts and baked foods. The "Utility Timer" was apparently also sold as the "Kitchen Timer" (**Model 8F50**). Designed by Raymond E. Patten.

The 1934-36 Telechron **Model 7F57** "Airlarm" ($9.95), 5-1/4" x 5-1/4" x 2-5/8", is the alarm version of the "Airman" (**Model 4F55**). It features a choice of maple case with brass bezel, etched in white numerals, and cream-white lacquered dial (shown) or walnut case with chrome-plated bezel, etched in black numerals, and black lacquered dial. Designed by Simon de Vaulchier. (10,611 sold). *Courtesy of Esther Cooperman.*

The Telechron **Model 7F57** "Sportsman" ($14.95), 5-1/4" x 5-1/4" x 3-1/16", was the alarm version of the "Airlux" (No. 4F55). It has a white onyx case, brass numeral band with etched in white numerals, and a white lacquered dial. Introduced as the 7F57 in 1935, almost 6,200 were sold before it was discontinued in 1940. The original "Sportsman" was also offered with a green onyx case. This variation is rare and commands a significantly higher price. The "Sportsman" (**Model 7H57**, $16.95) was reintroduced with an imitation onyx plastic case in 1947. Genuine onyx replaced the plastic in August 1948 and the price was increased to $19.95. The "Sportsman" was again discontinued in 1950. Designed by Simon de Vaulchier. (24,991 sold). *Courtesy of Esther Cooperman.*

The circa 1935 General Electric **Model 7F58** "Lumalarm" ($7.50), 5" x 5-1/2" x 3", has a black plastic case and base with fluted design on the sides. It has a mirror crystal with an arch motif and numerals applied directly to the surface by a special photographic process. The hands and numerals show as transparencies against the lighted, plain white recessed dial. Designed by Amos E. Northup.

The General Electric "Lumalarm" was also available in an ivory plastic case having a mirror crystal with a star motif and numerals applied directly to its surface. Case designed by Amos E. Northup.

The 1934-36 Telechron **Model 7F59** "Squarlarm" ($5.95), 4-15/16" x 4-15/16" x 3", has a lacquered metal case in choice of black, green, or ivory, all with chrome bezel and case band. The dial features black numerals on a light cream background with a cream-white center. Designed by John Nickelsen. (25,598 sold). *Courtesy of Peter J. Scagnelli.*

The circa 1936 General Electric **Model 7F60** "Morning Glory" ($7.95), 5-7/8" x 5" x 2-1/8", has a case of brown, striped mahogany accented by a base of light finished bird's eye maple. It has an ivory dial with Arabic numerals, a brass, telescope-type bezel and sweep second hand, and black hands.

The 1934-36 Telechron **Model 7F61** "Vedette" ($9.95), 5-1/8" x 5" x 3-5/8", was available in choice of (**A**) brass bezel and base with gold bronze lacquered metal back or (**B**) polished chrome bezel and base with silver lacquered back. The dial features etched-in gloss black numerals and alarm dots on a silver finished band with black outer band and etched gold finish center. (4,070 sold)

The 1934-39 Telechron **Model 7F63** "Quacker" ($6.50), 5-11/16" x 5-7/8" x 3", is the alarm version of the No. 8F01 "Smug" (pictured). It was offered in choice of yellow, black, or blue plastic case, all with orange beak and white and black eyes.
The 3-1/4" metal dial has a light blue background with yellow center and dark orange characters. The bezel is polished brass, the hands are blue on the yellow and blue models and dark orange on the black model. Designed by Belle Kogan. (10,422 sold). *Courtesy of Esther Cooperman.*

The General Electric **Model 7F62** "Englewood" ($7.95), 5" x 5" x 2-5/8", has a case of Honduran mahogany and light, natural finish satinwood with four brass stars. It has a brass bezel, ivory dial, black Arabic numerals, and black hands. Designed by John P. Rainbault.

The General Electric **Model 7F64** "Utility Timer" ($4.95 (black) or $5.50 (ivory)), 5" x 4-1/2" x 3-1/4", has the same case as the "Vedette" alarm (**Model 7F56**). It features a cream dial with black numerals and red alarm hand. Packed with every timer was a "handy oven chart which provides ready reference to the time required for most roast and baked foods." Case designed by Raymond E. Patten.

The 1935-37 Telechron **Model 7F65** "Deputy" alarm clock (Bk ($4.95) & I ($5.50)), 4-5/8" x4" x 3", comes in choice of molded black plastic case with antique ivory lacquered outer bezel and base (Bk) or antique ivory case with black lacquered outer bezel and base (I). Both have a 3" square dial with black and gray numerals on a light cream background. (73,056 sold).

With luminous painted hands and numerals on a black and light cream background, the "Deputy" became the 1935-37 **Model 7F65L** "Aladdin" (Bk ($5.95) & I ($6.50)). (56,091 sold). The "Aladdin" was briefly reintroduced in 1940 with brown plastic case and ivory colored feet (**Model 7F65 Br**). Designed by Irwin W. Kokins. (4,034 sold).

Not Pictured: The General Electric **Model 7F66** "Dawning" has the same case design as the "Morning Glory" (**Model 7F60**).

The 1935-36 Telechron **Model 7F67** "Carillon" ($9.95), 5-5/8" x 5-1/2" x 3-5/16", was available in choice of (A) polished brass bezel with gold bronze lacquered back and onyx base or (B) polished chrome bezel with silver lacquered back and onyx base. The dial features gloss black numerals on a silver band with a black outer band and gold center. (3,404 sold)

The General Electric **Model 7F68** "Beau" alarm has a traditional design with wood case, black lacquered base, and brass top handle and bezel.

The 1936-42 Telechron **Model CF769** "Constable" ($4.75 (Bk) & $5.25 (Iv)), 4" x 4-5/8" x 2-15/16", has a molded plastic case in choice of black with ivory lacquered front plate and brass bezel or ivory case with gun metal color front plate and brass bezel. (55,295 sold). Add luminous features and the "Constable" has earned a promotion to "Sheriff" (**Model CF769L**, $5.75 (Bk) & $6.25 (Iv)). The cream lacquered metal dial has radium treated numerals on a black band. The blued metal hands are also radium treated. Designed by Frank W. Green. *Courtesy of Jay Kennan.*

Catalog photo of the 1936-42 "Sheriff." (66,290 sold)

Above: The 1936-40 Telechron **Model 7F71** "Gendarme" alarm clock (Bk ($4.95) & I ($5.50)), 4-9/16" x 4-5/16" x 3", was available in choice of black (Bk) or Ivory (I) molded plastic case with polished brass bezel and side ornaments. The 3-1/4" dial features black characters on a gray numeral band and a cream center. The hands are blued metal. (51,774 sold). In 1940-41, the "Gendarme" was offered with a brown molded plastic case (**Model 7F71 Br**), adding almost 34,000 more sales. With luminous Radium-painted hands and numerals on a black and cream dial, the "Gendarme" became the 1936-40 **Model 7F71L** "Sparkler" (MBk ($5.95) & LI ($6.50)). (78,843 sold). Add a kitchen timer to the "Gendarme" and it becomes the "Advisor" (**Model 8F51**). Designed by Jacques Bars. *Courtesy of Jay Kennan.*

Right: The General Electric **Model 7F70** "Overseer," 4-7/8" x 8" x 2-5/8", has a striped mahogany case of modern design with pilasters of the same wood. A double brass bezel surrounds an ivory dial with black Arabic numerals. The hands are black with a brass sweep second hand. Designed by John P. Rainbault.

Time, September 28, 1936.

MARCH INTO SPRING WITH *Telechron* TIME

(Above) **GENDARME,** an attractive, efficient alarm. Molded plastic case in either black or ivory colors, gold-colored metal ornaments on sides. Black case **$4.95**
Ivory case $5.50.
SPARKLER, same design with luminous dial. Black case $5.95. Ivory molded case $6.50.

CONSORT, a popular clock for kitchen or bathroom wall. A really practical gift. Chrome-plated case, with molded bezel, in a choice of ivory, white, black, blue, green or red colors. Only **$4.95**

GRACEWOOD. This graceful modern tambour model has a brown mahogany case and a cherry base. For mantel or desk. Priced at **$8.95**

Telechron
(Reg. U. S. Pat. Off. by Warren Telechron Co.)

Soon you'll be living in a gay new world. Day by day, every one is feeling livelier, more alert.

Why not liven up your home (and your family) with Telechron electric clocks in every room? They'll brighten their corners and make every one prompt. Four or five Telechrons, plugged into regular electric outlets, provide your home with a complete timekeeping system. The right time, the same time, upstairs and down.

Every Telechron clock, regardless of price, contains the same fine self-starting Telechron motor—sealed in oil for quietness and longer life. Years ago, Telechron created the synchronous electric clock industry. Now millions of satisfied users have made Telechron the most famous name in electric clocks. Styled by America's foremost designers, Telechrons are sold as low as $3.50 by good jewelry, electric, gift and department stores.

WARREN TELECHRON COMPANY
Ashland   Massachusetts
(In Canada, the Canadian General Electric Company)

Schools, hotels, hospitals and office buildings are synchronizing their time with efficient Telechron commercial systems.

SELF-STARTING ELECTRIC CLOCKS

"March Into Spring With Telechron Time" featuring the "Gendarme." (*Saturday Evening Post*, April 3, 1937)

The General Electric **Model 7F72** "Heralder," 4-1/4" x 4-1/8" x 2-5/8", was available in choice of striped Honduras mahogany ($5.95) or molded black Textolite ($4.95) set on two tubular brass feet. The ivory and gold dial has black numerals.

Catalog photo showing the alternative dial for the **Model 7F72** "Heralder."

The 1936-37 Telechron **Model 7F73** "Meadowlark" alarm clock ($6.95), 5-3/8" x 5-3/8" x 3-1/4", came in choice of brown mahogany or cherry case, both with black wooden base, brass bezels, blued hands, and light cream dial with black numerals. Designed by Walter Dorwin Teague. (12,344 sold). *Courtesy of Jay Kennan.*

The General Electric **Model 7F74** "Heralder" ($4.95 (black), $5.95 (mahogany)), 4-3/8" x 4-1/8" x 2-5/8", is the same as the Model 7F72 except that the case is mounted on a square brass base divided into seven sections. Designed by John P. Rainbault.

The 1937-42 Telechron **Model 7F75** "Mayfair" ($7.95), 6-1/4" x 5-1/4" x 3-3/4", is the alarm version of the pictured **Model 4F67** "Embassy." It has a black plastic base, brass case and numeral band, and satin gold color dial. Add a luminous dial and the "Mayfair" becomes the **Model 7F75L** "Nocturne" ($8.95). (40,064 combined sales)

The General Electric **Model 7F76** "Geneva" ($5.95), 5-3/4" x 5-1/2" x 2-1/2", is available in choice of blue, gunmetal gray, or silver mirror glass with a 3-1/2" ivory dial encircled in a double brass bezel. It has Arabic numerals on a black ring.

The 1937-42 Telechron **Models 7F77** and **7H77** "Mirolarm" ($6.95), 4-3/4" x 4-3/4" x 2-3/4", was available in choice of blue or rose mirror glass, both with polished brass bezels, blued hands, and dial with black characters on a light cream background. The early "F" series versions of the "Mirolarm" had a separate, light gray, alarm disk set by lining up the alarm time with the center of the opening in the hour hand. Later versions have an alarm hand. (51,518 sold). *Courtesy of Esther Cooperman.*

The General Electric **Model 7H78** "Acorn" ($3.95), 4-5/8" x 5" x 2-5/8", is available in choice of black or walnut plastic case with a chrome bezel and sweep second hand. The dial is ivory, silver, and black with black hands. The "Acorn" was also available in walnut or black plastic case with ivory front panel and decorative stripes. The **Model 7H78L** "Luminous Acorn" ($4.95) is available in the same case choices as the Acorn but has a luminous ivory and black dial, luminous hands, and brass sweep second hand. *Courtesy of Jay Kennan.*

The Telechron "Mirolarm" in rose mirror glass.
Courtesy of Esther Cooperman.

The 1937-39 Telechron **Model 7H79** "Butler" alarm clock ($3.95), 4-1/2" x 4-1/4" x 2-7/8", has a molded plastic case in choice of black or mottled brown, brass bezel, blued hands, and dial with satin silver background, light cream numeral band, and silver and black numerals. (43,649 sold).
With luminous Radium painted numerals on a black numeral band and light cream background, the "Butler" became the **Model 7H79L** "Sexton" ($4.95). Without the alarm and luminous features, the "Butler" becomes the "Domino" (**Model 3H78**). Designed by Frank W. Green. (25,147 sold). *Courtesy of Jay Kennan.*

Catalog photo showing slight variation in the dial of the "Butler."

The General Electric **Model 7H80** "Julep" ($4.95), 4-1/2" x 4-1/4" x 2-5/8", has a fluted ivory, black, or veined rose "Fiberlon" case with integral molded feet. It features an ivory dial with black hands and numerals. The bezel and sweep second hand are brass. The black and rose versions are harder to find and command higher prices.

The General Electric **Model 7H82** "Sophist" ($9.95), 5-1/4" x 7-1/4" x 2-5/8", has a mahogany case with gold numeral band, bezel, and feet. It has an Enameloid Cloisonné dial in rippled gold.

The 1937-38 Telechron Special Campaign **Model CH783L** "Kleertone" ($5.95), 4-5/16" x 4-3/8" x 2-7/8", has a cast "Fiberlon" case in black, ivory, or brown, polished brass inner and outer bezels, and a dial with cream center, black numeral band, and luminous painted hands and numerals. Introduced in 1937 during a special campaign offering $1.00 off with trade-in of an old clock, sales totaled 15,530.

FALL AND WINTER 1938-1939

Telechron

SELF-STARTING ELECTRIC CLOCKS

Cover to the 1938-39 Telechron clock catalog.

Popular singers Gladys Swarthout and Frank Chapman display some of their General Electric clocks in this December 1937 *House and Garden* advertisement. Models include the "Julep," "The New Lotus," "Kitchen Hostess," "Hanover," "The Gladiator," "The Sophist," and an unidentified tall case clock.

The General Electric **Model 7H84** "Gladiator" ($7.50), 5-1/4" x 6-1/4" x 2-5/8", has a mahogany case with black side panels, a gold bezel, and a black dial with white numerals and hands.

The 1938-41 Telechron **Model 7H85** "Attendant" alarm clock (Br ($2.95) & I ($3.50), 5" x 4-3/4" x 2-3/4", was available in choice of brown plastic case with buffed Nicral bezel or ivory with polished brass bezel. The dial features tan characters on a light ivory background and black hands. (130,817 sold). With luminous hands and numerals, the "Attendant" became the pictured "Dispatcher" (**Model 7H85L** Br ($3.95) & I ($4.50)). Designed by Leo Ivan Bruce. (31,061 sold)

The Telechron "Attendant" was available for a short time in a black case as the 1939 Special Campaign **Model CH785**. (4,888 sold)

The General Electric **Model 7H86** "Warburton" ($5.95), 5" X 4-3/4" X 2-5/8", has a case of glossy molded tortoise shell or alabaster "Fiberlon" case with a brass bezel and gold Enameloid cloisonné dial. The "Warburton" was also available with a gray "Fiberlon" case, chrome bezel, and silver dial.

Not Pictured: The 1938-39 Telechron **Model 7H87** "Mentor" ($6.95), 5-3/4" x 6-3/4" x 2-7/8", has a walnut-finished wood panel with rounded sides, tan dial, and skeleton numeral band with polished brass inner bezel. It is the alarm version of the **Model 4H83** "Naples." (2,521 sold)

The General Electric **Model 7H88** "Dawning" ($6.95), 5-3/4" x 5-3/4" x 3", is similar in design to the "Ecstasy" (**Model 5F60**) but has an alarm and added decorative design around the middle of the dial. It is available in choice of blue or gunmetal gray mirror glass, both with white stick numerals and exposed hands.

The 1939-42 Telechron **Model 7H89** "Guest" alarm clock ($6.95), 5-1/4" x 5-11/16" x 3", has a dark brown wood case covered with pigskin-grained "Textileather" striped with brown lines. It has a polished brass bezel and hands, and the dial features medium brown characters on a light cream numeral band and tan background. Designed by Robert W. Goulet. (37,978 sold). *Courtesy of Jay Kennan.*

The General Electric **Model 7H90** "Eldorado" ($8.50), 6-1/4" x 5-3/4" x 3-1/8", is a round mirror glass alarm clock on a matching glass pedestal base. It is available in blue glass mirrored with white moderne numerals or rose glass mirrored with gold and having cream numerals. The exposed hands on both models match the color of the numerals.

The prewar Telechron **Model 7H91** "Secretary" ($3.95), 4-1/4" x 5-3/16" x 3", has a mottled brown Bakelite case. The light cream dial has medium brown numerals on a tan numeral band. The bezel is tan lacquer and the hands are lacquered medium brown. In 1940, an ivory-cased version was added. Add luminous painted hands and numerals and the "Secretary" became the **Model 7H91L** "Cordial" ($4.95). (211,608 sold). After the war, the "Secretary" was reintroduced as the Model **7H91LI** "Telalarm" ($6.50) with an ivory case, tan color bezel and dial, and brown numeral band. Between 1945 and 1951, sales totaled almost 665,000, making the "Telalarm" one of the most successful Telechron models. Designed by Leo Ivan Bruce. *Courtesy of Esther Cooperman.*

The General Electric **Model 7H92** "Circe" ($9.95), 7" x 8" x 4-1/4", is an arched white glass clock on a stepped chrome base. A silver design and numerals are etched into the glass and mirrored. The clock offers two levels of illumination from a small bulb in the rear. The exposed hands are chrome plated. Although the design was not patented, other patents awarded to John P. Rainbault cover both the center design and numerals.

The 1939-40 Telechron **Model 7H93** "New Telalarm," 4-7/8" x 4-3/4" x 3", was available in choice of (**A**) brass with brown Bakelite band and base ($5.95) or (**B**) butler nickel with black Bakelite band and base ($4.95). The 3-1/4" dial features black characters on a cream white background. (16,149 sold).

Shortly before the brass and nickel versions were discontinued, the "New Telalarm" was introduced in (**I**) ivory lacquered metal with brown plastic base and band ($4.95). It was discontinued less than a year later with sales totaling 15,463. With the addition of a translucent electrically illuminated dial, the "New Telalarm" became the **Model 7H93K** "Talisman" (**A** ($6.95), **B** ($5.95) & **I** ($5.95)). Designed by Leo Ivan Bruce. (26,259 sold)

The "New Telalarm" in brass.

The 1939-41 Telechron **Model 7H95** "Colonade" alarm clock ($6.95), 5-1/4" x 4-5/8" x 3-1/8", has a wood case with a fluted lower section finished in dark brown contrasting with a lighter top, polished brass bezel and hands, and a light cream dial with black numerals. (7,993 sold). Take away the alarm and the "Colonade" becomes the "Virginian" (**Model 3H81**).

The circa 1938 General Electric **Model 7H94** "Sergeant" ($2.95-$3.50), 5-1/4" x 4-1/2" x 2-1/2", was touted as "the lowest price alarm in General Electric history" and produced "without sacrificing one iota of quality in its essential parts." It was offered in choice of black or brown plastic case with chrome bezel or ivory case with brass bezel. All featured ivory and black dials with Arabic numerals. All variations were also available with luminous dials (**Model 7H94L**, $3.95-$4.50).

The circa 1938 General Electric **Model 7H96** "New Gladiator," 5-1/2" x 5-3/4" x 2-3/4", is touted as a "real man's alarm clock" with its covering of grained mahogany-toned facsimile leather. A brass bezel encircles an ivory dial with black numerals and gilt decoration.

The 1940 Telechron Special Campaign **Model CH797**. Designed by Norman F. Lockwood. (3,008 sold)

The General Electric **Model 7H98** "Corporal," 5-1/4" x 5-3/8" x 3-1/4", was available in choice of brown ($3.95) or ivory ($4.50) plastic case with brass bezel, and sweep second hand. The ivory and white dial featured black Arabic numerals.

The 1940-41 Telechron **Model 7H99** "Steward" alarm clock ($6.95), 6-1/2" x 5-7/8" x 3-3/4", has a brass case, brown plastic base, brown hands, and shaded brown dial with brown numerals on a cream white numeral band. Designed by Leo Ivan Bruce. (6,974 sold)

The General Electric **Model 7H100** "New Dawning" ($7.95), 5-1/16" x 5-1/16" x 3-3/8", has a brass easel-type case, white dial with diagonal gold stripes and black numerals, and brass hands.

The 1940-42 Telechron **Model 7H101** "Imp" alarm clock ($5.95), 4-5/16" x 4-5/8" x 2-7/8", was available in choice of ivory, rose, or brown molded plastic case, all with a double bezel of polished metal and dial with brown numerals on a light cream numeral band. (61,118 sold). After the war, the "IMP" was reintroduced in 1946-48 with a mottled gray plastic case, blue inner and white outer bezel, gray hands with luminous tips, and gray dial with white characters and luminous painted hour dots (**Model 7H101L**, $7.50). Designed by Leo Ivan Bruce. (117,195 sold)

The General Electric **Model 7H102** "Ashby" ($6.95), 4-3/4" x 5-1/8" x 3-1/4", has a blue mirror frame with an arched top. It features a tan and ivory dial with brown numerals and brass bezel and hands. The "Ashby" is also available in rose-colored glass with a golden hue. The dial on both is tan and ivory with brown numerals.

The 1940-47 Telechron **Model 7H103** "Conductor" alarm clock (Br ($3.95) & Iv ($4.50)), 5-1/8" x 5" x 3", was available in choice of mottled brown or ivory plastic case, brown hands, polished brass bezel, and dial with dark cream border, brown numerals, and light cream numeral band. Although production was halted for 3 years during World War II, production resumed in July 1945. Designed by Leo Ivan Bruce. (246,719 sold). *Courtesy of Jay Kennan.*

The Telechron "Conductor" in brown.

The General Electric **Model 7H104** "Hesperus" ($14.95), 5-3/8" x 5-3/8" x 3-1/4", has a case of genuine white onyx, brass numeral plate with etched numerals filled in with white enamel, a gold color dial, and white hour and minute hands.

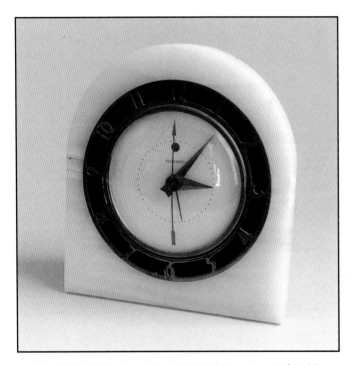

The 1940-42 Telechron **Model 7H105** "Legislator" ($14.95), 6-1/2" x 6" x 3-15/16", is the alarm version of the "Statesman" (**Model 4F81**). Introduced in 1940, the "Legislator" remained in production until 1942. (3,457 sold). *Courtesy of Esther Cooperman.*

The circa 1939-41 General Electric **Model 7H106** "Morning Glory" ($4.95), 4-11/16" x 4-13/32" x 3", has a metal case with "lustrous butler nickel finish," set on a black plastic base. It has a light cream dial with black numerals, "storm blue" hour and minute hands, green alarm hand, and silver second hand. Also available in mahogany brown enamel and gold color cases ($5.95). The "Morning Glory" was available with an illuminated dial in choice of butler nickel, ivory, or gold-colored case. Designed by Leo Ivan Bruce. *Courtesy of Jay Kennan.*

The 1940-42 Telechron **Model 7H107** "Supervisor" ($3.50), 4-1/2" x 4-1/2" x 2-3/4" and 1941-42 **Model 7H107K** "Warden" ($4.95), 4-1/2" x 4-9/16" x 3", were available in choice of mottled brown or ivory plastic case. The dial on the "Supervisor" has a light cream numeral band, darker center, and brown characters. The bezel is brass on the ivory version and brown lacquer on the brown case. The translucent dial on the "Warden" is light ivory with brown characters. The "Supervisor" is a redesigned "Butler" (7H79), having new feet and dial. (Sales—51,279 Supervisors, 67,968 Wardens). *Courtesy of Peter J. Scagnelli.*

The General Electric **Model 7H108** "Serf" ($6.95), 4-3/4" x 5" x 3-1/8", has a walnut-finished solid wood case with contrasting horizontal inlays and black base. It has a light ivory dial with black numerals, brass bezel and hour, minute, and second hands, and green alarm hand.

The 1940-41 Telechron **Model 7H109** "Flotilla" ships' wheel alarm clock ($6.95), 6-3/4" x 7-1/2" x 3-1/2", has a case of black oxidized metal, brass spokes, bezel, case cover, and easel foot rest. The dial has blue numerals and gold stars on a cream-white background. After June 18, 1942, this clock was shipped with an ivory plastic rather than brass case. (18,672 sold)

The General Electric **Model 7H110** "Orpheus" ($6.95), 6-3/8" x 5-3/4" x 3-1/2", has a case of polished and satin finish brass, a white dial with gold-colored band and brown moderne numerals, and brass bezel and hands. Designed by John P. Rainbault.

The 1941-42 Telechron **Model CH7111** "Semester" ($4.95), 5" x 6-3/8" x 3", was a special campaign model featuring a brown plastic case with a plain arched front panel and laterally grooved sides. The dial features brown numerals and a tan center against a light cream background. Both hands and bezel are brass. Designed by Leo Ivan Bruce. (20,062 sold). *Courtesy of Jay Kennan.*

The General Electric **Model 7H112** "Gallant" ($7.95), 5-1/16" x 5-1/16" x 3-3/8", has a brass case, polished in the front and satin on the back. The dial is light cream with tobacco brown numerals and outer band. The outer band is decorated with gold striping. The bezel and hands are brass.

The 1941-42 Telechron **Model 7H113** "Custodian" ($5.95), 4-7/8" x 5-1/4" x 2-7/8", has a brown wood case with black striped base, brass bezels, brown hands, and dial with brown characters on a light cream background. (12,179 sold)
Not Pictured: The General Electric Special Campaign **Model 7HX114** "Norse" has the same case design as the "Morning Star" (**Model AB7F52**) without the star motif and with a redesigned dial.

The 1940 General Electric **Model 7H116** "Orderly" ($3.50 (Br), $3.95 (Iv)), 4-1/4" x 4-1/4" x 3", was available in choice of walnut brown or ivory plastic case. It features a brass bezel, light cream and tan dial, brown numerals, hour, and minute hands, silver second hand, and green alarm hand. With an electrically illuminated dial, the "Orderly" becomes the **Model 7H116K** "Twinkle." Designed by Jacques Bars. *Courtesy of Jay Kennan.*

The 1941-42 Telechron **Model 7H115** "Fortress" alarm clock ($6.95), 6-5/8" x 5-13/16" x 3-3/16", has a brass case ring supported on an ivory plastic base, brass hands, and 5-1/2" dial with satin gold background, brown relief numerals and hour dots, and gold decorations. (6,050 sold)

The 1941-42 Telechron **Model 7H117** "Reporter" alarm clock (Br ($2.95) & Iv ($3.50)), 4-3/4" x 4-1/2" x 2-7/8", has a plastic case in choice of ivory with gold color bezel or brown with silver color bezel. The dial features brown characters and hands on a light ivory background with a dark cream center. (100,072 sold). *Courtesy of Jay Kennan.*

The circa 1945 General Electric **Model 7H118** "Troubadour" ($3.95(Br), $4.50 (Iv)), 4-1/16" x 5" x 3", was available in choice of antique ivory or walnut brown plastic case with brass bezel. The two-toned cream dial has rich brown numerals. The "Troubadour" was also available as pictured with luminous hands and numerals (**Model 7H118L**, $4.95). The tan dial has a dark brown numeral band, luminous numerals, and tobacco brown luminous hour and minute hands. Designed by Leo Ivan Bruce.

The 1941-42 Telechron **Model 7H119** "Governor" ($6.95), 5-3/8" x 5-11/16" x 3", has a case of light brown wood. The dial has brown characters on a light ivory background and a dark cream center. Hands and bezel are brass. Designed by Leo Ivan Bruce. (10,187 sold). *Courtesy of Jay Kennan.*

The General Electric **Model 7H120** "Tweed" ($6.95), 4-7/8" x 4-7/8" x 2-3/4", has a pigskin-grained facsimile leather case cradled between base strips of walnut. The bezel and all hands are brass; the dial is tan and ivory with skeleton numerals.

The 1941-42 Telechron **Model 7H121** "Serene" ($7.95), 6-13/16" x 6" x 3-7/16", has a case of transparent plastic tinted blue or rose supported on an ivory plastic base. (The same base used in the Model 7H115 "Fortress.") The dial has a cream-white background, brown numerals and dark cream dots. Bezels and hands are brass. (13,716 sold) **Not Pictured:** The General Electric **Model 7H122** "Informer" (5-1/8" x 5-1/2" x 3") is the alarm version of the Model 4H92 "New Ballard." Although the case design is the same as the "New Ballard," it has a square numeral band on an ivory background. It was also available with luminous hands and numbers (**Model 7H122L**). Designed by Jacques Martial.

The General Electric **Model 7H124** "Annapolis" ($6.95), 6-5/8" x 7-5/8" x 3-1/2", has a tan plastic case with brass spokes, bezel, and star decoration. The dial is light ivory with brown numerals and gold-color nautical motif.

The 1944-48 Telechron **Model 7H125** "Dispatcher" alarm clock ($4.95), 4-1/2" x 4-9/16" x 3", has an ivory colored plastic case, dark tan bezel, brown hands, and 3-1/4" dial with brown characters on a light ivory background. Introduced in October 1944, the "Dispatcher" has the same case as the prewar "Supervisor" (**Model 7H07**) but has a redesigned dial. (950,980 sold). *Courtesy of Jay Kennan.* **Not Pictured:** The General Electric Special Campaign **Model 7HX126** "Envoy."

The General Electric Special Campaign **Model 7HX130** has a plastic case with decorative metal fluting on the sides. With luminous features, it becomes the **Model 7HX130L**. *Courtesy of Jay Kennan.*

The General Electric Special Campaign **Model 7HX128** "New Lumalarm" ($3.95), 5" x 4-1/2" x 2", is shown in this March 15, 1941, *Saturday Evening Post* advertisement. It is basically an alarm version of the **Model 3H76** "Ithaca." It features a brown plastic case with luminous dial and hands.

Above: The General Electric **Model 7H134** "Helper" has a brass case/bezel set on an ivory plastic base.

Left: The General Electric **Model 7H132** "Brisk" has a mahogany finish case with black lacquer base and sides.

The 1945-50 Telechron **Model 7H133** "Embassy" alarm ($6.85), 5-1/2" x 5-1/4" x 3" has a mahogany-finished "authentic Colonial design" wood case, brass hands and bezel, and metal dial with dark cream center, light ivory numeral band, and brown characters. (173,73 sold). *Courtesy of Esther Cooperman.*

Three variations of the "Telalarm." *Courtesy of Esther Cooperman.*

The 1946-50 Telechron **Model 7H135** "Telalarm Jr." ($3.95), 3-3/4" x 4-1/2" x 2-3/4", has an ivory color plastic case and a 3 inch metal dial with dark tan background and brown characters on an ivory numeral band. It is the same case design as the earlier "Secretary" (**Model 7H91**) but is slightly smaller and came with a "control-a-tone" alarm that adjusts from loud to soft. (4,066 sold).
The "Telalarm, Jr." was also available with fully luminous hands and hour dots (**Models 7H135L & 7H135LI**). (700,602 sold). Finally, the "Telalarm, Jr." was available with a phosphorescent case (**Model 7H135LP**, $6.50) that glows in the dark. Original case design by Leo Ivan Bruce. (257,803 sold). *Courtesy of Esther Cooperman.*

The 1946-49 Telechron **Model 7H139** "Talisman" ($6.85), 4-3/8" x 4-3/4" x 2-3/4", has a wood case with mahogany finish and two vertical maple finish inlay bands, brass bezel, and brown hands. The 3" metal dial features brown characters on a light cream background. (287,224 sold). In 1950, a Special Campaign Model "Talisman" (**Model 7HC139**, $4.99) was offered with a redesigned dial. (50,342 sold)

Yet another variation of the Ivan Bruce design, the 1947-55 Telechron "Little Tel" (**Models 7H137, 7HA137, 7HB137, 7HD137, 7HE137, & 7H137LI**, $3.95-$6.50), 3-1/2" x 4-1/4" x 2-3/4", came in choice of brown or ivory plastic case and with or without luminous hands and hour dots. In addition, midway through its production life, it was redesigned with a white dial and brass hands. (2,360,733 combined sales). *Courtesy of Esther Cooperman.*

The General Electric **Model 7H138** "Chipper."

The General Electric **Model 7H136** "Gay Hour."

The postwar General Electric **Model 7H140** "Delegate" ($6.95), 5-3/16" x 5" x 3", has a golden mahogany case with brass bezel and hands. The dial has a light cream background with tobacco brown numerals. Hands and bezels are brass.

The General Electric **Model 7H142** "Contact."

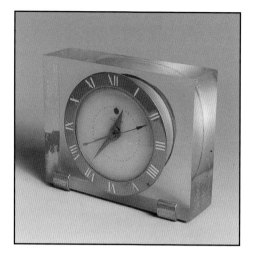

The 1946-57 Telechron Model **7H141L** & **7H141CP** "Airlux" alarm ($22.50), 5-1/4" x 6-1/2" x 3-1/4", has a case of "crystal clear optical plastic," brass numeral band with etched and filled characters, brass hands, and cream white metal dial. When introduced in March 1946, the case was set on four Lucite feet, two on each side. By November of that year, however, a single brass foot on each side had replaced the Lucite feet. It was described in the 1949 catalog as "America's favorite gift clock." (117,786 sold)

The General Electric **Model 7H144** "Nymph." **Not Pictured:** The General Electric Special Campaign **Model No. 7HX146** has the same case design as the "Ashby" (**Model 7H102**) but the dial features Roman rather than Arabic numerals.

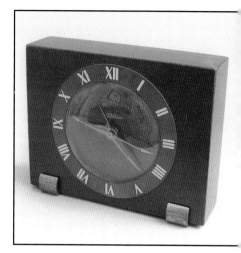

In September 1947, the "Airlux" was made available in a hand-rubbed mahogany case and mahogany colored dial with gold color dots (**Model 7H141M**, $14.95). Between 1947 and 1958, sales totaled 125,927. In 1953, the "Airlux" (**Model 7HA141**, $17.95-$36.95) was reintroduced with a white textured dial with tan hour markers. It was available in both mahogany and Lucite cases. *Courtesy of Esther Cooperman.*

The 1947-48 Telechron **Model 7H147** "Pinwall" ($7.95), 7-1/2" x 4-3/4" x 2-3/4", is a combination wall "pin-up" and table model alarm clock. The case is ivory plastic set on a detachable brown plastic base. The dial features ivory characters on a brown background. Hands and bezel are ivory. (52,930 sold). *Courtesy of Jay Kennan.*

The "Pinwall" with its wall bracket.

The 1948-49 Telechron **Models 7H149K & 7HC149** "Sparkler" (4-1/2" x 4-3/4" x 3") have an ivory plastic case. It features a translucent dial, "Control-a-Tone" adjustable alarm, and built in night light. (101,947 sold). In 1950, a phosphorescent, glow-in-the-dark, case was added and the "Sparkler" became the 1950-52 **Model 7HP149** "Shoreham" ($6.95). (40,171 sold)

The 1948-52 Telechron "Serene" or "Starlet" (**Models 7H153, 7HB153, & 7H153LP**, $4.95-$6.50), 3-1/2" x 4-3/8" x 2-3/4", features "petite and dainty, smart feminine styling" in an ivory plastic case with "stylish curtain tie back effect." The dial is chocolate brown. (333,044 sold)

The General Electric **Model 7H154** "Chantilly" (4-1/2" x 4-1/4" x 3") has a molded plastic case in choice of "gleaming ivory" or "warm brown." The light ivory dial with brown numerals is surrounded by a tan bezel. Hands are dark brown. *Courtesy of Jay Kennan.*

The 1949-51 Telechron **Model 7H155** "Telebell" ($4.95), 4" x 5" x 3", has an ivory plastic case and cream and tan dial. It features a new "rhythmic bell" alarm. The **Model 7H155L** ($5.95) adds luminous features. Original case design by Leo Ivan Bruce. (99,072 sold of 7H155, 1,956 of 7H155L)

The 1949-54 Telechron **Model 7H157 & 7HA157** "Colonade" ($7.95), 4-3/16" x 4-7/8" x 3", is a "boudoir clock" in a light mahogany case with "Grecian fluting." It features a "control-a-tone" alarm that adjusts loud or soft. (132,727 sold). *Courtesy of Jay Kennan.*

The 1949-52 Telechron **Model 7H159** "Nocturne" ($7.95), 4-1/2" x 4-7/8" x 3", was touted in 1949 as a "new design styled for modern bedrooms." The case was available in choice of ivory or brown plastic. The case design is the same as the **Model 7H09** "Nocturne." The center of the hands and the alarm dots are luminous. Designed by Leo Ivan Bruce. (57,948 sold, brown; 112,723 sold, ivory). *Courtesy of Jay Kennan.*

The 1947-52 General Electric **Models 7H160 & 7HA160** "Heralder" ($4.95), 4-1/2" x 4-1/8" x 2-3/4", has a case of antique ivory plastic and luminous hands and hour dots. The dial features light ivory numerals against a chocolate brown face. The bezel and sweep second hand are brass. The "Select-A-Larm" feature makes possible alarm volume control from a "soft purr to a loud shout." The "Heralder" was also available with luminous hands and hour dots (**Model 7H160L**) and with brown case (**Model 7H160BR**). *Courtesy of Jay Kennan.*

The 1949-53 Telechron **Models No. 7H161 & 7H161LI** "Tempo" ($5.95), 3-5/8" x 4-1/4" x 2-7/8", was Telechron's lowest price alarm clock in 1949. It has an ivory plastic case with "modern, slip stream styling," luminous features, and contrasting chocolate brown dial. (371,081 sold). *Courtesy of Jay Kennan.*

The 1948-52 General Electric **Models 7H162 & 7HA162** "Gay Hour" ($4.95-$8.95), 4-9/16" x 4-5/16" x 2-1/4", has a wood case and features "Select-A-Larm." Also available with luminous hands and hour dots as the **Model 7H162L** "New Gay Hour" ($7.95).

The 1949-53 Telechron **Models 7H163 & 7HA163** "Kirkwood" ($9.95), 4-3/4" x 4-11/16" x 3", has a hand-rubbed mahogany case and fully luminous features. It features a brass "picture frame" bezel. (98,929 sold). *Courtesy of Jay Kennan.*

Another of the numerous Telechron Christmas advertisements. *Courtesy of Jay Kennan.*

Advertisement for the "Beau."

The General Electric **Model 7H164** "Beau" ($3.95), 3-7/8" x 3-17/32" x 2-11/16". The case is mottled mahogany plastic.

The 1949-51 Telechron **Model 7H165** "Coronado" alarm ($12.50), 4-5/8" x 7-1/4" x 3-1/8", has a dark mahogany case, brass case ornament, twin bezels, and hands, and dial featuring black numerals against a white background. (36,873 sold)

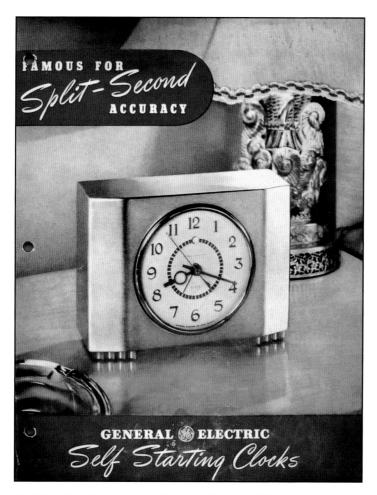

The "Morning Glory" was the "cover girl" on the 1949 General Electric clock catalog.

The 1949-53 General Electric **Model 7H166** "Morning Glory" ($12.50), 4-3/4" x 6-1/2" x 3", has a metal case with a "soft, satiny butler silver finish" and fluted polished brass feet. The dial has a satin silver finish with polished gold numerals, hands, and bezel. (36,873 sold)

The 1950-51 Telechron "Yachtsman" (**Models 7H167, 7HA167, & 7HB167** $7.95), 6-1/8" x 7" x 3-1/4", has a brown plastic case, polished brass bezel, rim, and spokes, and an instrument-like dial. Shown is the 7HB167. (50,155 sold). *Courtesy of Ashland Historical Society.*
Not Pictured: The General Electric **Model 7HA168** "Chantilly" (4-1/2" x 4-1/2" x 3") has the same case design as the earlier "Chantilly" (**Model 7H154**) but has a dark dial with luminous features. The bezel matches the body color.

The 1950-53 Telechron **Models 7H169** & **7HC169** "Guest" ($4.50), 3-15/16" x 4-3/4" x 3", has a streamlined ivory plastic case and new "wide angle vision" plastic crystal. The cream color dial features brown numerals and hands. (149,311 sold). From 1951-53, the "Guest" was also available with dark dial and luminous features (**Model 7H169L**). Designed by Rudolph Max Babel. (150,837 sold)

Rudolph Max Babel was awarded a design patent (D163,162, May 8, 1951) for the "Guest."

Catalog photograph of the luminous "Guest."

The 1947-52 General Electric **Models 7H170K** & **7HA170K** "Morning Star" ($7.95), 4-7/16" x 4-5/16" x 2-1/4", has an ivory plastic case with 3-1/2" round crystal. The dial is illuminated.

August 1947 advertisement for the "Morning Star."

The 1950-54 Telechron **Models 7HP171 & 7HAP171** "Bancroft" ($4.95), 4-3/8" x 4-7/8" x 3-1/8", has an ivory plastic case and clear dial. (48,647 sold)

The General Electric **Models 7H174 & 7HA174L** "Informer" ($7.75), 4-9/16" x 5" x 2-7/8", has an ivory plastic case with wide polished brass bezel and tan dial. *Courtesy of Esther Cooperman.* **Not pictured:** The 1949-50 General Electric **Model 7H176** "Deb" ($5.50) has a rectangular ivory plastic case with 2-5/8"x 3-3/8" dial. **Not pictured:** The 1950-51 General Electric **Model 7H178** "Orderly" ($4.95) has an ivory plastic case with 2-9/16" round crystal.

The 1950-53 Telechron **Model 7H173LP** "Tel-A-Glow" ($6.95), 4" x 5-1/4" x 3-1/8", was advertised as "America's most completely luminous clock—case and dial glow at night." (147,766 sold)

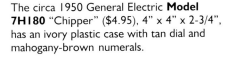

Cover to the 1953-54 Telechron clock catalog.

The circa 1950 General Electric **Model 7H180** "Chipper" ($4.95), 4" x 4" x 2-3/4", has an ivory plastic case with tan dial and mahogany-brown numerals.

The 1950-56 Telechron **Model 7H179 & 7HA179** "Tribute" ($9.95), 5-1/8" x 6" x 3-1/16", has a buffed brass cylindrical base, "modern diamond-cut sun tint dial," and full vision plastic crystal. Designed by Rudolph Max Babel. (241,926 sold)

The 1950-53 Telechron **Model 7H181** "Mentor" alarm ($8.95), 5-1/4" x 5-1/2" x 2-1/2", was touted as a "triumph of modern design—'dial framed in polished brass'—pierced numerals on wide gold color bezel." Introduced in August 1950, a General Sales Letter was issued January 24, 1951 withdrawing the design from sale. By February 1952, stock had been exhausted and the design was formally discontinued on May 30, 1953. (44,826 sold). *Courtesy of Jay Kennan.*

The 1950-52 General Electric **Model 7H182** "Twinkle" ($8.95), 5-7/16" x 5-1/2" x 3-1/8", is described in the 1950 catalog as "modern as tomorrow." Its maroon plastic case sets off an ivory color dial and polished brass bezel and base. *Courtesy of Jay Kennan.*

The 1950-53 Telechron **Model 7H183** "Imp" ($4.95), 3-7/16" x 5-1/4" x 3-1/16", has a plastic case in choice of ivory or brown, an anti-glare wide angle vision crystal, and clear dial. (192,057 sold)

The 1950-52 General Electric **Model 7H184** "Warbler" ($12.50), 5" x 5-3/4" x 3", has a grained mahogany case with brushed brass bezel.

The 1951-55 Telechron **Models 7H185, 7HA185,** & **7HB185** "Tiara" ($7.95), 4-1/2" x 5-1/8" x 2-7/8", has a clear dial "framed with sparkling jewel-like beads." Available in pastel pink, green, and blue pearlescent or ivory cases that reflect through the beads. The "Tiara" was also available with luminous features (**Model 7H185L**). Designed by Carl Otto. (295,949 sold)

The cover to the 1951-52 Telechron catalog featured the **Model 7H187** "Personality" ($9.95), 5-13/16" x 8" x 3-1/8". It has a clear frame that you can "change to suit your interests, hobbies, or décor." Simply slip in wallpaper, fabric, or photos. It features a fawn-color plastic case and gold hands and numerals. (47,268 sold)

The 1950-58 General Electric Telechron **Model 7H188** "Candlewick" ($18.95), 5-7/16" x 7-3/4" x 3", has a mahogany case with polished gold-bronze bezel and base. The ivory dial has raised gold-color numerals. (81,012 sold). *Courtesy of Jay Kennan.*

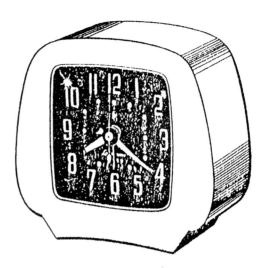

Drawing of the 1950-51 General Electric **Model 7H190** "Gay" ($4.95) from a parts manual. The "Gay" has a plastic case and crystal. The brown hands have luminous features.

The 1951-53 Telechron **Model 7H189** "Aladdin" ($6.95), 3-3/4" x 4-5/8" x 2-7/8", has a neon light at the bottom of the dial that glows when the alarm is set. The pyramidal shape of the ivory plastic case is intended to prevent tipping. Light color hands and numerals are contrasted against a chocolate brown dial. (36,953 sold)

The 1950 General Electric **Model 7H192** "Wink" ($3.25), 3-3/4" x 4-1/4" x 2-1/16", has a "carnation pink" plastic case with clear plastic crystal. The hands are maroon; the sweep second hand is gold.

Left: The General Electric "Nudger" (**Models 7H194, 7HA194, 7HB194, 7H194-LI**, $5.95), 4" x 4-7/16" x 2-5/8", has an ivory plastic case with wide, brushed bronze bezel and luminous hands and hour dots. Give it a new dial and the "Nudger" becomes the **Model 7HA194L** "Morning Star." The "Morning Star" has a "jewel" on the dial that lights when the alarm is set.

Above: The 1951-53 Telechron **Model 7H195** "Mirolarm" ($12.95), 5-1/8" x 5-1/2" x 3", has a plastic case, white numerals on a polished mirror dial, brass bezel and ball feet. (18,778 sold)

The 1952-53 Telechron "Parliament" alarm (**Models 7HA195** & **7HB195**, $12.95), 4-5/8" x 7-1/4" x 3-1/8", has the same case as the "Mirolarm" but the dial features raised gold color numerals and bands against a textured background. (18,609 sold)

The 1950-52 General Electric **Model 7H198K** "Lumalarm" ($6.95), 4-5/8" x 5" x 2-7/8", has an illuminated, edge lit dial in an ivory plastic case. The "handsomely textured bezel lends distinction." *Courtesy of Jay Kennan.*

The 1950-54 General Electric **Model 7H196I** "Heralder" ($4.95) and "New Heralder" (**Models 7HA196** & **7H196-L**), ($5.50-$6.50), 3-3/4" x 3-7/8" x 2-3/4", have ivory plastic cases with integral tubular feet, clear plastic crystals, and luminous hands and numerals. Shown here on the cover of the 1950 catalog.

Above: The 1951-53 Telechron **Model 7H199** "Minstrel" ($5.95), 3-1/2" x 4-3/8" x 3-3/8", has an ivory plastic case with "winged back that adds beauty and conceals controls." The hands are ivory; the sweep second hand is red. (34,894 sold).
Not Pictured: The 1951-53 General Electric **Model 7H200I** "Cue" & **Model 7H200L** "New Cue" ($6.95), 3-7/8" x 4-3/8" x 2-7/8", have plastic cases and crystals. The dial is chocolate brown and the luminous hands are ivory. The sweep second hand is red.

Left: The 1952-56 Telechron **Model 7H203** "Enhancer" ($4.99), 4-1/4" x 5" x 3", made the cover of the 1952-53 catalog. It has a beige plastic case and crystal. The numeral band is accented by gold color rings on a textured gray background. Substitute an ivory dial, black hour and minute hands, red sweep second hand, and tan alarm hand and the "Enhancer" becomes the General Electric Telechron **Model 7HC203** ($6.95). Designed by Carl Otto. (121,377 sold)

The 1953-55 Telechron **Model 7H197K** "Illuminette" ($9.98), 4-1/2" x 5-1/4" x 2-3/4", is an illuminated alarm that can be regulated from low to bright. Plastic case with gold-color front grille. (78,237 sold). *Courtesy of Jay Kennan.*

The 1952-55 Telechron "Telegrain" (**Models 7H201** & **7HA201**, $7.95), 4-5/8" x 5" x 2-7/8", has a plastic case with quartered-wood effect around the dial. (86,839 sold).
Not pictured: The 1951-52 General Electric **Model 7H202** "Brisk" ($5.95). Both the case and crystal are plastic. The hour and minute hands are ivory; the alarm and sweep second hands are red.

The "Enhancer" is also featured in this early 1950s advertisement. Note the higher price $8.95. *Courtesy of Jay Kennan.*

The 1951-53 General Electric **Model 7H208** "Riser" ($4.95), 3-9/16" x 3-9/16" x 2-7/8", has an ivory plastic case and shatter-proof crystal. The white dial features horizontal stripes and brown numerals and hands. Add luminous features and the "Riser" becomes the **Model 7H208LI** "PurrAlarm" ($5.95).

The 1953-55 Telechron **Model 7H209** "Gracewood" ($9.95), 4-1/4" x 3-3/4" x 2-1/8", was available in blond, provincial maple, and brown mahogany (shown) finishes. All have polished brass feet and bezels. The "Gracewood" was also available with luminous hands (**Model 7H209L**). Although I found no reference to the "Gracewood" being available with a Lucite base, the indentations in the pictured base match the ball feet on the clock. The base may have been offered as a promotional item. (102,523 sold)

The 1951-56 General Electric "Tweed" (**Models 7H204, 7HA204, & 7HB204**, $10.95), 5-1/4" x 6" x 2-7/8", has a "massive brass bezel" and "rich metal-finish" case. The hands are gold. The original dial on the "Tweed" features raised gold color numerals on a textured white background. The dial was redesigned twice between 1953-56. (138,384 sold)

The 1952-54 Telechron "Lullaby" (**Models 7H207 & 7HA207**, $4.95), 3-1/2" x 3-5/8" x 3", has an ivory plastic case with vertical ribbed base. The crystal is genuine plastic. The "Lullaby" was also available with luminous features. Designed by Philip Garland, Jr.

The "Lullaby" was also available in 1952-53 with luminous features (**Model 7H207L**). (87,651 sold)

The "Gracewood" in maple.
Courtesy of Jay Kennan.

Parts catalog sketch of the 1951-53 General Electric **Model 7H210** "Beau Alarm" ($7.50), 3-1/2" x 4" x 2-3/4", has a plastic case and crystal and luminous hands and hour dots. The dial is wood-grained. Like the "Drummer," the crystal "rolls graciously over top of clock."

Catalog photograph of the 1953-54 General Electric Telechron "Dorm" (**Models 7H211 & 7HA211**, $3.98 & $4.98), 3-1/2" x 4" x 2", has a hexagonal ivory plastic case with "maximum vision dial." Also available with luminous dial and hands. The luminous "Dorm" also came in a brown plastic case (**Model 7H211L & 7H211LBr**, $4.98).

The 1951-54 General Electric "Woodsman" (**Models 7H212 & 7HA212**, $8.95), 4-1/8" x 5-7/16" x 2-7/8", has a brown mahogany finished wood case and dial, plastic crystal, and wide bronze-finished numeral bezel with brown numerals. The hour and minute hands are white; the alarm and sweep second hands are red.

The 1953-56 General Electric Telechron **Model 7H213** "Perspective" ($17.95), 6" x 7" x 3-1/8", has a gold color concave dial with a white numeral band set in a black plastic case. The case sits on a gold color tripod with tiny ball feet. (35,256 sold)

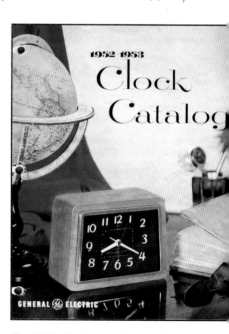

The 1953-54 General Electric "Serenade" (**Models 7H214 & 7HA214**, $13.50), 4-1/8" x 5-7/16" x 3-1/8", has a light birch case and jet black dial. The numerals, hour, and minute hands are white; the alarm hand is red; and the sweep second hand is gold. Seen here on the cover of the 1952-53 catalog.

Left: The 1953-58 General Electric Telechron **Model 7H215** "Décor" ($6.95), 3-3/4" x 6" x 2-5/8", has a plastic case and crystal. The numerals are applied to the crystal rather than the textured dial. The case was available in beige, blue, ivory, pink, and sea mist. The Décor was also available in a beige case with dark brown dial and luminous features (**Model 7H215L**, $7.98). (745,873 sold)

The 1953-60 General Electric Telechron **Model 7H216K** "Brite Dial" ($9.98), 4-1/4" x 5-1/4" x 2-3/4", is an electrically illuminated alarm clock with a light intensity control knob on the front of the clock. Black plastic case with glass crystal, and gold texture metal bezel. Dark brown hands with vermilion sweep second hand.

The 1954-56 General Electric/Telechron "Telecrat" (**Models 7H217 & 7HC217**, $5.98 & $6.98), 4" x 4-1/2" x 2-1/2", has a plastic case and crystal with gold color metal trim on the top and sides. It has a numerated crystal.

Parts catalog drawing of the 1952-54 General Electric "Beckoner" (**Models 7H218 & 7HA218**, $6.95), 3-3/4" x 3-7/8" x 2-3/4", has an ivory plastic case and shatterproof crystal. The hour and minute hands are ivory, the alarm hand red, and the sweep second hand gold.

The 1953-55 General Electric Telechron "Starter" (**Models 7H220 & 7HA220**, $3.98 & $4.98), 3-3/16" x 3-1/4" x 2-3/4", was "exquisitely designed with a woman in mind." It has an ivory "dynaline" plastic case, clear plastic crystal, ivory dial with brown hands, and a red sweep second hand.

Above: The 1954-55 General Electric **Model 7H221** "Turn-about" ($19.95), 7" x 5" x 5-1/2", has a plastic case, wood base, and 4" crystal. The hands are red, the alarm hand gray, and the sweep second hand white. "A pert, practical table or wall alarm clock with the modern touch." A part of the ill-fated designer line, the price was cut to $8.50 after the "Turn-about" was discontinued in October 1955. About three-fourths of the sales occurred after the price cut. (2,507 sold)

Left: The "Starter" was also available with luminous features on a dark brown dial and choice of ivory or brown plastic case (**Models 7H220L & 7H220LBr**, $4.98).

215

The General Electric Telechron **Model 7H223** "Room-mate" ($3.98), 3-1/4" × 3-3/8" × 2-3/4", has a plastic case in choice of pink, ivory, and a number of other colors. It was also available with luminous features (No. 7H223L, $4.98).

Featured in the upper left hand corner of this General Electric advertisement is the 1953-55 **Model 7H222** "Boudoir" ($7.95), 4-1/2" × 5-1/4" × 3". The "Boudoir" has a plastic case and dark dial and features luminous hour and minute hands, gold alarm hand, and red sweep second hand. The case was available in choice of coronation blue, carnation pink, willow green, and antique white. The wide bezel is textured "with quality of old cut glass." Other models pictured in the ad are, clockwise from the "Boudoir," the "Starter" (7H220), "Concord" (3H184), "Brite-Dial" (7H218), "Serenade" (7H214), "Jackstraw" (2H42), and the "Adams" (309).

Parts catalog drawing of the 1953-55 General Electric Telechron **Model 7H224L** "Partner" ($7.98), 4-1/8" × 4" × 2-1/2". The "Partner" has a gold color aluminum case, white dial, and 3-1/2" glass crystal. It features gold color numerals and luminous hour and minute hands trimmed with gold, gold alarm hand, and red sweep second hand.

The 1955-58 General Electric Telechron **Model 7H225L** "Luminary" ($5.98), 3-1/2" × 4-1/4" × 2-1/2", has an ivory plastic case and luminous numerals, hour dots, and hands. (405,687 sold)

The 1954-55 General Electric **Model 7H226** "Urban" ($9.98), 5-3/8" × 6" × 2-1/2", has an ebony black plastic case with fluted gold color border and clear plastic crystal. The face and hands are set back in a shadow box effect. It features silver numerals, black hour and minute hands, and gold alarm and sweep second hands.

The 1954-56 General Electric Telechron **Model 7H228** "Architect" ($7.98), 4-1/8" × 4-1/2" × 3", has a wood case with dark mahogany finish. The non-luminous version was available only in dark mahogany case, white dial with gold center, and deep maroon numerals and hands. The "Architect" was also available with luminous features (**Model 7H228L**, $8.98) and dark brown dial. The luminous version offered light mahogany and natural birch in addition to the dark mahogany finish. The alarm and sweep second hands on both models are gold color. *Courtesy of Jay Kennan.*

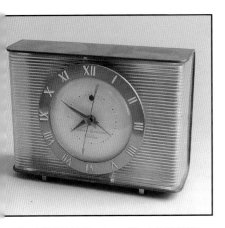

The 1955-57 Telechron **Model 7H229** "Replica" ($24.95), 5-3/4" x 7-3/4" x 3", has a solid brass case and 3-1/2" crystal. It features a white dial and wide gold numeral band. The front and sides are covered by ribbed translucent plastic. All hands are gold color. (17,877 sold). *Courtesy of Esther Cooperman.*

The 1954-55 General Electric **Model 7H230** "New Debutante" ($19.95), 3-3/8" x 3-1/8" x 2-1/2", has a case and base with classic bead design that is "luxuriously silver plated." The dial is blue with silver numerals. The hour and minute hands are pink, the alarm hand green, and the sweep second hand gold. *Courtesy of Jay Kennan.*

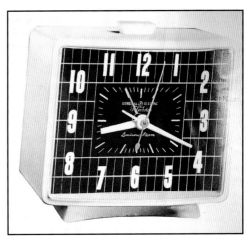

The 1954-55 General Electric Telechron **Model 7H232L** "Caller" ($6.98), 4-1/4" x 4-1/4" x 2-5/8", has an antique white plastic case, midnight blue dial, and clear plastic crystal. It features luminous hour and minute hands, red alarm hand, and gold sweep second hand. The "Caller" features a top shut off. (73,859 sold)

Above: The 1955-1958 General Electric Telechron **Model 7H233** "Circlewood" ($7.98), 4-1/2" x 5" x 2-3/4", was available in choice of light or dark mahogany case. Also available with luminous features (**Model 7H233L**). (199,568 combined sales)

Right: The 1954-57 General Electric Telechron "Harlequin" (**Models 7H234 & 7H234L**, $4.99-$6.98), 3-5/8" x 5-5/8" x 3", was "gracefully designed with distinctive feminine appeal." It was available with (260,212 sold) and without (197,989 sold) luminous features.

Left: The 1955-58 General Electric Telechron **Model 7H235** "Fidelity" ($9.98), 4-1/4" x 7" x 3", has a light or dark mahogany case and gold color feet. (134,860 sold). The "Fidelity" was also available from 1957-59 with luminous features (**Model 7H135L**, $12.95). (27,337 sold).
Right: The Model 7H233 "Circlewood."

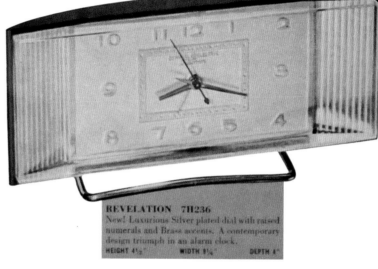

The circa 1955-58 General Electric Telechron **Model 7H236** "Revelation" ($12.95), 4-1/2" x 9-1/4" x 4", has a "luxurious Silver plated dial with raised numerals and Brass accents." (60,413 sold)

The 1944 Telechron **War Alarm Model 1** ($4.95) has an ivory plastic case, 3-1/4" metal dial with light ivory background and brown characters, dark tan bezel, and brown hands. (211,479 sold). At the end of the war, it continued in production as the "Dispatcher" (**Model 7H125**).
Courtesy of Jay Kennan.

Telechron announced that it was making alarm clocks again in this February 10, 1945, *Saturday Evening Post* advertisement. Note the post-war "Dispatcher" name.

The Telechron **War Alarm Model 2** ($4.95), 4-1/2" x 4-1/4" x 3", has an ivory plastic case, tan bezel, light ivory dial, brown numerals, dark brown hour and minute hands, and green sweep second hand. At the end of the war, it reentered production as the "Chantilly" (**Model 7H154**).

Chapter 12

Cyclometers, Day/Date Clocks, Clock Timers, Clock Radios, Novelty Clocks, and Barometers

Cover to the Fall/Winter 1937-38 Telechron clock catalog.

Cyclometers

The 1933-34 Telechron **Model 8B01** "Minitmaster" cyclometer clock ($10.95), 6-5/16" x 4-3/16" x 3-11/16", has a molded black plastic case, gold finished ornaments, and a front metal panel with an etched design. It features three lacquered metal drum type dials and sweep second disc with printed numerals. A miniature lamp illuminates the dial. Designed by Edgar Bourquin. (13,419 sold)

"NOW I can tell time, Daddy!"

Telechron "Minitmaster" is as practical as it is novel and dependable. PRACTICAL, because it tells time as simply as "A-B-C." At only $9.95 list, your market is tremendous . . . your selling Job easy . . . . your profit in dollars and good-will great.

A 1933 promotion for the newly developed cyclometer clock that first appeared in the *Telechronicle*.

The 1933-36 Telechron **Model 8B03** "Minitman" cyclometer clock ($9.95), 6-1/8" x 4-3/8" x 3-11/16", has a brown mahogany case with Satinwood ornamental front and top panels, statuary bronze escutcheon panel, and three drum type dials with black characters. The poor condition of the wood in the pictured example significantly lowers its value. (6,452 sold). *Courtesy of Jay Kennan.*

The 1933 General Electric **Model AB8B02** "Executive," 6-1/2" x 4-1/8" x 3-5/8", has a case of black or brown Textolite with inlays and faceplate of oxidized silver and bronze, respectively, with an engraved decoration. Ad copy for this "NEW TYPE Handless Clock" reads "Today's busy executive now has a clock that talks his own language! His time tables, appointment cards and cost sheets read in numerals, as '10:45,' '6:27.' This clock tells time the same way, by giving the exact second of the hour at all times with unvarying accuracy by means of changing numerals." Designed by Edgar Bourquin.

The General Electric **Model 8B04** "New Executive" ($8.95), 8" w, was touted in sales literature as a "new and moderately priced, better-type, cyclometer model in moulded case designed by one of the foremost men [Walter Dorwin Teague] in the field." It was available in mottled walnut with gold metal trim and black with chrome dials and trim. *Courtesy of Sara Hassan.*

The 1934-36 Telechron **Model 8B05** "New Minitmaster" ($9.95), 6-5/16" x 4-3/16" x 3-11/16", replaced the "Minitmaster" in May 1934. It featured a black plastic case with buffed nickel silver ornaments and white numerals on three black drum type dials and sweep second disk. A miniature lamp illuminates the clock. The "New Minitmaster" was also available in an ivory plastic case with black numerals on light cream dials. The ivory version had no metal ornamentation. (15,194 sold)

The General Electric **Model 8B08** "Executive."

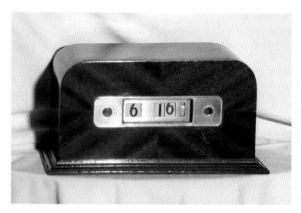

The General Electric **Model 8B06** "Budgeteer" ($12.50), 5-1/2" x 8-3/4" x 4-1/4", was cited in company literature as a "new, deluxe cyclometer model in a richly finished, matched wood case of simple, tasteful design." The dial is illuminated with a tiny MAZDA lamp. A polished brass escutcheon sets off an ivory dial with large black Arabic numerals. Designed by John P. Rainbault. *Photo by Stephen Kruft. Courtesy of Stephen Kruft.*

The 1936-39 Telechron **Model 8B07** "Baron" cyclometer clock ($8.95), 3-3/4" x 8-1/16" x 3-7/8", was available with (1) black molded plastic case, maroon base, chrome-plated escutcheon, and maroon band, (2) brown plastic case and base, brass escutcheon, and ivory band, and (3) ivory case, maroon base, polished chrome escutcheon, and maroon band. The dials are ivory with black characters. The brown and black models were introduced in 1936, the ivory a year later. All were discontinued in 1939, although a few were shipped from stock after the war. Designed by Walter Dorwin Teague. (26,226 sold)

The 1936-40 Telechron **Model 8B09** "Tribute" cyclometer clock ($12.50), 4-1/4" x 8" x 3-3/4", has a walnut case with horizontal ornament overlays in light maple. The dial features black characters on a light cream background. Designed by Walter Dorwin Teague. (7,762 sold)

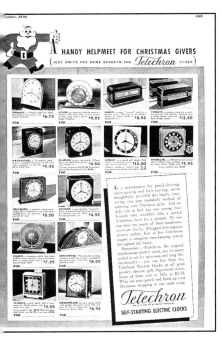

Esquire, December 1936.

The General Electric **Model 8B10** "Framingham" ($9.95), 4" x 8-9/16" x 3-5/8", has a brown walnut case with brass escutcheon plate, light cream numeral drums, and black numbers.

The 1938-42 Telechron **Model 8B11** "Granada" cyclometer clock ($7.50), 3-3/4" x 8-1/16" x 3-7/8", was available with a (1) black molded Bakelite case, maroon base, chrome-plated escutcheon, or (2) brown case and base with brass escutcheon. The dials feature black numerals on a light cream background. (26,514 sold)

The 1939-42 Telechron **Model 8B13** "Register" cyclometer ($9.95), 3-7/8" x 8-5/8" x 3-5/8", has a brown walnut veneer front and back, solid brown walnut top and sides, brass escutcheon plate, and light cream numeral drums with black characters. (11,855 sold)

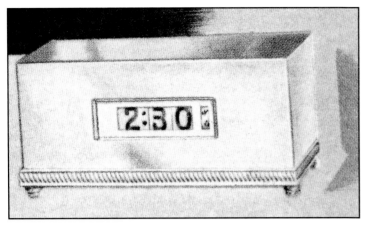

The circa 1948 General Electric **Model 8B22** "Executive," 3-1/2" x 7-3/4" x 3-1/8", has a butler silver finish.

The 1946-48 Telechron **Model 8B23** "Register" ($28.00), 3-1/2" x 7-1/4" x 3-9/16", has a gun metal finished case with gold color ornaments and brass feet. The numeral drums have a light ivory background and black characters. Introduced in October 1946 for $28.00, by the time it was discontinued at the beginning of 1948, the price had risen to $37.00. (4,780 sold)

Day/Date Clocks

Circa 1946 Telechron advertisement.

The circa 1940 General Electric **Model 8H14** "Almanac" ($9.95) is a calendar clock with mahogany case with brass feet, bezel, and hands. The light cream dial features black numerals. The day and date characters are red.

The 1940-41 Telechron **Model 8H15** "Instructor" ($9.95), 5-1/2" x 5-1/4" x 3-1/8", is an automatic calendar clock in a brown wood case with contrasting wood inlays and brass feet, bezels, and hands. The 3-1/2" dial has a light cream background, black characters, and gold lines. The cream color calendar dial has red characters. (8,806 sold)

The 1941-42 Telechron **Model 8H17** "Registrar" ($9.95), 5-1/8" x 5-3/4" x 3-1/16", is an automatic calendar clock in a brown wood case with quartered grain front and metal feet and brass bezels and hands. The dial is light cream with black numerals and gold lines. The day and date dials have red characters. (6,326 sold)

The 1954-56 General Electric Telechron **Model 8H24** "Almanac" ($9.98), 5-7/8" x 5-7/8" x 3-1/8", is a calendar kitchen clock with 60 minute timer. It has a plastic case in choice of coral, blue, turquoise, white, or yellow and a numerated crystal. The case will hang on the wall or stand on a shelf. *Courtesy of Jay Kennan.*

The 1954-55 Telechron **Model 8H29** "Tele-jour" ($14.95), 5-3/4" x 5-3/4" x 2-3/4", is a day-date clock in a brushed brass frame and plastic case. A polished brass bezel surrounds a white dial. (47,999 sold)

Design patent 175,458 awarded to Leo Ivan Bruce on August 30, 1955.

Clock Timers

Above: Circa 1954 advertisement announcing new Telechron models, including the "Tele-jour." *Courtesy of Jay Kennan.*

Right: The circa 1935 General Electric **Model 8F50** "Kitchen Timer" (5" x 4-1/2" x 3-1/4") has a black plastic case, chrome band, ivory dial, and blued steel hands. The "Kitchen Timer" was also available in ivory and gold. Designed by Raymond E. Patten.

The circa 1935 General Electric **Model 8B50** "Select-O-Switch" ($12.50), has a walnut-finished case with metal ornaments. The dial is light cream with black numerals. The bezel is bronze and the hands blued steel. A time switch mechanism enables the clock to be used "to turn on and off favorite radio programs, switch on and off lights." Designed by Raymond E. Patten. *Courtesy of Jay Kennan.*

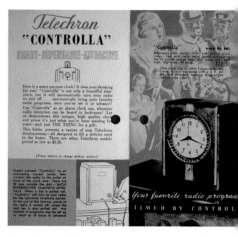

The "Controlla" received a two page spread in the sales catalog when it was introduced in 1935.

Raymond E. Patten designed the "Kitchen Timer" (D97,781, awarded Dec. 10, 1935). The same case was also used for the "Utility Timer" (No. 7F64) and "Vedette" (No. 7F56).

The 1935-39 Telechron **Model 8B51** "Controlla" ($12.50), 6-3/4" x 5-5/8" x 3-15/16", has a mahogany case with walnut finish and eight wood vertical inlays. Two brass bezels surround 15 minute period keys. The light cream dial has black characters. Designed by Belle Kogan. (11,262 sold)

Above: Sales literature for the General Electric **Model 8B52** "Radio Traveler" ($9.95), 6-1/4" x 5-1/4" x 3-1/4", notes that, "designed for use by radio fans, this clock features a dial that indicates the time in important parts of the globe. A radio receiver, plugged into the back, will be switched on about $\frac{1}{2}$ minute before the program desired starts." The "Radio Traveler," also sold as the "Voyageur," has a molded plastic case in mottled walnut and a double brass bezel. Designed by Jacques Bars.

Jacques Bars received a design patent (D104,012, April 13, 1937) for the "Advisor." The same case was used for the "Pageant" (No. 3F67), the "Sparkler" (No. 7F71), and the "Gendarme" (No. 7F71L).

The 1936-40 Telechron **Model 8F51** "Advisor" (Bk ($4.95), I ($5.50)), was billed as a "new style reminder clock." It was equipped with a special hand permitting setting of alarm in 5 minute intervals up to 3-1/2 hours. It was available in choice of (1) black plastic with buffed Nicral bezel and side ornaments or (2) ivory plastic with brass. Designed by Jacques Bars. (9,536 sold)

Left: The 1936-42 Telechron **Model 8B53** "Organizer" household timer ($9.95), 6-3/8" x 5-1/4" x 3-5/8", features a walnut color molded plastic case with a 3-1/4" metal dial. Forty-eight keys surround the dial, each representing a 15 minute interval. The sales literature contains instructions for connecting a radio to the outlet in the back of the clock. It notes that "When a key is pulled out, it will turn on the radio for the indicated 15 minute period. When more than one successive key is pulled out, the radio will operate for the corresponding number of 15 minute periods. At the end of an interval, power to the radio is turned off. Any number of programs may be set up as much as 10 hours in advance." Designed by Walter Dorwin Teague. (25,999 sold). *Courtesy of Jay Kennan.*

The General Electric **Model 8B54** "Radio Traveler" ($12.50), 7" x 6-3/4" x 3-1/2", is a deluxe time-switch model with mahogany case and double bezel. The sales literature notes that it is "useful to radio fans—particularly those who seek distant programs on the short waves." Designed by John P. Rainbault.

The 1945-53 Telechron **Models 8H55** and **8HA55** "Selector" ($9.95-$19.95), 5-1/8" x 5-3/4" x 3-5/8", has a mottled brown plastic case. It automatically switches lights and other appliances on and off and allows user to pre-select radio programs 11 hours in advance. Designed by Francesco Collura. (123,309 sold). *Courtesy of Jay Kennan.*

The 1945-50 Telechron **Model 8H57** "Lite-Call" ($8.95), 4-1/2" x 4-3/4" x 3-1/4", has an ivory plastic case, 3-1/2 inch ivory dial, gold color numeral band with maroon characters, and maroon hands. The "Lite-Call" was also available with a walnut brown plastic case. Designed by Francesco Collura. (78,270 sold)

The 1945-52 General Electric **Models 8H58** and **8HA58** "Select-O-Switch" ($9.95-$17.50), 5-3/16" x 6-1/2" x 2-3/4", has a mottled chestnut brown plastic case with fluted base, an ivory dial with dark maroon numerals, and modernistic hands in deep mahogany with a vermilion second hand. The selection keys and selection ring are finished in bronze.

The 1947-50 General Electric **Model 8H60** "Beam Alarm" ($6.95-$8.95), 4-7/8" x 4-7/16" x 2-1/2", makes a lamp plugged into the back of the case flash intermittently at wake-up time. It has an ivory case and alarm face, clear dial, and ivory numerals on chocolate bronze bezel. The hands are chocolate brown except the sweep second hand, which is vermilion.

The circa 1945-52 Telechron **Model 8H61** "Switch-alarm" ($5.95-$9.95), 5" x 5" x 3-1/8", will turn on radio, lights, or other light appliances at pre-selected times. It also houses a conventional alarm. It has a walnut brown plastic case. Designed by Francesco Collura. (283,461 sold). *Courtesy of Esther Cooperman.*

Left: The 1947-48 Telechron **Model 8H63** "Minitmaster, Jr." ($5.95), 3-9/16" x 4-5/16" x 3-1/4", is a combination clock and kitchen timer in a white plastic case. The dial features gray numerals and characters on a white center and white alarm characters on a red band. There is a red arrow on the white signal hand. (88,267 sold)

The 1948-50 General Electric **Model 8H64** "Tune-A-Larm" ($5.95), 4-3/4" x 5-9/16" x 2-5/16", turns on a radio plugged into the rear of the case at alarm time. The case is mottled mahogany plastic. The dial features maroon numerals on "warm grey pearl essence" background and light tan alarm face. *Courtesy of Jay Kennan.*

The 1948-50 General Electric **Model 8H66** "Little Chef" ($5.50), 3-3/4" x 4" x 2-7/8", has a plastic case. It "times any household task up to 30 minutes." *Courtesy of Jay Kennan.*

This circa 1948 Telechron **"Minitmaster"** timer, 4-5/8" x 5-1/4" x 2-1/4", bears no model identification. The bottom of the dial is marked "Telechron, Inc., Ashland, Mass."

Circa 1948 General Electric **Model 3T63BAA2** "Electric Range Time Switch" (Catalog No. TM-52), 3-1/2" x 6" x 2-1/2", white plastic case, chrome bezel and knobs, and beige dial. The dial is marked "Telechron Movement."

The 1956-63 General Electric Telechron **Model 8S69** "Video-clock" ($14.95), 3-1/8" X 7" X 2-1/2", has a brown plastic case. (86,898 sold). *Courtesy of Jay Kennan.*
Not Pictured: The General Electric **Model 8H70** "New Tune-A-Larm" ($8.95), 4-1/8" x 4-1/4" x 2-3/4", is "styled to perfection" with its brown plastic case. The alarm turns on the bedside radio and, 7 minutes later, sounds its own alarm.
Not Pictured: The 1950-51 General Electric **Model 8H72** "Tune-A-Larm" ($7.95) has the same ivory plastic case design as the "Beam Alarm" (8H60). The dial and hands also appear identical to the "Beam."

Novelty Clocks and Clock Radios

The General Electric **Model 8F02** "Traveler" (5" x 5" x 1-7/8") is described as a "unique and useful clock for short-wave fans, exporters, etc., who need to know the time in various parts of the world. Set for local time, the revolving dial shows the corresponding time in 24 sections of the globe." The "Traveler" has a molded black plastic case with rectangular chrome bezel, ivory dial, and chrome hands.

The Telechron **Model 8F01** "Smug" ($5.25) was introduced in September 1934 and discontinued at the beginning of 1939. It was offered with yellow, black, or blue cases, orange colored beak, and white and black eyes. The cream white dial has indigo blue characters. The bezel is brass, the hands dark orange lacquer. Designed by Belle Kogan. (18,569 sold). *Courtesy of Esther Cooperman.*

The 1937-39 Telechron **Model 8F03** "Explorer" or "Globetrotter" ($7.50), 6-3/8" x 6-3/8" x 3", has a walnut case with bronze back and footrest. The 5" square dial has black characters on a brown background with a revolving world band of light and dark sections denoting A.M. or P.M. This "world time" clock has a 24 hour band showing time in different cities around the globe. Designed by Walter Dorwin Teague. (11,874 sold)

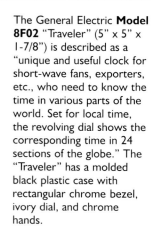

Walter Dorwin Teague was awarded the design patent (D108,586, Feb. 22, 1938) for the "Explorer."

The 1954-55 General Electric Telechron **Model 8H27** "Innovation" ($16.95) is a hanging occasional clock with an exposed dial. The tail assembly is wood. Designed by Rudolph Max Babel. **Not Pictured:** The 1957-58 General Electronic Telechron **Model 8H28** "Trixie." (59,441 sold)

The 1935-41 Telechron Fisk™ **"Time to Re-Tire"** advertising clock. (5,293 sold)

The 1928-31 General Electric Telechron **"Monitor Top"** refrigerator clock. At least two types of "Monitor Tops" were produced. On the earliest clocks, the General Electric nameplate is 3-3/8" long and the condenser has 16 circular (horizontal) cooling fins. The condenser is permanently attached to the top of the case. In the later model, the GE nameplate is only 1-9/16 inches long and the condenser has 14 circular cooling fins and 11 pairs of vertical fins. The condenser is bolted to the top of the case.

The "Monitor Top," which was prolifically advertised, brought the convenience of electric refrigeration to the middle class.

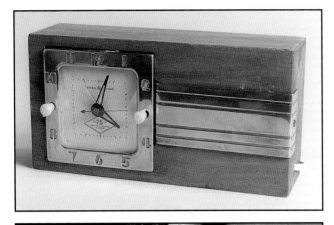

The 1953 double-faced General Electric **Model 1803**, 4-1/4" x 8-1/4" x 2-1/4", marking the company's 75th anniversary. It has a solid wood case with brass trim.

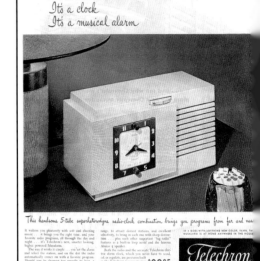

The new "Musalarm" as featured in the October 4, 1947 *Saturday Evening Post*.

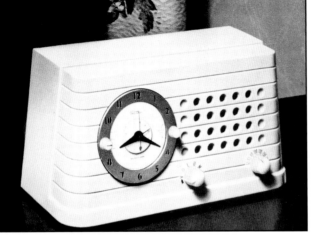

The 1946-49 Telechron **Model 8H59** "Musalarm" ($27.35), 5-3/4" x 10-5/8" x 4-3/4", was a combination radio and conventional alarm clock in a maroon plastic case. The dial is ivory with gold numeral band and maroon characters. The hands are maroon lacquer. It was later offered with walnut brown and ivory plastic cases. Designed by Francesco Collura.

The Telechron **Model 8H67** "Musalarm" ($39.95), 6-1/4" x 11-1/4" x 6-1/4", is a combination radio and conventional alarm clock in choice of "rich fawn" or brown plastic case. The dial features a white background with pierced numerals. Both bezels and hands are bronze color. (134,081 sold)

General Electric introduced its own version of the clock radio as shown in this 1946 *Saturday Evening Post* advertisement. The advertisement does not identify the model number.

Left and far left: Although radio manufacturers were initially reluctant to introduce clock radios, by 1955, at least 30 manufacturers were using Telechron "Electric Memory Timers" in their clock radios. Among the companies using Telechron timers were Crosley, Philco, Admiral, Magnavox, Westinghouse, Motorola, and Sylvania.

Barometers

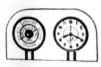

Label for the General Electric **Model 8H16** "Barotime," a ship's wheel barometer/clock combination.

The 1940-42 Telechron **Model 8030 and 8030T** "Quartermaster" ($16.50), 7-1/4" x 15-1/8" x 4-15/16", is a combination barometer and clock. It consists of the No. 3H85 Telechron clock and a Telechron barometer set on a wood base panel. The cases are brass and the dials have cream white backgrounds with blue characters. The 1940 catalog notes that "Owners of this combination set will be 'time and weather warned.'" (5,059 sold)

The 1940-42 Telechron **Model 8027 and 8027T** "Forecaster" ($7.95), 6-3/4" x 7-1/2" x 2-7/8", is the barometer companion to the Resolute. It has a brass case with six spokes and cream white dial with blue characters. (9,898 sold). *Courtesy of Esther Cooperman.*

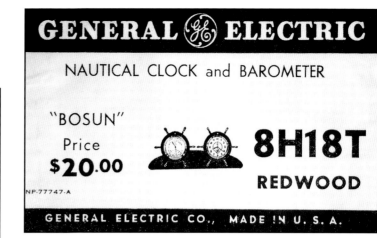

Label for the General Electric **Model 8H18** "Bosun" ($20.00), 7-1/8" x 17-1/4" x 3-1/8", a combination nautical clock and barometer. The base is of burl redwood, the bezels and spokes are brass, and the case of brown plastic.

The 1940-42 Telechron **Model 8H19T** "Prophet" ($20.00), 7-3/8" x 15-3/8" x 3-1/8", is a combination clock and barometer in a ship's wheel design. The brass ships' wheel cases sit on a redwood burl base. The dials have a light cream background with blue characters. (2,509 sold)

Appendix I.

Tips for Repairing and Restoring Telechron and General Electric Clocks

By Jay Kennan

Jay Kennan, an apprentice clocksmith and creator of the popular web site, Pappy's Telechron Clock Page, prepared this appendix. While the fairly straightforward repairs outlined below can be accomplished without special training, neither the author, the publisher, nor Mr. Kennan, accepts any responsibility for losses that result from efforts by nonprofessionals to repair or restore a clock. If you are at all uncertain about what repair(s) need to be performed or your mechanical abilities to complete the repairs, it is better to pay a professional clocksmith to perform the repairs than risk damaging the clock.

A "Death in the Family"

In a three ring binder, on a shelf at the Ashland Historical Society, there is a letter addressed simply to the Warren Telechron Company, Ashland, Massachusetts. The letter begins with the author saying that she had had a "death in the family today." She explained that the Telechron clock that had hung in her kitchen for as long as she cared to remember had suddenly stopped working. She inquired as to whether the model was still available. In its response, Timex, which acquired the former Telechron plant from General Electric in 1978, told her that the model was no longer made and enclosed a Timex clock catalog, assuring her that their new quartz clocks were built to the same quality standards as the Telechron she had recently lost.

I sometimes wonder what that woman did after she got her reply from Timex. At the time she wrote, Telechron "H" rotors were still being produced at the factory and were cheap. Her clock probably needed only a new rotor and a good cleaning. I like to think that her inquiries did not stop at that first letter and that she learned that any clocksmith could get her a new H rotor for a few dollars, a fact that was not volunteered by Timex.

That 3 ring binder is full of letters like hers, from people wondering where they could find a clock as reliable as the Telechron that had recently broken. I thought about what it is about a Telechron clock that would make someone not only want a replacement but also express sorrow over their loss. Although no other letter used the term "death in the family" (one does start "a very dear friend of ours passed away yesterday"), many use similar terms and yes, emotion to describe what you would think would be just another broken appliance.

Whether you're a thriving little family of Telechrons already or are thinking about adopting your first one, this appendix is meant to help you keep them looking and running their best. I will take you through a series of steps in the restoration process, using a Telechron Model 7F71 "Sparkler" as the patient.

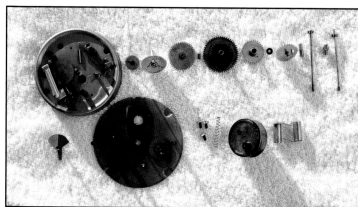

"Sparkler" parts Top row, left to right: base plate assembly, sweep second hand shaft, minute hand sleeve, setting gear, set pinion spacer, hour hand sleeve, alarm hand sleeve, cam gear hub washer, cam gear, alarm set shaft spacer, alarm set shaft, time set shaft sleeve, time set shaft. Bottom row, left to right: reset indicator, front plate assembly, front plate screws (3), time set shaft spring, "H" rotor, and spreader post (2).

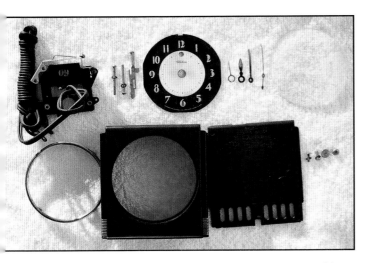

"Sparkler" parts continued Top row, left to right: field coil assembly with attached cord set and alarm vibrator assembly, field screws (2) w/ lock washers, shutoff lever, dial, alarm hand, hour hand, minute hand, sweep second hand, crystal. Bottom row, left to right: bezel, case front, case rear, case screws (2) w/ attached lock washers, alarm set knob, time set knob.

Tip 1: How to Take a Clock Apart

Tools and supplies needed

- Thick towel
- Slot head screwdriver (1/4 inch)
- Needle nose pliers
- Regular pliers
- Small pieces of suede or similar material

Step 1: Position the clock—Place the clock face (crystal side) down on the towel.

Step 2: Remove screws—Remove the two or three slot head screws in the back of the movement. On some models, the screw goes through a spring and grommet, which should be removed.

Step 3: Remove knobs—If the holes for the set knob(s) are large enough, remove the back of the case. If the knob(s) will not pass through the back, they will have to be removed. Place a piece of suede around the shaft of the knob and grip it with the needle nose pliers. To avoid scratching the case, keep the suede between the tool and the case. Grip the knob itself with the other pair of pliers, using a piece of suede to protect the knob. Now, turn the

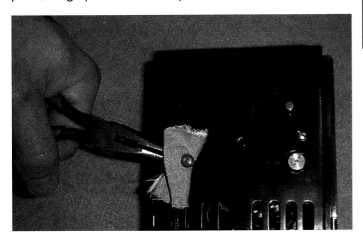

Using a small piece of suede helps protect the case from damage when removing the knobs. A second piece of suede should be used to protect the knob.

knob in the direction indicated below while keeping the shaft from turning.

To unscrew the time-set knob, turn it in the direction opposite to the way you turn the knob to move the hands clockwise (it is *usually* reverse-threaded). While most time-set knobs unscrew by turning them clockwise, the time set knob on the Model 454 unscrews *counter*-clockwise.

Follow the same procedure to remove the alarm-set knob. The alarm-set knob typically unscrews in the direction opposite to that used to remove the time-set knob. (**Hint: If there are arrows molded into the case back to indicate the direction in which to turn the knob to set the hands, turn the knobs in the opposite direction shown by the arrows to unscrew the knob**). If the clock has a tone adjustment knob (for controlling the pitch of the alarm), it can be removed by turning it in a counter-clockwise direction.

Step 4: Remove back—Remove the case back, allowing access to the movement.

Clock Tales for You—Roach Motel

It is warm, dark, and relatively quiet inside an electric clock. I thought it was a fluke when I took a kitchen clock apart one day and found a pile of dead roaches inside. But, I've since found three other clocks with roaches (none living, thank goodness) within and have resigned myself to this sad truth: People aren't the only ones who get a warm feeling from having a Telechron in the house. And if that clock is in the kitchen near all the food, that makes it an even better place to find roaches. The point is, be prepared for the unexpected when you remove the back cover. Otherwise, you may end up dropping the clock or flinging it across the room during what the roaches might consider a home invasion.

How an Alarm Clock Works

Telechron experimented with several alarm mechanisms before finding one it liked. There was a very subtle, awful-to-adjust mechanism in the "Electrolarm" (No. 711) and a tiny "electric jackhammer" in the "Autolarm" (Nos. 7B01 and 7B02). Beginning with the "Announcer" (No.7F01), Telechron found a winner with the vibrator-arm type alarm. The designs may look different but they all work on the same principle: alternating current passing through the coils creates a magnetic force in the field arms. The direction of the force changes 120 times a second (in clocks made for the U.S.) and alternately repels and attracts a steel arm that makes noise (or powers a tiny jackhammer against a bell).

Tip 2: How to Adjust the Alarm

After many years of service, the violent action of the alarm often throws the alarm out of whack. (This same effect can be achieved in shorter time by repeatedly knocking the alarm clock off the night stand or tossing it across the room.) The sound of any Telechron or GE alarm will invariably get quieter over the years but they are relatively simple to adjust, at least in theory.

The alarms on Telechron clocks can usually be fixed. In fact, I have never worked on one that I have been unable to fix even after someone else had clearly been in to muck things up. The alarm is not dependent on the clock's rotor, and will continue to operate even if the clock appears dead.

Clock Tales for You—Silence Please

One of the strangest things I found when I removed the back cover of a clock was stick-on felt applied to virtually every available spot on the inside of the case with tiny holes cut out for the knobs. Presumably, the felt was added to make the alarm quieter. It must have taken the owner an hour to do with the felt (with questionable success) what they could have done in five seconds with pliers.

Two Deaths May Be Better Than One

An alarm clock that has both a dead movement *and* a dead alarm is often easier and less costly to repair than one with a working alarm but dead movement. If the alarm and movement are both dead, the culprit is often a bad cord or coils, both of which are readily available and relatively inexpensive. However, if the alarm still works, the dead movement probably needs a new or rebuilt rotor. Because rotors are no longer being manufactured, many clocksmiths will not repair Telechron or GE clocks that need new rotors.

If you have not already removed the back of the case, follow the directions in Tip 1 before proceeding. The only tool needed for adjusting the alarm is a pair of needle nose pliers.

Step 1: Check for obstruction—If the clock is running but the alarm does not trip, check first to see if the vibrator arm is trapped by the alarm hook. If the arm is trapped, merely swing the hook back to the left and let the vibrator arm return to its normal position.

Step 2: Bend vibrator arm—If the alarm trips but is too quiet or does not sound at all, then some minor bending adjustments are all that is needed. With a buzzer alarm (no bell), bend the vibrator arm toward the coils until it sounds. Remember that it is the sound of the vibrator arm striking the coils that produces the buzz; if it is too close to the coils it will not move and there

will be no or muffled sound. On the other hand, if the vibrator arm is bent too far from the coils, no contact will be made and the alarm will not sound.

Adjusting a bell alarm is a bit more challenging. You want to hear the bell, not the buzzer (unless you are a heavy sleeper and you want to hear both). Getting this right often involves dozens of small bends both to the vibrator arm and the bell arm. To get the sound right you want the vibrator arm to miss the coils but still cause enough movement to the bell arm so that the hammer hits the bell. Achieving the proper adjustment can be extremely frustrating. I have spent hours adjusting a few troublesome alarms until I got it right, but the results are rewarding. Although there will always be a slight buzzing while the alarm is sounding, the primary sound should be the ringing bell.

Tip 3: How to Replace the Cord

<u>Tools and supplies needed</u>
• screwdriver
• wire strippers
• new cord (about 6 feet)
• new plug (optional)

<u>Additional tools and supplies for F, H and S rotor clocks</u>
• vice
• soldering iron
• flux
• solder
• wet sponge for cleaning soldering iron

Whether for repair, safety, or just appearance, most electric clocks will eventually need a replacement power cord. To my knowledge, all of the early, B rotor Telechron and General Electric models had external plugs or, like the "Electrolarm," had the cord attached by screws so that soldering is not required to replace the cord. For the remaining models, however, a soldering iron is needed to properly replace the cord.

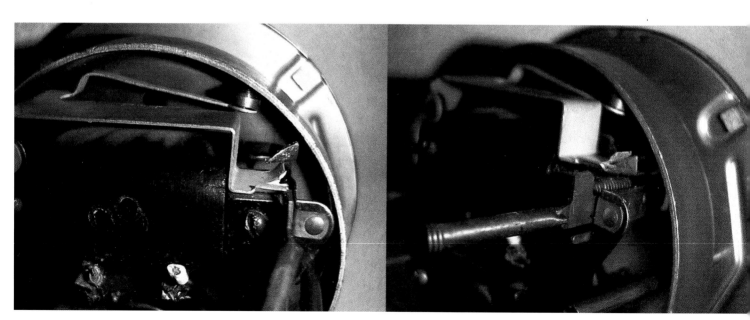

Fixing the alarm is a simple matter if the alarm hook, as shown in these photos, traps the vibrator arm.

When should the cord be replaced? If you plan to use your vintage clocks, they should have cords free of chips, cracks, fraying, or bare wires for safety reasons. You may also want to replace cords that have heavy scuffs or discoloration just for the aesthetics. If you do not plan to use the clock, then replacing the cord is simply a matter of aesthetics.

What kind of cord should I use? General Electric and Telechron clocks produced before 1939 usually had artificial silk-wrapped cords. These were attractive and safe but once the outer wrapping began to fray, there was no stopping it, revealing two, cloth-covered inner wires. In the mid 1930s, rubber brgan to replace silk cords on GE models and, by 1941, rubber cords became the standard. They could stand being dragged and scraped around corners much better than cloth but they had two problems. First, they dried out, became brittle, and cracked. Second, they were incompatible with the Plaskon cases that replaced good, old Bakelite in the 1940s. The rubber would (and still will) melt right into those cases, permanently marring them. (You fishermen who have ever had a rubber worm dissolve right into the bottom of your tackle box know what I'm talking about.) Finally, by the 1950s, power cords on most everything (and all Telechron and General Electric clocks) were made of vinyl.

CAUTION: It is imperative that heavy gauge appliance cord be used for radio and appliance timers (like models 8B50, 8B51, 8B52, 8B53, 8H55, 8H58, and 8H61). Such clocks are meant to control high-wattage tube radios and kitchen appliances and the cords may carry several times the amount of current that can safely be carried on a standard lamp cord. If you have a timer or are thinking of buying one with a replacement cord, check to make sure that proper gauge cord was used. Light duty rayon cord should not be used to rewire timers. It may look good but it is not safe for use on an appliance timer.

If you use new, rayon cord, you must keep the braided outer covering from fraying after you expose the inner wires. This can be done by using shrink-wrap or by spreading epoxy or white glue on the ends of the braided cover. One trick I use is to put an old-style Bakelite plug on the cord *first*. Then I put epoxy on thickly around the end of the cord. This prevents fraying and keeps the wires from being pulled off of the screws if someone gives the cord a good yank.

Step 1: Remove the Old Cord—Cut off the cord where it enters the case. If the plug is in good condition and has screw connectors, it can be reused.

Step 2: Remove the Field Coils—For an F or H rotor clock, take the field coils out of the movement. Open the case (See Tip 1) to expose the rear of the movement. Take the screws out of the standoffs on either side of the rotor. **DO NOT** try to loosen the screws on either side of the coils. They do not hold the field coil in and their removal could throw the alarm out of adjustment.

Step 3: Mount the Field Coil in a Vice—Once the field coil has been removed, it should be mounted in a vice.

Step 4: Prepare the Wire—Separate about an inch of the two wires in the new cord and expose about 1/4 inch of each with wire strippers. Roll the ends of each wire between your fingers to twist the strands together.

Step 5: Remove the Old Wires from the Coil—With a hot soldering iron heat each pole of the coil until the old solder melts and the old cord ends can be removed. Leave the holes in the center of each pole open (free of solder) so that the new cord can be inserted.

Step 6: Run the New Wire Through the Case—If the plug is already attached to the other end of the cord, pass the wires through the rear case or movement cover **before you solder**. Otherwise, you will be unable to reassemble the case without removing the plug. This step can be skipped if the plug has not been attached.

Step 7: Solder the Connections—Poke one end of the new cord through each of the holes in the poles (See step 5) and bend the ends back. With the hot soldering iron apply enough flux and solder to secure the wires—just a drop. Unplug the soldering iron and clean the tip on a wet sponge. After it cools, wipe off any excess flux with a paper towel.

Attaching a new plug is a simple repair even with an old Bakelite plug with screw connectors.

Replacing the cord on a B rotor clock is a cinch, particularly if the clock has an external plug-in connector for the power cord. Simply open the connector by loosening the one screw, detach the old cord from the screw terminals, and attach the new cord to the screws on each pole of the plug. Attach a wall plug to the other end of the new power cord (pictured). The same basic procedure is followed for "B" rotor clocks that do not have an external power cord connector, such as models 715 and 8B52, except that the case must be opened to find the screw connectors. Be sure to remember to run the new cord through the case before attaching the wires.

Tip 4: Cleaning the Crystal

It is tough to tell what will be needed to clean the glass and dial. The crystals on Telechron and G. E. clocks come apart in so many different ways that all I can do is provide general guidelines based on the 7H71.

Step 1: Removing the Bezel and Crystal—On our project clock, the glass crystal and dial are held onto the front plate of the movement by a brass bezel. The bezel is attached to the front plate by four brass tabs. **Very carefully** bend the tabs away from the front plate to allow the bezel to pass over the dial. Bending two adjacent tabs out all the way (in line with the bezel) and the other two just slightly allows the bezel to swing off like a door and keeps from bending the tabs too much. The tabs are thin brass and there are only so many times you can bend them before they crack and fall off. Bending the tabs slowly helps prevent their breaking.

Most General Electric and Telechron clocks have a bezel with tabs to hold the glass similar to the bezel described above. There are, however, a number of other methods used to attach the bezel. For example, in clocks with flat glass crystals, like models 711 and 356, the crystal is sandwiched between the dial and case. Similarly, in early wooden Telechrons like models 370 and 324, the bezel is held in place by threaded rods that secure the bezel to the back plate. Some of the later plastic crystals just pop off the front or are sandwiched between the movement and the case. Whatever clock you are working on, just remember to go slowly, work carefully, and think before you use force.

Step 2: Remove Scratches—To remove fine scratches on plastic crystals, use a scratch remover like Novus 2™. It also works magic on fine scratches in those 1950s plastic cases. If a scratch is too deep to be effectively removed by Novus 2, rub a little toothpaste over the scratch in a circular motion with your fingertip or a soft cloth until the scratch disappears. Do not use a paper towel as it may add new scratches as quickly as it removes the old ones. Application of toothpaste to a clear plastic crystal will fog the crystal and **must** be followed by application of Novus 2 in accordance with the manufacturer's directions.

Removing scratches on glass that are so bad you can not ignore them are best left to a professional. Here, a professional does not necessarily mean a clocksmith. Most clocksmiths do not have the type of buffing equipment needed to remove deep scratches. Other places to try include plate glass companies, jewelry stores, and opticians. The big "eyeglasses-while-you-wait" stores located in many shopping centers might be willing to help you out particularly if you are a regular customer.

Step 3: Cleaning the Crystal—Once any major scratches have been removed, clean the crystal with a good glass cleaner. Use a lint free towel or cloth to avoid leaving dust on the inside of the crystal. Some glass cleaners tend to leave a residue if not completely removed, so check to make sure the crystal is completely clear. Once the crystal has been cleaned, handle it by the edges or outside. Nothing is more annoying than finding a big fingerprint on the inside of the crystal after the clock has been reassembled.

Tip 5: Cleaning the Dial

No part of a Telechron has caused me personally so much grief as the dial. It is literally as well as figuratively the face of your clock. Scars and discoloration on the dial are among the first things you notice about a clock. Sadly, the dial is also the part of a clock that is most casually damaged and the hardest to restore.

Paper or Plastic? The Things that Dials are Made Of

The majority of Telechron dials are painted steel. But some dials, even in early Telechrons, were made of paper. According to Dick Fannon, a former engineer at Telechron, clocks were made with paper dials and sold at bargain "campaign" prices during periods of slow sales. For example, the "Butler" (No. 7H79) was available with a paper dial. Other dials were made of semi-transparent plastic to allow illumination from behind, examples being the "Announcer" (No. 7F01) and "Morning Glory" (No. 7H106). By the 1950s, most dials were made of plastic just to save money. Some dials on 1950s and 1960s clocks were even made of painted aluminum foil (the 7H253 "Little Snooz Alarm" comes to mind).

CAUTION: Improper Removal of the Hands Can Damage the Dial

Step 1: Removing the Hands—To remove the hands, you will need a 1/8 inch slot head screwdriver and a small piece of cardboard like a matchbook cover. Place the cardboard on top of the minute hand along its length, completely covering the hand. Put the screwdriver on the cardboard with the tip beneath the base of the second hand. Give the screwdriver a slight twist and the second hand should pop right off. Repeat this process for the minute hand, putting the cardboard on the hour hand. To remove the hour hand, put the cardboard on top of the alarm hand and a piece of paper under the alarm hand as it is often too close to the dial to press upon without scratching the dial. To remove the alarm hand put the cardboard under and a little to one side of the hand. Leave enough room to safely get the screwdriver in without taking a chance of scratching the dial.

Do You Really Want to Clean the Dial?

Before you do anything to the dial, keep in mind that most clocksmiths do not restore dials or even clean them. The clocksmith for whom I apprentice sends his dials out to a specialist ("the dial doctor," George calls him) and then only if the customer insists. Dial work beyond a simple cleaning is more artistic than technical and if you do not have the artistic talent, its better to leave such dial work to an expert. Otherwise, a cleaning project can turn into a restoration project.

CAUTION—
Do not mess with luminous paint.

Luminous paint has a tendency to turn dark and crumbly over time. Any attempt to clean it, however, will likely create a bigger mess. Besides, luminous paint is radioactive!

CAUTION—
The Telltale Signs of WD-40™ Poisoning

If, upon close examination, the dial of a clock has an oil stain around the hands that looks like a brownish circle or a big, green streak that goes from the center of the dial down to the bottom, some prior owner has likely treated the clock to a healthy dose of WD-40 or some other penetrating oil. And that is just what it has done. It has penetrated between the metal and the paint causing irreparable damage. Over time, most of the remaining paint will probably flake off of the dial.

Not much can be done to repair a dial damaged by oil. Once the oil penetrates beneath the paint, any attempt to clean the dial will just result in further damage as a damp towel will cause the numerals to wipe off and large chunks of paint to be removed.

CAUTION—
WD-40™ and Clocks do not Mix

WD-40™ is a great lubricant for most everything, but it can do serious damage to clocks. Spraying WD-40 on a clock will probably make the clock run quieter that it has in years. But this benefit is only temporary while the damage to other parts is permanent. A good shot of WD-40 can leave oil stains on the dial and penetrate under the paint leading to eventual flaking. It can also dissolve rubber power cords and certain types of plastic cases. After a quick spray of WD-40, dust now finds it can stick to every part of the movement and work its way into the moving parts. The most damaging effect, however, is on brass. WD-40 permanently discolors and reacts with brass to form little crystals that are abrasive to the movement.

Step 2: Wipe the Dial with a Soft Dry Cloth—This is the safest way to clean a dial but is also likely to have limited effect.

Step 3: Spot Test the Paint—Before any further attempts to clean the dial, it is absolutely critical that the soundness of the paint be tested. Dip the corner of a towel in watered down glass cleaner and gently rub a small, inconspicuous, area at the edge of the dial away from any printing. If the paint is removed, stop immediately and progress to step 5. Otherwise continue to step 4.

Step 4: Clean the Dial—If the test showed the paint to be sound, move inward, changing the towel frequently to avoid spreading the dirt around. Avoid all contact with luminous features, they are usually just waiting to fall off. If there is no sign that the "General Electric" or "Telechron" logo is starting to fade, you can try a stronger solution, but never spray anything directly onto the dial. If this cleaning provided satisfactory results, skip down to step 6, replacing the hands. Otherwise, let the dial dry thoroughly before proceeding to step 5.

Step 5: Dry Cleaning the Dial with an Eraser—One of the gentlest methods of cleaning a dial is to use a soft pencil eraser. Because it is dry it is less likely to damage the paint, but it is still advisable to test an inconspicuous area for both results and damage before proceeding to clean the whole dial. The pencil eraser has the added advantage of being easy to control. One disadvantage to its use, however, is that the whole dial will have to be cleaned, not just the dirtiest parts. Otherwise, the dial will have an uneven finish. With the eraser, it is all or nothing, and I only use it on dials that are wrecks anyway. It works great on most of those green oil stains I mentioned if the damage to the dial is not too severe. The pencil eraser may also leave beige dials a little lighter than the original color.

Restoring Missing Paint

Frequently, dials have damage to the paint resulting from an improperly installed hand or errant screwdriver scraping the dial. Although it is fairly easy to touch up these flaws, an improperly matched paint can result in a dial that highlights rather than hides its flaws. It is highly unlikely that you will achieve a perfect match with off the shelf paint. The computerized color matching equipment at auto parts, paint, and hardware stores, however, can do an excellent job of color matching. Just take the dial with you to the store and they can mix a near perfect match. The down side is that you will have a quart of paint when only a few drops are needed. The results, however, can be impressive as the scratches disappear.

Step 6: Putting the Hands Back On—The key to reinstalling the hands is to remember to put the hands back on at the 12:00 position. Beginning with the alarm hand, reinstall the hands in the reverse order in which they were removed.

Reinstalling the hands on an alarm clock is a little bit trickier:

(1) Move the alarm knob slowly until you hear and feel the alarm trip. (To test whether the alarm has properly tripped, try to turn the alarm knob backward. It should not go back more than a mite.)

(2) Put the alarm then the hour hand on, both pointing at the 12.

(3) Move the alarm hand to 2:00 (it moves much quicker than the hour hand).

(4) Move the time-set knob until the alarm trips, hopefully, right as it hits the 2. If the hour hand reaches 2 before the alarm trips, you can hold it there while continuing to turn the time-set knob until the alarm trips. If the alarm trips before the hour hand reaches 2, it is difficult to try and move the hour hand forward the right amount because you cannot tell how much the hand is moving on the shaft versus how much the time is advancing. This can give rise to a few angry moments, but just be patient and keep trying. The trick is to trip the alarm s-l-o-w-l-y the first time before you put the hands on and make sure you don't move any knobs or hands while you put each hand on.

(5) Put the minute hand on pointing at the 12.

(6) Put the second hand on. The position of the second hand is not important because its motion is not tied to that of the minute and hour hands.

A Primer on the Rotor

The rotor is the heart of every G. E. and Telechron clock. For that matter, it was the heart of every Revere, Guild Crest, NuTone, and Pam advertising clock. Telechron rotors drove virtually **EVERY** clock radio made in the 1950s as well as the timers in washing machines, dryers, and stoves of every description. Similarly, a Telechron promotional brochure notes that

> "Thousands of Telechron motors are also being used in many types of devices other than clocks with unusual success. Such devices include demand meters, elapsed time indicators, gas analyzers, humidity recorder controllers, power factor meters, recording pyrometers, temperature regulators, time stamps, time switches, traffic signals, vacuum gauges and regulators, voltage regulators, recording watt hour meters, etc."

The rotor is the feature that most easily distinguishes Telechrons from every other electric clock. It had and has a number of advantages over other electric clock motors. It is sealed in oil so it runs quietly and free from dust and other contamination. Because the main shaft of the rotor is whizzing around at 3600 RPM, the permanent oil bath is the difference between a rotor that lasts 30 years and one that lasts only 1 year. The inside of the rotor is little more than a group of gears designed to slow the frantic spinning of the main shaft to a more sober 3.6 RPM for "F," "H," and "S" rotors and 1 RPM for "B" rotors. Two round, steel vanes on the end of the main shaft ride down in the tail of the rotor right where the magnetism of the field arms can act on them

Capillary action lets the oil reach all of the parts as long as the rotor is correctly oriented. Every rotor has the word "TOP" stamped on the outside so it can be correctly placed in the clock. Marking the top in this way is essential for the 'B' rotors which are outwardly the same all the way around. On 'H' rotors, the top is found near the off-center external gear and it cannot be installed if it is not oriented correctly. If the rotor is not properly aligned, oil will not be distributed properly and the rotor will begin to wear out and run loudly.

You will often hear the term *synchronous* when talking about electric clocks. The motor is synchronized to the frequency of the alternating current changes at the power station. The direction of the current changes 120 times a second (in the United States) and the Telechron rotor is designed to take advantage of that frequency. The arms of the field assembly extend from either side of the coils. Because of the electrical energy, a magnetic field is created with one arm or pole *pushing* and one pole *pulling* the vanes in the rotor. But because of the alternating current, the direction changes and each pole alternately pushes and pulls the vanes of the rotor 120 times a second. A double spoke that holds the pivot bisects the vane. That spoke marks the point on the vane that is pulled halfway around every cycle making 60 RPM.

If each arm of the field assembly were pushing and pulling the rotor equally, it would remain stationary no matter how many times the force changed direction if it were not for the "shading coil," the metal ring around one "finger" of each field arm which cancels out the magnetic field and with it, the push or pull from that field arm. The two "fingers" without the shading coil work to move the rotor vanes in the same direction; one is pushing while the other pulls.

Telechron rotors from A to S. From left to right: Four "B" rotors in brass and steel, a cast steel "F" rotor, an early "H" rotor with stabilizing wings and brass standoffs, and a regular "H" rotor with the spreader posts. Front and center is the "S" rotor.

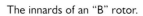

The innards of an "B" rotor.

236

Tip 7—Quieting a Noisy Rotor

Tools and supplies needed

- small baby food jar
- round piece of felt cut to fit bottom of the jar
- sewing machine oil (NOT WD-40 or motor oil!)
- double boiler (one pot inside another will do)
- pot holder
- water

Step 1—Place the felt in the bottom of the baby food jar and fill the jar with sewing machine oil.

Step 2—Cap the jar and place it in the freezer for at least an hour.

Step 3—If you have not already done so, remove the rotor from the clock.

Step 4—Fill the lower section of a double boiler with about an inch of water, place the rotor in the top section, and bring the pot to a boil. Boil until the rotor is too hot to touch, being careful not to get burned by the steam.

Step 5—Remove the jar from the freezer and the double boiler from the heat. Using the potholder, pluck the rotor out of the double boiler and quickly drop it, gear-side-up, into the oil-filled jar.

Step 6—Cap and return the jar and rotor to the freezer. As the air inside the rotor cools, a partial vacuum is created inside the rotor. The cold oil will go down the rotor's gear bearing and fill the vacuum.

Step 7—Remove the rotor from the jar after 1 hour and wipe off any oil.

Step 8—Return the rotor to the coils and plug them in. The rotor should now be noticeably quieter.

Step 9—Repeat the above steps as needed to bring the noise down to a tolerable level. Keep in mind, though, that too much oil will slow or stop the rotor altogether. While it is true a good rotor does run "as quiet as moonlight," it is usually not possible to achieve absolute quiet again once a rotor has become loud.

Why Rotors Stop

A rotor will stop if the oil inside gets sludgy enough to keep the vanes from turning or because a lack of oil has caused the pivots or gears inside to wear to a point that they wobble out of orbit and bind. The latter is a rare occurrence as a rotor will usually make a noise like somebody stepped on the cat when the oil gets that low.

CAUTION--There is no good or easy way to take a rotor apart. Rotors were not meant to be repaired; it was intended that the rotor be replaced when it became loud or quit working. Unfortunately, replacement rotors are no longer being manufactured. There are some master clocksmiths who specialize in repair of electric clocks who routinely perform rotor surgery, but most clocksmiths will not attempt such repairs. Such invasive repairs are both challenging and expensive and best left to a specialized clocksmith.

The non-invasive method described below can often achieve the same results at lower cost and requires far less skill.

Tip 8—How to Breathe New Life Into Dead "B," "F," and "H" Rotors

Equipment and supplies needed

- ultrasonic cleaner
- lacquer thinner
- well-ventilated area
- spare field coil(s) with cord attached

Step 1—Set up the ultrasonic cleaner—Place the cleaner in a well-ventilated room, or, weather permitting, outside.

Step 2—Place rotors in cleaner and fill—Place one or more dead rotors in the basket and fill with lacquer thinner until the rotors are covered. A small ultrasonic cleaner uses about a quart of lacquer thinner and will accommodate five or six rotors.

Step 3—"Cook" the rotors—Turn the ultrasonic cleaner on and simply "cook" the rotors for about 10 minutes. The pummeling sound waves from the cleaner will help to break up any sludge so that the lacquer thinner can more effectively dissolve it back into something more like oil.

Step 4—Test the rotor—Take the rotor out of the cleaner and attach it to a field coil. Plug in the field coil to see if the motor starts to turn.

Step 5—Manually assist the rotor—If the motor does not start on its own, try turning the gear with **just your thumb and forefinger** to get it going. (Turn the gear clockwise for "B" rotors and counter-clockwise for "F" and "H" rotors) If it starts to turn, let it run a few minutes. (Hint: It helps to have extra field coils hanging around for this project if you are working on multiple rotors at the same time.)

Step 6—Add clock oil—If the rotor runs but is loud, follow the steps in Quieting A Noisy Rotor (Tip 7).

Step 7—Repeat as needed—If the rotor seems to be turning too slowly or will not turn at all, return it to the tank for another 10 minutes and then begin again at step 4.

It is critical that *the rotor be kept running* once it has started and that some proper clock oil be introduced inside the rotor if it is loud. Otherwise, the rotor is very likely to seize up again.

Naturally, the above method will not work for every frozen rotor. Rotors with worn-out bushings or sprung plates will need more invasive medicine to get them running again. Expect about an 80 percent success rate with "B" and "H" rotors. "F" rotors, because of their thick, pot metal cases, are harder to revive ultrasonically and odds are about even that they will work.

New, nylon-geared Telechron rotors cost about $35 (plus shipping). The above method could save your original, higher quality, rotor at a fraction of the cost. The savings could also help cover the cost of the ultrasonic cleaner

---

Turning Back Time

Former Telechron engineer Dick Fannon recalls that a popular prank played by the engineers at the Telechron plant was to flip the field arms so that the shading coils are reversed. This made the clock run backwards. My long-time barber—PeeWee—took this prank one step further. In addition to reversing the coil, he put new numerals on the dial in reverse-order. Now his clients can read the time on the clock behind them just by looking in the mirror.

The Case for Restoration

There are two schools of thought about antique clocks. The first treats an antique clock like a piece of 18th Century French furniture and says it should be left in original or as-found condition. The other school must have been taught by classic car buffs. That is, do anything it takes to get the object of your desire back into new-looking and working shape. In the antique family tree, electric clocks are on the same branch as tube radios. Tube radio collectors in general have no misgivings about replacing capacitors, line cords, and speaker cloths. They use reproduction dials, knobs, escutcheons and (horror of horrors!) they chemically strip and refinish the cases on those old beauties until they look impossibly new.

I fall more closely in line with the Zenith tombstone radio collector than with the Louis XIV chair collector. Although I appreciate a perfect, original finish as much as anyone, I will usually do what I can to improve a scruffy one. If you are of the feeling that any refinishing is too much, this section is not for you.

The idea, however, is to restore the clock to its original condition not to build a new clock out of the old. That means no quartz movements, no new colors for painted metal cases, no painting of stained wooden cases, and no transparent vinyl cords. Any such changes decrease the value of the clock. Similarly, putting a General Electric dial in a Telechron clock, or putting Session's hands on a General Electric clock will lower the value of the clock. To maintain its maximum value, the clock must be accurately restored. When antique automobiles are judged, points are deducted for any variation from original equipment and finish. The same is true of clock restorations.

Tip 9—How to Cover Scratches on a Wooden Case

More books have been written about restoring, stripping and refinishing wood than will ever be written about clocks—electric or otherwise. If the clock case has deep scratches, gouges, or loose or missing veneer, I recommend using a book like *The Weekend Refinisher* by Bruce Johnson as your guide to restoration. Just remember to restore the case to as close to original condition as possible.

Before deciding that the clock needs to be refinished, however, you might try a couple of applications of *Howard RestorAFinish*™. For damage to your wooden clock that is limited to the finish, just rubbing *Restor-AFinish* on with a soft cloth is just short of magic. And, for damage that goes through the finish to expose unstained wood, *RestorAFinish* is available with a variety of stains to darken the wood. Repeat the application as needed. The manufacturer recommends application of paste wax over the restored finish. Restor-AFinish may improve the appearance of the clock enough that stripping and refinishing is deemed unnecessary.

Tip 10—Repairing Chips in Plastic Cases

Not much can be done to restore a plastic case with chips unless the missing piece is located. If the clock was already chipped when you bought it, there is not much that can be done. Although there are a number of companies that advertise Bakelite and Catalin repair, they are expensive and often yield disappointing results. If

you broke the clock yourself, the "chip" can probably be located and glued back in place. Glue the piece back in place from the *inside* of the case using quick setting epoxy designed for use on plastic. Gluing from the inside will help prevent excess epoxy from getting on the outside of the case. If it is not possible to apply epoxy from the inside, apply Super Glue™ or some other quick setting glue recommended for use on plastic to the surfaces to be joined. The edges of broken plastic are porous and Super Glue works very well. Apply sparingly from the inside to avoid having the excess glue ooze out onto the exterior of the clock.

Tip 11—How to Clean Cracks in Plastic Cases

Step 1: Wash the case—The trick with cracks is to get the dirt out before dealing with the crack itself. With brown or black cases, dirt does not really show, but with a white or other light color case, any dirt in the crack shows up like a pimple on prom night. With a plastic case, there is nothing wrong with a short bath in the sink after the movement, crystal, and dial have been removed. Do not use any harsh cleaners or scouring pads, just a hemp or jute vegetable brush and a mild dishwashing soap like Dove™. Be sure to scrub the inside of the case at the same time. Remove or avoid excessive scrubbing of brass trim to avoid damaging the protective layer of lacquer.

Step 2: Clean the Case in an Ultrasonic Cleaner (Optional)—Nothing cleans cases quite like an ultrasonic cleaner. I bought a white Bakelite Telechron "Hostess" (No. 454) for $5 at a flea market that had probably been passed over by many collectors because of the numerous minute cracks in the white Bakelite, each filled with dirt. Scrubbing did not begin to get the grime out of those cracks but just a few minutes in the ultrasonic tank and the dirt disappeared and with it the cracks. I still marvel at the job it did whenever I see that $5 clock that looks like a million dollars now.

Tip 12—Repairing Cracks in Plastic Cases

<u>Equipment and supplies needed</u>

- clear, two-part epoxy
- glossy piece of cardboard or similar material
- toothpicks
- clamp

Step 1: Prepare epoxy—Once the case is cleaned and dried, mix a dab of epoxy on a piece of cardboard, following label directions. To repair cracks up to two inches long, a dollop of epoxy about the size of a nickel is plenty.

Step 2: Adjust case—Working with one crack at a time, line the two sides of the crack up so that the case wall is as smooth as possible. You can think of this almost like setting a broken bone. You may have to wiggle or even spread the crack a little to get the sides to line up again.

Step 3: Clamp Case—Clamp the sides in place, being careful not to apply the clamp too tightly. If the clamp is set too tight, it could crush the case. (pictured)

Use a clamp to close the crack in preparation for applying the epoxy. Exercise caution to avoid applying excessive pressure to the case.

Step 4: Apply epoxy—Set the case crack side down. Working from the inside of the case, spread epoxy on the crack and at least 1/8th inch on each side, being careful not to cover screw holes or block parts of the case that must fit together with other parts. Do not let the epoxy drip over the edge of the case or spread over any holes.

Step 5: Remove clamp—Allow the epoxy to dry for as long as the maker recommends before removing the clamp and reassembling the clock or moving on to another crack.

Tip 13—How to Remove Surface Scratches in Plastic Cases

Scratches in a plastic clock case are easy to overlook as just part of the patina—until you come across a perfect case, gleaming like the day it came out of the box. Whether its Bakelite, Catalin, Textolite, Vinylite, or Plaskon, every plastic-cased General Electric and Telechron clock left the factory with a perfect, glassy sheen. Restoring that sheen is really pretty simple given the right "tools" and a little hard work. Giving the case a facelift involves the same process used to remove scratches from a plastic crystal.

For visible scrapes and scratches put a little toothpaste or Novus 3™ scratch remover on the scratch and rub in a circular motion with a soft cloth. Check periodically to determine whether the scratch has been totally removed. After removing scrapes and scratches, clean the entire case with Novus 2 as discussed above. Turpentine, an oil, can also be used to clean Bakelite and is particularly effective in removing price stickers.

CAUTION—It is easy to drop a clock case during the polishing process. It is best to work on a countertop with the case resting on a towel.

CAUTION—Although it is only mildly abrasive, excessive rubbing with toothpaste or Novus 3 can remove raised printing or decorative ridges.

CAUTION—Power polishing tools like the Dremel Mototool™ can quickly remove scratches, but they are hard to control and may also remove decorative detail from the case.

CAUTION: Bakelite May Change Color

Polishing too much patina off your plastic case may yield more than just a new finish—it may yield a new color. Bakelite, like bronze and wood, tends to darken and change color over time. An ivory Bakelite case tends to take on a rich butterscotch color after 60-70 years. If you are too fervent in your attempt to rub out a particularly deep scratch in a Bakelite case, you will get to see that original color—in a patch that is now more visible than the original scratch.

Unless there is noticeable variation in color caused by a price sticker or other foreign object that "protected" a portion of the surface from exposure, it is probably best to limit the cleaning of Bakelite to washing or applying Novus 2.

Tip 14—Polishing Brass Cases and Trim

Brass cases, bezels, and trim were given a coat of clear lacquer to preserve the polished finish and prevent tarnish. Clear lacquer, however, turns yellow over time eventually hiding the beauty of the brass. In addition, wherever portions of the lacquer coat have been rubbed, scrubbed, scraped or washed off exposing the brass to air, the brass tarnishes, resulting in dark brown spots. A quick way to tell whether brass or copper has a protective coating of lacquer is to apply a little Brasso™ or Tarn-X™. If nothing happens, or if only the brown spots are brightened, there is a coat of lacquer preventing the polish from working. Restoring the original finish to brass is time consuming but rewarding.

Step 1: Remove the lacquer—This is not as easy as it sounds and involves a lot of hard work. The care instructions included with Chase™ copper and brass giftware items suggests the use of ordinary rubbing alcohol to remove lacquer. If possible, the piece should be soaked in alcohol to allow the alcohol to soften the lacquer. If this approach is not successful, try wetting the surface with alcohol and follow immediately with application of a good brass and copper polish applied with a rag soaked in alcohol.

CAUTION—Under no circumstances should steel wool be used to remove lacquer from or polish brass, copper, nickel, or chrome cases and trim. **Even the finest steel wool will permanently scratch the metal**.

CAUTION—Trim should be removed from Bakelite cases before attempting to remove the lacquer. **Alcohol will permanently stain Bakelite**.

If the above did not remove all of the lacquer, you can move on to something more toxic like lacquer thinner, an acetone-based nail polish remover, or even paint remover. Just be sure to use with adequate ventilation and wait to light up that cigarette until after you are done.

An ultrasonic tank filled with lacquer thinner can make quick work of lacquer removal and cleans the brass at the same time.

Step 2: Polish—Once the lacquer is removed, brass is an

easy metal to polish and virtually any metal polish like Brasso™ or Simichrome™ will do a good job. One of the best brass cleaners is L & R's™ Clock Cleaning Solution.

Restoration Kits

Many stores, including discount department stores like K-Mart, sell brass polishing "kits" consisting of a bottle of lacquer thinner and a can of spray lacquer, together with instructions on how to use them. The price is usually about the same as the cost of the items if bought separately.

Step 3: Lacquer (Optional)—To avoid the need to frequently polish the brass, a new coat of lacquer can be applied. Applying spray lacquer, however, takes some practice and any errors will put you back at step 1. It is advisable to rehearse your spraying technique on scrap metal before applying lacquer to the clock parts. Avoid spraying in dusty rooms and follow the manufacturer's directions on the can. Maintain the same distance between the can and the parts as you spray and spray each coat from a different axis (that is, if you sprayed the first coat moving the can from north to south, then spray the second coat moving the can from east to west).

> ### Tip 15—How to Strip and Paint a Metal Case

Choosing the Right Paint and Color

Paints now come in a dizzying array of types and colors. Just about any type of paint can be used on a metal case if the case is properly primed. Latex and alkyd acrylic enamels have the advantage of quick drying and easy clean up but generally lack the sheen and depth of color achieved through use of lacquer and oil based enamels.

Many auto supply stores, paint stores, and hardware stores have computerized paint matching that can exactly duplicate the original color of your clock. Obviously, its your clock and you can paint it any color you want, but just as the value of a classic car is reduced if it is painted a non-factory color, so too is the value of a clock decreased if it is painted other than a factory color.

Step 1: Remove the old paint—When a metal case is in such poor shape that only a fresh coat of paint will make it presentable, it is important that the old paint be removed right down to the bare metal. Almost any commercial paint stripper will do on a job this small. Follow the manufacturer's instructions (including ventilation and rubber gloves). An old toothbrush and a nylon scouring pad are often helpful in removing paint from all the nooks and crannies. As long as you are planning to repaint the case, extra fine steel wool can also be used to aid the removal.

Step 2: Apply a primer—Use a primer appropriate to the type of paint you plan to use. The primer prevents the metal from rusting and provides a sound base for the paint. Follow the directions on the can with respect to number of coats and drying time. If you lack experience in applying spray paints, there are a number of guides and internet sites (www.krylon.com is a good one) that offer spray painting tips. Like so many things in life, practice makes perfect.

Step 3: Apply the paint—It is important that the paint be sprayed rather than brushed to assure an even coat with no brushstrokes. Allow the recommended time between coats and apply a second, and if needed, third coat. Darker colors generally do not cover as well and multiple coats may be needed.

Step 4: Allow to dry—Allow the paint to thoroughly dry before attempting to reassemble the clock. Although paint may dry to the touch in a few minutes or hours, it takes several days for enamels to cure.

> ### Tip 16—How to Touch Up a Metal Case

If the paint on the case is sound, but there are noticeable scratches to the surface, the paint can be matched and the case touched up without going to the trouble of stripping and repainting the whole case.

Step 1: Have the paint matched—Although the paint sample at the hardware store may appear to be the same color as your clock, even a slight difference will be noticeable. Take your clock in to an auto parts, paint, or hardware store that does computer paint matching and have it matched. Buy the smallest quantity available.

Step 2: Mix and transfer paint—Thoroughly mix the paint. Mixing is particularly important for oil based paints that tend to separate. Even with latex paints, however, some separation occurs. Transfer a little paint to a smaller container like a film canister or soda bottle cap.

Step 3: Adjust consistency—Using a small sable brush, test the consistency of the paint on a piece of scrap (like a quartz clock). At the proper consistency, the paint should flow right into the scratches. If the paint is too thick, thin according to label directions, adding just one or two drops of the appropriate thinner and stirring with a toothpick. Repeat until the paint is thinned to the right consistency—almost like cream.

Step 4: Apply paint—Using the sable brush, carefully apply the paint to the scratches. Do not overload the brush as this could result in too much paint being applied. It is better to apply several light coats if necessary than to risk the paint running if too much is applied.

> ### Tip 17—How to Clean and Polish Chrome, Nickel, and Nicral™ Cases

Chrome, nickel, and Nicral (an alloy of chrome, nickel, and aluminum) cases are easy to clean and polish. Just wash them with lukewarm soapy water, rinse with clear water, and dry with a soft towel. If you have a case that is so caked with dirt that just a quick cleaning is not sufficient, try a little Brasso™ or other nonabrasive chrome polish on a soft cloth.

CAUTION—Never use any kind of steel wool, including soap pads like Brillo™ to clean brass, copper, nickel, or chromium finishes. Even the finest steel wool will permanently scratch the finish.

Chromium and nickel cases that are pitted or have flaking chromium can be replated, but this is a task best left to a professional. The cost of replating, however, will in all likelihood, exceed the value of the clock.

> **CAUTION**--Always keep your clocks--running or not--in an upright position. If a General Electric or Telechron clock is left on its face for any length of time, oil may leak out of the rotor bearing and into the works.

Telechron and General Electric Design Patents

The following list includes all known design patents issued for General Electric and Telechron clocks between 1925 and 1956.

Model No.	Patent No.	Designer	Date	Model No.	Patent No.	Designer	Date	Model No.	Patent No.	Designer	Date
326	D84,953	Shepard Pond	Aug. 25, 1931	3H97	D133,501	Eugene J. Lux	Aug. 18, 1942	7F64	D97,781	Raymond E. Patten	Dec. 10, 1935
356	D82,424	Eroll W. Goff	Nov. 4, 1930	3H161	D163,676	Ivan Bruce	June 19, 1951	7F65	D97,488	Irwin W. Kokins	Nov. 12, 1935
357	D84,595	Harry C. Richardson	July 7, 1931	3H163	D166,590	Ivan Bruce	Apr. 29, 1952	CF769	D99,711	Frank W. Green	May 19, 1936
358	D84,595	Harry C. Richardson	July 7, 1931	4F05	D104,011	Jacques Bars	Apr. 13, 1937	7F70	D102,919	John P. Rainbault	Jan. 26, 1937
431	D82,548	Paul T. Frankl	Nov. 18, 1930	4B07	D124,830	Ivan Bruce	Jan. 28, 1941	7F71	D104,012	Jacques Bars	Apr. 13, 1937
454	D83,789	Edgar Bourquin	Mar. 31, 1931	4F52	D92,976	John P. Rainbault	Aug. 7, 1934	7F73	D103,837	Walter Dorwin Teague	Mar. 30,1937
528	D84,754	Harry Richardson	July 18, 1931	4F53	D86,474	Harry C. Richardson	Mar. 8, 1932	7F74	D102,763	John P. Rainbault	Jan. 19, 1937
528A	D84,754	Harry Richardson	July 18, 1931	4F55	D92,950	Simon DeVaulchier	Aug. 7, 1934	7H79	D107,039	Frank W. Green	Nov. 16, 1937
530	D83,627	George M. Long	Mar. 10, 1931	4F57	D92,949	Simon DeVaulchier	Aug. 7, 1934	7H85	D112,595	Ivan Bruce	Dec. 20, 1938
605	D83,992	Harry Richardson	Apr. 21, 1931	4F58	D97,782	Raymond E. Patten	Dec. 10, 1935	7H89	D115,620	Robert W. Goulet	July 11, 1939
711	D85,094	George Graff	Sept. 15, 1931	4F60	D97,780	Raymond E. Patten	Dec. 10, 1935	7H91	D117,895	Ivan Bruce	Dec. 5, 1939
712	D85,095	George Graff	Sept. 15, 1931	4F61	D94,868	Jacques Bars	Mar. 19, 1935	7H93	D117,897	Ivan Bruce	Dec. 5, 1939
715	D85,094	George Graff	Sept. 15, 1931	4F64	D104,047	John P. Rainbault	Apr. 13, 1937	CH797	D122,316	Norman F. Lockwood	Sept. 3, 1940
716	D85,095	George Graff	Sept. 15, 1931	4F65	D97,753	Jacques Bars	Dec. 10, 1935	7H99	D122,309	Ivan Bruce	Sept. 3, 1940
TM-2	D81,068	Raymond E. Patten	Apr. 29, 1930	4F66	D104,046	John P. Rainbault	Apr. 13, 1937	7H101	D122,307	Ivan Bruce	Sept. 3, 1940
TM-8	D83,642	Raymond E. Patten	Mar. 3, 1931	4F69	D105,599	Eugene J. Lux	Aug. 10, 1937	7H103	D124,828	Ivan Bruce	Jan. 28, 1941
2F01	D89,236	Edgar Bourquin	Feb. 7, 1933	4F73	D105,472	Ivan Bruce	Aug. 3, 1937	7H106	D119,372	Ivan Bruce	Mar. 12, 1940
2F03	D97,775	Eugene J. Lux	Dec. 10, 1935	4H78	D120,012	Jacques Martial	Apr. 16, 1940	7H110	D118,834	John P. Rainbault	Feb. 6, 1940
2F04	D94,561	Raymond E. Patten	Feb. 12, 1935	4B79	D107,004	Jacques Bars	Nov. 16, 1937	CH71111	D131,802	Ivan Bruce	Mar. 31, 1942
2F06	D96,410	Raymond E. Patten	July 30, 1935	4B85	D112,596	Ivan Bruce	Dec. 20, 1938	7H116	D125,557	Jacques Bars	Mar. 4, 1941
2H07	D107,406	Leo Ivan Bruce	Dec. 14, 1937	4H86	D122,308	Ivan Bruce	Sept. 3, 1940	7H118	D127,367	Ivan Bruce	May 20, 1941
2H08	D118,835	John P. Rainbault	Feb. 6, 1940	4H87	D115,905	Ivan Bruce	Aug. 1, 1939	7H119	D131,800	Ivan Bruce	Mar. 31, 1942
2H09	D117,916	Findley Williams	Dec. 5, 1939	4H89	D115,195	Ivan Bruce	June 13, 1939	7H135	D117,895	Ivan Bruce	Dec. 5, 1939
2H10	D124,980	John P. Rainbault	Feb. 4, 1941	4H89	D115,195	Ivan Bruce	June 13, 1939	7H137	D117,895	Ivan Bruce	Dec. 5, 1939
2H13	D131,801	Ivan Bruce	Mar. 31, 1942	4H91	D115,196	Ivan Bruce	June 13, 1939	7H155	D117,895	Ivan Bruce	Dec. 5, 1939
2H19	D163,565	Ivan Bruce	June 12, 1951	4H92	D120,012	Jacques Martial	Apr. 16, 1940	7H157	D163,567	Ivan Bruce	June 12, 1951
2H21	D158,929	Ivan Bruce	June 13, 1950	4H93	D117,896	Ivan Bruce	Dec. 5, 1939	7H159	D163,930	Ivan Bruce	July 17, 1951
2H25	D163,566	Ivan Bruce	June 12, 1951	4H95	D118,143	Findley Williams	Dec. 19, 1939	7H163	D162,929	Ivan Bruce	Apr. 17, 1951
2H27	D163,363	Ivan Bruce	May 22, 1951	4H97	D124,827	Ivan Bruce	Jan. 28, 1941	7H169	D163,162	Rudolph Max Babel	May 8, 1951
2H31	D166,069	Ivan Bruce	Mar. 3, 1952	4H99	D124,843	Harry C. Richardson	Jan. 28, 1941	7HP171	D166,297	Ivan Bruce	Apr. 1, 1952
2H33	D165,133	Ivan Bruce	Nov. 13, 1951	4B151	D124,831	Ivan Bruce	Jan. 28, 1941	7H179	D165,357	Rudolph Max Babel	Dec. 11, 1951
2H39	D172,266	Ivan Bruce	May 25, 1954	4B153	D124,829	Ivan Bruce	Jan. 28, 1941	7H181	D166,026	Ivan Bruce	Feb. 26, 1952
2H41	D175,242	Rudolph M. Babel	Aug. 2, 1955	4B155	D124,832	Ivan Bruce	Jan. 28, 1941	7H185	D164,594	Carl Otto	Sept. 18, 1951
2H45	D174,986	Robert O. Fletcher	June 21, 1955	5F03	D93,228	Belle Kogan	Sept. 4, 1934	7HA1	95 D174,214	Ivan Bruce	Oct. 26, 1954
2H47	D174,895	Ivan Bruce and Philip Frederick Huy	June 7, 1955	5F50	D104,048	John P. Rainbault	Apr. 13, 1937	7H201	D173,302	Ivan Bruce	Oct. 26, 1954
				5F52	D104,049	John P. Rainbault	Apr. 13, 1937	7H203	D169,453	Carl Otto	Apr. 28, 1953
2H49	D175,294	Ivan Bruce and Philip Frederick Huy	Aug. 9, 1955	5B53	D107,401	Jacques Bars	Dec. 14, 1937	7H207	D169,432	Philip Garland, Jr.	Apr. 28, 1953
				5F54	D105,714	John P. Rainbault	Aug. 17, 1937	7H211	D174,244	Rudolph Max Babel	Mar. 22, 1955
2H51	D112,594	Ivan Bruce	Dec. 20, 1938	5B55	D107,405	Ivan Bruce	Dec. 14, 1937	7H217	D174,742	Robert O. Fletcher	May 15, 1955
2H101	D175,293	Ivan Bruce	Aug. 9, 1955	5H57	D122,309	Ivan Bruce	Sept. 3, 1940	7H221	D176,407	Robert O. Fletcher	Dec. 20, 1955
2H103	D174,615	Ivan Bruce	May 3, 1955	5F61	D93,228	Belle Kogan	Sept. 4, 1934	8B01	D89,741	Edgar Bourquin	May 2, 1933
3F01	D92,551	John Nickelsen	June 19, 1934	5H65	D173,142	Ivan Bruce	Oct. 5, 1954	8F01	D93,662	Belle Kogan	Oct. 23, 1934
3F02	D91,086	John P. Rainbault	Nov. 21, 1933	5H66	D118,834	John P. Rainbault	Feb. 6, 1940	8B02	D89,742	Edgar Bourquin	May 2, 1933
3F03	D97,494	Eugene J. Lux	Nov. 12, 1935	5H67	D175,665	Ivan Bruce	Sept. 20, 1955	8F03	D108,586	Walter Dorwin Teague	Feb. 22, 1938
3F51	D90,213	Kurt Rettich	June 27, 1933	5H69	D175,501	Robert O. Fletcher	Sept. 6, 1955	8B04	D103,749	Walter Dorwin Teague	Mar. 23,1937
3F52	D89,790	Francis W. Pike	May 2, 1933	5H71	D175,665	Rudolph Max Babel	Sept. 27, 1955	8B06	D102,840	John P. Rainbault	Jan. 19, 1937
3F53	D91,240	Harriet Heile	Dec. 26, 1933	6B03	D107,405	Ivan Bruce	Dec. 14, 1937	8B07	D103,748	Walter Dorwin Teague	Mar. 23, 1937
3F54	D91,085	John P. Rainbault	Nov. 21, 1933	6B05	D107,401	Jacques Bars	Dec. 14, 1937	8B09	D103,747	Walter Dorwin Teague	Mar. 23,1937
3F56	D94,560	Raymond E. Patten	Feb. 12, 1935	6B11	D117,896	Ivan Bruce	Dec. 5, 1939	8H29	D175,458	Ivan Bruce	Aug. 30, 1955
3F58	D94,774	Shepard Pond	Mar. 5, 1935	7B01	D84,837	George Long	Aug. 11, 1931	8B50	D97,952	Raymond E. Patten	Dec. 24, 1935
3F59	D93,993	John Nickelsen	Dec. 4, 1934	7B02	D84,837	George Long	Aug. 11, 1931	8F50	D97,781	Raymond E. Patten	Dec. 10, 1935
3F61	D97,453	Jacques Bars	Nov. 12, 1935	7F03	D103,836	Walter Dorwin Teague	Mar. 30,1937	8B51	D97,939	Belle Kogan	Dec. 25, 1935
CF363	D99,711	Frank W. Green	May 19, 1936	7H09	D163,930	Leo Ivan Bruce	July 17, 1951	8F51	D104,012	Jacques Bars	April 13, 1937
3F66	D102,918	John P. Rainbault	Jan. 26, 1937	7F52	D92,677	John P. Rainbault	July 3, 1934	8B52	D104,013	Jacques Bars	Apr. 13, 1937
3F67	D104,012	Jacques Bars	April 13, 1937	7F53	D92,007	Irwin Kokins	Apr. 17, 1934	8B53	D103,838	Walter Dorwin Teague	Mar. 30,1937
3F68	D101,285	John P. Rainbault	Sept. 22, 1936	7F54	D92,977	John P. Rainbault	Aug. 7, 1934	8B54	D103,162	John P. Rainbault	Feb. 9, 1937
3F69	D106,130	Ivan Bruce	Sept. 21, 1937	7F56	D97,781	Raymond E. Patten	Dec. 10, 1935	8H55	D145,352	Francesco Collura	Aug. 6, 1946
3F70	D101,286	John P. Rainbault	Sept. 22, 1936	7H57	D92,950	Simon DeVaulchier	Aug. 7, 1934	8H57	D145,351	Francesco Collura	Aug. 6, 1946
3F71	D105,471	Ivan Bruce	Aug. 3, 1937	7F58	D97,204	Amos E. Northup	Oct. 15, 1935	8H59	D145,996	Francesco Collura	Dec. 3, 1946
3H77	D115,620	Robert W. Goulet	July 11, 1939	7F59	D93,993	John Nickelsen	Dec. 4, 1934	8H61	D145,353	Francesco Collura	Aug. 6, 1946
CH387	D124,963	Ivan Bruce	Feb. 4, 1941	7F62	D101,287	John P. Rainbault	Sept. 22, 1936				
3H89	D127,786	Ivan Bruce	June 17, 1941	7F63	D93,662	Belle Kogan	Oct. 23, 1934				

The "Time" That Got Away:
Designs That Did Not Enter Production

For every clock design that entered production, there were likely many others that were considered and rejected. The following pages illustrate some of the design patents assigned to Warren Telechron and General Electric that are not known to have reached production. If you have a clock based on one of these designs, please contact the author so that it can be included in future editions.

Emma M. Thomas assigned her rights to design patent 86,066, awarded January 19, 1932, to the Warren Telechron Company, but the clock never reached production. The design is very similar to a design patented two years later by Irwin Kokins for the "Telebell."

Robert W. McLaughlin assigned his rights to design patent 86,041, awarded January 19, 1932, to the Warren Telechron Company. This was the only clock patent awarded to McLaughlin.

George M. Long assigned his rights to design patent 84,838, awarded August 11, 1931, to the Warren Telechron Company. Only two of Long's designs apparently entered production, including the design for the "Autolarm" (7B01).

George R. Kraber of Newtonville, Massachusetts assigned his rights to design patent 86,317, awarded February 23, 1932, to the Warren Telechron Company, but I found no record of the design entering production.

George M. Long assigned his rights to design patent 86,172, awarded February 9, 1932, to the Warren Telechron Company but I found no record of the clock entering production.

George R. Kraber assigned his rights to design patent 86,318, awarded February 23, 1932, to the Warren Telechron Company, but I found no record of the design entering production.

George R. Kraber assigned his rights to design patent 86,319, awarded February 23, 1932, to the Warren Telechron Company, but I found no record of the design entering production.

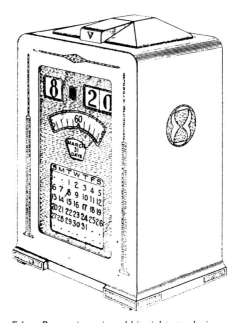

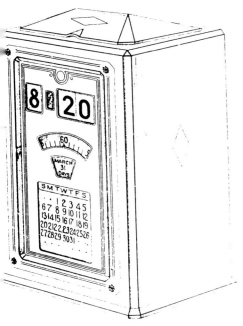

Edgar Bourquin assigned his rights to design patent 89,743, awarded May 2, 1933, to the Warren Telechron Company. Bourquin designed four variations of the cyclometer clock, two of which entered production as the 8B01 and 8B02. This design was for a day-date calendar cyclometer clock. Bourquin designed the case and the mechanics of the clock, obtaining a separate mechanical patent.

A variation of Edgar Bourquin's day-date cyclometer clock (D89,744 awarded May 2, 1933). One of the two models was probably intended to be a General Electric model.

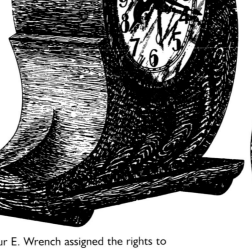

Right: Arthur E. Wrench assigned the rights to design patent 90,749, awarded September 26, 1933, to the Warren Telechron Company. The graining in the patent drawings suggests that Wrench intended for the clocks to have oak cases.

Above: Another of Arthur E. Wrench's designs (D90,791, awarded Sept. 26, 1933). None of Wrench's designs reached production.

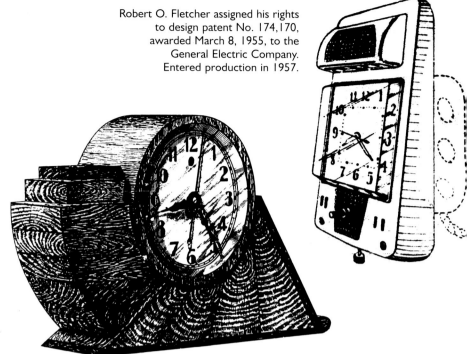

Robert O. Fletcher assigned his rights to design patent No. 174,170, awarded March 8, 1955, to the General Electric Company. Entered production in 1957.

Wrench's fourth and final design (D90,793, awarded Sept. 26, 1933). The four design patents Wrench assigned to Telechron are the only patents he holds.

Like his other designs, Wrench assigned the rights to this clock case (D90,792, awarded Sept. 26, 1933) to Telechron.

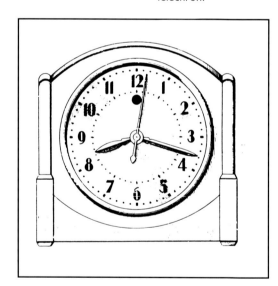

Belle Kogan assigned the rights to design patent 93,114, awarded August 21, 1934, to the Warren Telechron Company.

Belle Kogan assigned the rights to design patent 93,663, awarded October 23, 1934, to the Warren Telechron Company. Awarded at the same time as the design for the "Smug" and "Quacker," Telechron apparently chose to produce only the one version. Too bad as this would undoubtedly have become one of the most collectible Telechron clocks had it reached production.

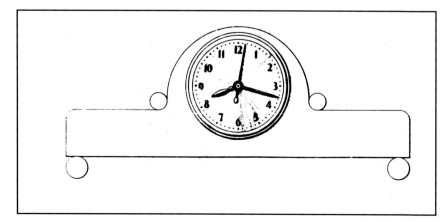

Jacques Bars assigned the rights to design patent 93,602, awarded October 16, 1934, to the Warren Telechron Company.

A Gallery of Telechron Commercial Models

During the 1920s and early 1930s, the Warren Telechron Company focused primarily on commercial installations of clocks and central control systems. The following illustrate the variety of commercial models available in 1931 for both indoor and outdoor applications. A wide range of other commercial models is illustrated on Jay Kennan's *Pappy's Telechron Clock Page*.

Outdoor Models

Outdoor models include single and multiple face clocks, with illuminated or non-illuminated dials. Cases were available for mounting on the face of a building, on posts, on suspension brackets, in signs, or in towers. Outdoor models typically came with a statuary bronze finish and could be installed individually or as part of a central control system. In addition to a wide range of sizes, a variety of bracket designs and illumination options were offered. Displayed below are the outdoor models available in 1931, with the exception of tower and sign clocks.

Telechron double face suspension type, illuminated, outdoor clocks were available with case diameters of 18" (No. 1502), 22" (No. 1503), 29" (No. 1504), 37" (No. 1505), 44" (No. 1506), 51" (No. 1507), and 57" (No. 1508). The standard finish is statuary bronze. A variety of bracket styles were available.

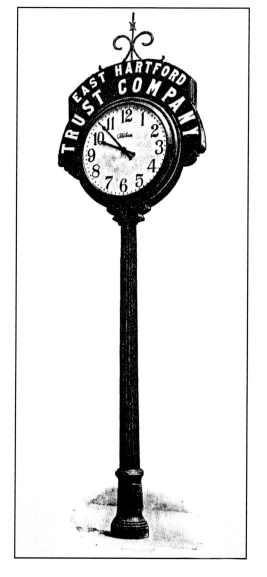

Far left: Telechron Post Clock available in dial sizes of 18, 24, 30, 36, 42, and 48 inches. Posts were available in custom sizes. The sign unit was sold separately.

Left: Telechron illuminated double face knee bracket outdoor clocks were available in three sizes—75" x 44" x 18", 86" x 48" x 20", and 105" x 54" x 22". The standard finish is statuary bronze. The signs and dials are illuminated from the interior.

Telechron illuminated surface mounted outdoor clocks were available in case diameters of 16-3/4" (No. 2212), 19-3/4" (No. 2215), 24" (No. 2218), 30-3/4" (No. 2224), 36-1/4" (No. 2230), 42-1/2" (No. 2236), 48-1/2" (No. 2242), and 54-1/2" (No. 2248). The last two digits of the model number are the diameter of the dial. Standard finish was statuary bronze.

Telechron illuminated recess-type clocks were available in case diameters of 14-3/8" (No. 1076), 16-7/8" (No. 1077), 20-1/8" (No. 1078), 26-1/2" (No. 1080), and 33-1/2" (No. 1081). Standard finish was statuary bronze.

Telechron illuminated semi-flush outdoor clocks were available in case diameters of 15" (No. 1056), 17-1/2" (No. 1057), 20-3/4" (No. 1058), 27-3/4" (No. 1060), 33-5/9" (No. 1061), 39-5/8" (No. 1062), 45-5/8" (No. 1063), and 51-5/8" (No. 1064). Available with either illuminated or non-illuminated dial. Standard finish was statuary bronze.

Telechron non-illuminated surface type clocks were available in case diameters of 12" (No. 2108), 14" (No. 2110), 16-3/4" (No. 2112), 19-3/4" (No. 2115), 24" (No. 2118), 30-3/4" (No. 2124), 36-1/4" (No. 2130), 42-1/2" (No. 2136), 48-1/2" (No. 2142), and 54-1/2" (No. 2148). Standard finish was statuary bronze. The last two digits of the model number are the diameter of the dial.

Interior Models

In 1931, Telechron offered a wide range of interior models for individual installation or installation as part of a central control system. When clocks were installed as part of a central system, control could be either manual or automatic depending on the type of system installed. Interior models were available in a wide range of marble, wood, and metal cases.

Marble Dial Clocks were custom made in any specified domestic or imported marble. In addition to a variety of styles and sizes, some metal case models were available with illuminated dials.

Telechron marble dial clocks with bronze ring-type cases for surface mounting were available in diameters of 13-1/4" (No. 1361), 15-3/4" (No. 1362), 18-3/4" (No. 1363), 25" (No. 1364), 31" (No. 1365), and 37" (No. 1366).

Telechron marble dial clocks with wood cases were available in case diameters of 16-3/8" (No. 1381), 18-7/8" (No. 1382), 21-7/8" (No. 1383), and 27-7/8" (No. 1384). To be surface mounted. Choice of solid oak, mahogany, or walnut case.

Telechron marble dial clocks with ogee edge were available with outside diameters of 12-1/2" (No. 1371), 15" (No. 1372), 18" (No. 1373), 24" (No. 1374), 30" (No. 1375), and 36" (No. 1376). To be surface mounted.

Telechron plain, square-edge type, marble dial clocks were available in outside diameters of 12-1/2" (No. 1391), 15" (No. 1392), 18" (No. 1393), 24" (No. 1394), 30" (No. 1395), and 36" (No. 1396). To be surface or recess mounted.

Metal Case Commercial Clocks came with a standard statuary bronze finish, but many of the cases were also available with white, mahogany, or walnut grained finishes. Some models had two faces.

Telechron surface mount metal case clocks were available in case diameters of 12" (No. 108), 14" (No. 110), 16-3/4" (No. 112), 19-3/4" (No. 115), 24" (No. 118), 30-3/4" (No. 124), 36-1/4" (No. 130), 42-1/2" (No. 136), 48-1/2" (No. 142), and 54-1/2" (No. 148). The last two digits of the model number are the diameter of the dial.

Telechron semi-flush metal case clocks were available in case diameters of 10-1/16" (No. 2308), 12" (No. 2310), 14-1/4" (No. 2312), 17-1/4" (No. 2315), 21" (No. 2318), and 27-1/8" (No. 2324). The last two digits of the model number are the diameter of the dial.

Telechron flush metal case clocks with convex crystals were available in case diameters of 6-5/8" (No. 444), 8-5/8" (No. 445), 13-1/8" (No. 446), 15-5/8" (No. 447), and 18-5/8" (No. 448). They were available with or without an outlet box.

Telechron dust and moisture proof boiler room surface clocks were available in case diameters of 12" (No. 2508), 14" (No. 2510), 16-1/8" (No. 2512), 19-3/8" (No. 2515), 23" (No. 2518), and 29-1/4" (No. 2524). The last two digits of the model number are the diameter of the dial.

Telechron single face Gymnasium Clocks were available in case diameters of 12" (No. 2608), 14" (No. 2610), 16-3/4" (No. 2612), 19-3/4" (No. 2615), and 24" (No. 2618). The last two digits of the model number are the diameter of the dial. The wire guard and clock are hinged to a wooden back.

Telechron double-faced ceiling saddle suspension clocks were available in case heights of 17" (No. 1810), 20-1/4" (No. 1812), 24" (No. 1815), 29" (No. 1818), and 37-1/4" (No. 1824). The last two digits of the model number are the diameter of the dial. Also available with an illuminated dial (2812 series).

Above: Telechron double face wall bracket suspension clocks were available in widths of 17" (No. 2010), 20-1/4" (No. 2012), 24" (No. 2015), 29" (No. 2018), and 37-1/4" (No. 2024). The last two digits of the model number are the diameter of the dial. Also available with an illuminated dial (3012 series).

Right: Telechron double face chain suspension clocks were available in case diameters of 14" (No. 1910), 16-3/4" (No. 1912), 19-3/4" (No. 1915), 24" (No. 1918), and 30-3/4" (No. 1924). The last two digits of the model number are the diameter of the dial. Also available with illuminated dial (2912 series).

Wood-Cased Commercial Clocks were offered in a variety
of models with up to four faces. In addition to a wide range of sizes,
many were available in choice of oak, mahogany, or walnut case.

This Telechron commercial wall clock has a hand-painted silver dial with corner ornaments of gold leaf and black hairline stripe. It was available with choice of Arabic or Roman numerals. The square case came in sizes of 12-1/2" (No. 1319), 17" (No. 1320), 19-1/2" (No. 1321), 22-1/2" (No. 1322), and 28-3/8" (No. 1323).

Telechron square wood cased wall clocks were available in heights of 10-3/4" (No. 908), 13" (No. 910), 15-1/2" (No. 912), 19" (No. 915), 23" (No. 918), and 30" (No. 924). The last two digits of the model number are the diameter of the dial. Available in oak, mahogany, walnut, and white finishes.

The tambour model with hand-carved mahogany or walnut case was available in lengths of 28-5/8" (No. 1408), 40-3/4" (No. 1412), 48-7/8" (No. 1414), 61" (No. 1418), and 81-1/4" (No. 1424). The last two digits of the model number are the diameter of the dial. Available with Arabic or Roman numerals. Also available in double face design and with illuminated dial. Some pictures show this clock in exterior as well as interior installations.

Double face knee bracket square case clocks for indoor use were available in heights of 24" (No. 1200), 31-1/2" (No. 1201), 38" (No. 1202), 45" (No. 1203), and 56" (No. 1204).

The double face saddle suspension square case clock was available in lengths of 30" (No. 1250), 42" (No. 1251), 50" (No. 1252), 60" (No. 1253), and 76" (No. 1254).

Four-face chain suspension square case clocks were available in heights of 18-9/16" (No. 1106), 22" (No. 1107), 27" (No. 1108), and 32-1/2" (No. 1110).

Three face knee bracket square case clocks were available in heights of 24" (No. 1210), 31-1/2" (No. 1211), 38" (No. 1212), 45" (No. 1213), and 56" (No. 1214).

Skeleton Dial Clocks were offered with dials up to 48 inches in diameter. Skeleton dials that were 18 inches in diameter or smaller were mounted on a silver plate while larger dials were mounted on a cast center rosette without the silver plate.

Skeleton dial clocks with minute dots were available with dial diameters of 8" (No. 755), 12" (No. 756), 14" (No. 757), 18" (No. 758), 24" (No. 760), 30" (No. 761), 36" (No. 762), 42" (No. 763), and 48" (No. 764).

Skeleton dial clocks without minute dots were available in dial diameters of 8" (No. 775), 12" (No. 776), 14" (No. 777), 18" (No. 788), 24" (No. 780), 30" (No. 781), 36" (No. 782), 42" (No. 783), and 48" (No. 784).

Appendix V.
Selected Bibliography

Books

Aked, Charles K. *Electrifying Time*. Ticehurst, Wadhurst, Sussex, Great Britain: The Antiquarian Horological Society, 1976.

Ball, Charlotte, ed. *Who's Who in American Art: Vol. III for the Years 1940-1941*. Washington, D.C.: The American Federation of Arts, 1940.

Battersby, Martin. *The Decorative Thirties*. New York: Walker and Company, 1971.

Battersby, Martin. *The Decorative Twenties*. New York: Walker and Company, 1969.

Byars, Mel. *The Design Encyclopedia*. New York: John Wiley & Sons, Inc., 1994.

Collins, Philip. *Pastime: Telling Time From 1879 to 1969*. San Francisco: Chronicle Books, 1993.

Crum, Elmer G. and William F. Keller, ed. *150 Years of Electric Horology*. Exhibit prepared for the 1992 Chicago Convention of the National Association of Watch and Clock Collectors.

DiNoto, Andrea. *Art Plastic: Designed for Living*. New York: Abbeville Press, 1984.

Fusco, Tony. *The Official Identification and Price Guide to Art Deco*. New York: House of Collectibles, 1988.

Gaston, Mary Frank, *Collector's Guide to Art Deco, Second Edition*. Paducah, Kentucky: Collector Books, 1997.

Grief, Martin. *Depression Modern: The Thirties Style in America*. New York: Riverside Books, 1975.

Hildebrand, George, ed. *The Golden Age of the Luxury Car: An Anthology of Articles and Photographs from "Autobody," 1927-1931*. New York: Dover Publications, Inc., 1980.

Hillier, Bevis. *The World of Art Deco*. New York: E. P. Dutton and Co., Inc., 1971.

Hillier, Bevis. *Art Deco*. New York: E. P. Dutton and Co., Inc., 1968.

Hope-Jones, F. *Electrical Timekeeping*. London: N. A. G. Press Ltd., 1949.

Jarvis, Everett G. *Final Curtain: Deaths of Noted Movie and T. V. Personalities*. New York: Citadel Press, 1992.

Johnson, Bruce. *The Weekend Refinisher*. New York: Ballantine Books, 1989.

Kimes, Beverly Rae, ed. *The Classic Car*. Des Plaines: Classic Car Club of America, Inc., 1990.

Linz, Jim. *Art Deco Chrome*. Atglen, PA: Schiffer Publishing Ltd., 1999.

Mandel, Leon. *American Cars*. New York: Stewart, Tabori & Chang, 1982.

Mandelbaum, Howard and Eric Myers. *Screen Deco: A Celebration of High Style in Hollywood*. New York: St. Martin's Press, 1985.

McDermott, Kathleen. *Timex: A Company and its Community 1854-1998*. Middlebury, CT: Timex Corporation, 1998.

Meikle, Jeffrey L. *Twentieth Century Limited: Industrial Design in America, 1925-1939*. Philadelphia: Temple University Press, 1979.

Palmer, Brooks. *The Romance of Time*. New Haven, CT: Clock Manufacturers Association of America, Inc., 1954.

Philpott, Stuart F. *Modern Electric Clocks: Principles, Construction, Installation, and Maintenance*. New York: Pitman Publishing Corporation, 1949.

Pile, John. *Dictionary of 20th Century Design*. New York: Facts on File, A Roundtable Press Book, 1990.

Rasmussen, Henry. *American Classic Cars: The Survivors Series*. Arroyo Grande, CA: Picturama Publications, 1977.

Sedgwick, Michael. *Cars of the Thirties and Forties*. New York: Beekman House, 1979.

Shenton, Alan and Rita. *Collectible Clocks, 1840-1940: Reference and Price Guide*. Woodbridge, Suffolk, England: Antique Collectors' Club Ltd., 1985.

Shipman, David. *Cinema: The First Hundred Years*. New York: St. Martin's Press, 1993.

Slater, Robert. *The New GE: How Jack Welch Revived an American Institution*. Homewood, IL: Business One Irwin, 1993.

Spencer-Jones, Harold. *Electrical Timekeeping*. London: N. A. G. Press, 1949.

Tichy, Noel M. and Stratford Sherman. *Control Your Destiny or Someone Else Will: How Jack Welch is Making General Electric the Worlds Most Competitive Corporation*. New York: Doubleday, 1993.

Wilson, Richard Guy, Dianne H. Pilgrim, and Dickran Tashjian. *The Machine Age in America 1918-1941*. New York: The Brooklyn Museum in association with Harry N. Abrams, Inc., 1986.

Articles

Aked, Charles K., undated, "Echoes of the Synchronous Clock." *Clocks*, 26-52.

Anderson, John M. 1991 "Henry Warren and His Master Clocks." *NAWCC Bulletin*, August, 375-395.

"A Brief History of the Herschede Hall Clock Company," unpublished and undated, NAWCC files.

Forman, Ethan. 1997. "Leaving Clocktown USA." *Wellesley Tab*. March 11.

"Body by Murray." 1974. *Special-Interest Autos*, Jan.-Feb., 36-56.

"Henry Ellis Warren: A Biographical Memoir," *The Encyclopedia of American Biography*. New York: American Historical Company, Inc.

"Henry E. Warren." *Horology*. July 1935, pp 27-28.

Robinson, Walter F. 1978. "1933 Reo Royale." *Special-Interest Autos*, Jan.-Feb., 50-56.

Archives

Ashland Historical Society. Ashland, MA: Telechron and General Electric catalogs and sales brochures, photographs, *Telechronicles*, *Synchronuses*, photographs, clippings, sales and distribution data, promotional materials, parts and repair manuals.

Hall of Electrical History, The Schenectady Museum: Telechron and General Electric parts and repair manuals.

National Association of Watch and Clock Collectors. Columbia, PA: Telechron and General Electric catalogs and repair manuals. Herschede Hall catalogs and correspondence.

Orsini and Frost, Inc., Manassas, Virginia: Telechron and General Electric catalogs and repair manuals.

United States Patent Office, Arlington, Virginia: design and mechanical patents.

Wright, Steven L. *Herschede Hall Clock Company Records, 1887-1964*. Historical Note, Business Archives, Cincinnati Museum Center, 12/9/99.

Appendix VI.
Price Guide and Index to Models

Factors that Affect Values

Many factors affect what sellers can expect to charge and what buyers can expect to pay for a Telechron or General Electric clock. These include the location and venue in which the clock is offered for sale, the condition of the clock both in terms of appearance and function, and the design of the clock. In setting prices, sellers also need to consider what they paid for the clock and how long they are willing to keep it in inventory to obtain the "best" price. Individuals seeking to sell clocks to a dealer or at a garage sale should expect to get no more than 30 to 50 percent of its value. Dealers incur significant selling expenses and cannot afford to acquire inventory at prices approaching what they expect to charge for an item.

Neither the author nor the publisher accepts responsibility for any losses that might occur through use of this guide.

Beware of False Advertising (Clocks)

Recently, the online auctions have been swamped with "vintage" advertising clocks. These clocks often sell for hundreds of dollars. Many of the clocks, however, are of recent manufacture and made specifically for the collector market. Others have a new advertising "decal" applied to an old school or business clock. Often, the company was not in business at the time the clock was made or had a different trademark or advertising slogan at the time. You know it is a fake if the "decal" is actually a peel and stick label. Even the old-fashioned decals that are soaked in water and then applied are being remanufactured and applied to common school clocks. When in doubt, consult a collector's guide to advertising memorabilia. Buyers should carefully examine advertising clocks at antique shops and flea markets and elicit a guarantee of authenticity from online sellers before buying an advertising clock.

Location and Venue. Regional variation in prices seems to be declining, in part because of the widespread availability of price guides and the proliferation of antique shows that draw dealers from around the country. Still, prices are likely to be higher in antique shops in major metropolitan areas and in "trendy" shopping districts like Melrose Avenue in Los Angeles.

Prices within a community also vary depending on the type of store. Thrift stores and church bazaars have low selling expenses— the goods were donated and many of the staff are unpaid volunteers—and can afford to offer items for rock bottom prices. Real bargains can still be found, but it is hit or miss. It may take 100 visits to a thrift store to find a treasure. Competition for thrift store bargains is also intense as casual dealers increasingly seek inventory for on-line auctions such as ebay™.

Bargains can also be found at the weekend garage sales. Homeowners running garage sales have culled out items that they no longer need or want and are often content to get a fraction of its true value. What does not sell is often carted off to the dump or (hopefully) donated to a thrift shop. Rarely do homeowners do the research to determine the true value of items that have been gathering dust in the attic for many years. The downside of garage sales is that you may have to wade through tons of baby clothes and furniture to find anything of interest to a collector.

Garage sales are generally a better source of bargains than estate sales. Although estate sales must, like the garage sale, dispose of vast quantities of merchandise in a short period, they are increasingly run by professional estate agents having a better idea of the value of items offered for sale. Expect prices to be much higher, sometimes exceeding what you might pay in a retail shop. Prices are almost invariably slashed by up to 50 percent on the final day of the sale, so bargains can still be found.

Auctions are another place to find bargains. Traditional estate auctions, such as those listed in *Antique Week* and any number of other antiques publications, provide the best opportunity to find bargains because they offer a wide array of merchandise and a limited number of competitors. Still, it takes only one other bidder to quickly drive the price of that clock up way beyond its true value. While this happens occasionally at estate auctions, it happens frequently in on-line auctions like ebay. With millions of users able to view and bid on items, rare clocks frequently sell for far more than what a dealer could expect to obtain in a retail shop. After such an item is first offered on ebay, however, subsequent auctions frequently draw significantly lower bids.

Ebay can also be a source of bargains, however, as the more common Telechron and General Electric models flood the market. Common models such as the "Airlux" (7H141) have decreased in value because of overexposure on ebay. This is also having a downward effect on retail prices.

Among the dealers charging the highest prices are those in the mega-malls located in close proximity to an interstate highway or a resort area. Dealers have to charge higher prices in such malls because of high booth rental fees. In addition, some of the malls collect 10 percent or more of the sale price. Most malls, however, will give a standard 10 percent off posted prices with payment by check or cash. Employees do not routinely offer the discount; you have to ask if the dealer does better on prices.

Prices are also generally higher at clock and art deco shops, but here you get added value. The clock has usually been cleaned and restored to good working condition. In the long run, paying a higher price for a restored clock may be appreciably less expensive than buying a non-working clock and paying to have it fixed.

Local weekend flea markets can also be a good source of bargains. Bargains can still be found at the larger, nationally advertised, markets like Renningers and Brimfield but they are increasingly populated by full-time dealers who travel from show to show with the same merchandise. Obviously, however, they are constantly adding new merchandise. While they avoid the high monthly rental of an antique mall, they still incur significant expenses for travel, lodging, and booth rental. Nothing, however, beats the ambiance and excitement of the early morning search for bargains at a flea market.

Condition. Values reflected in this guide are for clocks in excellent condition. This means:

• It is in good running condition and keeps accurate time. For alarm clocks, the alarm must work. For strike and chime clocks, these functions must also be operational.

• The case, dial, and movement are original. If the dial or movement have been repaired or replaced, only new original stock or remanufactured parts have been used.

• The case shows minimal wear. The finish on wooden cases is sound, veneered surfaces are intact, and there are no scratches or gouges in the wood. Bakelite and other plastics are free of cracks, chips, burn marks, and uneven coloration. Plated surfaces are intact with no base metal showing through.

• The dial is free of oil or water stains, peeling paint, or other damage.

• The crystal is intact and free from clouding.

• Painted surfaces are intact and free of stains, peeling, and flaking.

Because few clocks meet these stringent requirements, both sellers and buyers should take into consideration the actual condition of the clock in determining value. The effect on value depends on the type(s) and number of defects and their effect on the appearance of the item. As a general rule, deduct

• 2 to 5 percent if the cord is damaged but the clock works. Replacing the cord is among the easiest repairs and many owners are comfortable undertaking this "repair."

• 5 to 20 percent if the clock is not working properly. Although a clock that is not working has a lower value than does a clock in perfect working condition, in general, working condition is not as important as appearance in setting prices. Deduct less if the clock runs but is noisy or if some function, like the alarm, does not work.

• 50 to 75 percent if the clock has a replacement quartz movement. Substituting a quartz movement for the original Telechron movement essentially destroys the appeal of the clock to collectors.

• 10 to 30 percent for a cracked or missing crystal. Cracked or missing crystals significantly lower value because the purchaser will incur cost in finding a replacement. If the crystal is flat glass, it can often be replaced at a reasonable cost. The same is true for convex crystals as long as they are round. Deductions in the upper range apply to convex crystals in unusual shapes, which are virtually impossible to replace.

• 25 to 65 percent for chips or missing pieces of plastic cases. As a rule, the more visible the crack, chip, or gouge, the more it affects value. If there is significant damage to the case visible from the front or side, values drop at least 50 percent.

• 10 to 30 percent if the dial is damaged. The dial is the focal point of the clock and any significant damage, including stains, flaking paint, and scrapes from improperly positioned hands has a major impact on appearance and value. Other than cleaning and touch up of minor scrapes, dial restoration requires the help of a professional and is likely to cost more than the clock.

• 25 to 60 percent if the wood has gouges, scratches, or missing parts. Numerous products are available to fill and cover scratches and such defects can often be minimized at little cost and effort. Gouges and missing parts, however, require repairs that are more extensive and have a significant effect on value. If the wooden case has peeling or missing veneer or missing parts, cut its value by 30 to 40 percent.

• 10 to 25 percent if ornamental trim is missing.

• 10 to 25 percent if metal parts are dented, worn, or heavily scratched. Trim parts that are tarnished but otherwise in good condition do not significantly detract from value.

• 5 percent for each missing knob.

Under the above adjustments, clocks with multiple defects quickly lose most if not all of their value. Their value never, however, drops to zero. An insurer declares an automobile a total loss when the cost to repair the car exceeds its fair market value. Such cars, however, still have some salvage value. Similarly, clocks with multiple defects that would require more than a 100 percent adjustment can be sold for parts at 5 to 20 percent of value.

The Perfect Marriage?

Telechron movements often outlive their cases and mysteriously show up, dial and all, in either homemade cases, cases for another GE or Telechron clock, or as a replacement movement in another manufacturer's clock. Similarly, in those rare instances where the case outlives the movement, a Telechron or GE clock may have a replacement quartz movement or a movement taken from another electric clock. Because both types of "marriages" essentially destroy the value of the clock, buyers should carefully examine clocks before purchase to ensure that they are original. Even "same sex" marriages in which dials and cases of two Telechron or GE clocks are combined significantly lowers the value.

This clock has a leather case stamped "Eaton's" but a Telechron movement marked "7F57." Although the movement fits perfectly in the case and appears to be original, it is in all likelihood a marriage. While Telechron sold its clock movements to many companies, the dials to their clocks generally bore the company's name in addition to the "Telechron movement" on the lower half of the dial. In addition, clock cases made by other manufacturers should not bear a Telechron model number.

Design and Designer. Clocks by big name designers like Walter Dorwin Teague, Paul Frankl, and Russel Wright invariably bring higher prices than those by lesser know or anonymous designers. Some individuals focus their collections on the works of specific designers, like Russel Wright, rather than on a particular category of collectibles, like clocks. Expect clocks designed by John Rainbault and Raymond Patten to soar in value as more is learned about the work of these two extraordinary designers.

Ultimately, it is the quality of the design not the name of the designer that makes a clock collectible. In general, art deco designs are the most collectible and have higher values. Interpretations of period designs, particularly tambour style mantel clocks, are less collectible, and 1950s plastic alarm clocks have little current value.

CAUTION: Beware of False Attribution

Many sellers, particularly on ebay and other on-line auctions, use the line "attributed to…" followed by Rockwell Kent, Russel Wright, or some other famous designer in an attempt to increase the selling price of their clocks. Others simply use a randomly selected designer's name followed by a (?) to draw attention to their auction, having no real information to suggest that the designer had anything to do with the clock. The most flagrant abuse is on the series of etched glass clocks designed by John Rainbault. These designs have been "attributed to" Russel Wright, Rockwell Kent, Walter "Darwin" Teague, Gilbert Rohde, and Walter Von Nessen among others.

Challenge the seller to substantiate designer claims.

Rarity. In general, the laws of supply and demand apply to clocks just as they do to other collectibles. This book includes sales figures for many Telechron and General Electric models. Such figures should not, however, be used in isolation in determining the effect on value. A clock that did not sell well when it was introduced may have a dull case design that will not appeal to most collectors. Such clocks appeal to the small group of collectors whose collections are based on completeness more than aesthetics. They may be willing to pay a premium price for a bland but rare clock, but the clock may sit in inventory for months or years before the right collector comes along.

Where rarity has the greatest effect on value is in cases where initial sales were slow because of some external force, such as the Great Depression or World War II. For example, the "Modernique" was introduced shortly before the stock market crash in 1929 and the market for such luxury clocks quickly evaporated. Similarly, the four extraordinary onyx clocks Leo Ivan Bruce designed in 1940 are rare because production was halted when the United States entered World War II.

Current Values

Cat.No.	Model	Price	Pg.
Early Models (Ch. 7)			
101	Wood Case Telechron	$100-125	59
102	Executive	$55-65	62
103	Walton	$50-65	58
201	Wood Case Telechron	$125-150	59
301	Wood Case Telechron	$125-150	59
322	Vanity	$50-65	62
323	Petite	$50-65	62
324	Victoria	$55-65	63
325	Copley	$50-65	63
326	Bristol or Bruce	$45-55	63
327	Salisbury or Sudbury	$50-60	63
328	not named	$50-60	64
329	Colony	$50-60	64
330	not named	$60-70	64
331	Plymouth	$40-50	64
332	Duncan	$40-50	65
333	Beverly	$65-75	65
334	Jeffrey	$75-85	65
335	Englewood	$45-55	65
336	Trenton	$50-60	65
355	Cathedral	$40-55	66
356	Tudor	$35-45	66
357	Apollo	$135-160	66
358	Diana	$135-160	66
370	Clinton	$50-60	67
371	Auburn	$55-65	67
401	Wood Case Telechron	$150-175	59
402	Mantel Telechron	$115-130	67
403	Wall Telechron	$40-50	59
405	Metal Case Telechron	$30-40	60
406	Metal Case Telechron	$30-40	60
407	Metal Case Telechron	$30-40	60
408	Metal Case Telechron	$30-40	60
410	Metal Case Telechron	$30-40	60
415	Semi-flush Telechron	$35-45	59
416	Semi-flush Telechron	$35-45	59
417	Semi-flush Telechron	$40-55	59
418	Semi-flush Telechron	$45-55	59
420	Semi-flush Telechron	$55-65	59
431	Modernique	$1200-1500	68
452	Copley	$175-225	60
453	Constance	$50-65	60
454	Hostess	$55-60	60
455	Radio	$125-140	69
457	not named	$50-65	61
458	Unnamed	$45-55	61
501	Gothic Mantel Telechron	$65-75	69
502	Doric Mantel Telechron	$65-75	69
503	Gothic Mantel Telechron	$65-75	70
504	Mantel Telechron	$70-80	70
505	Queen Anne Mantel Telechron	$100-110	70
508	Mantel or Desk Telechron	$75-90	70
522	Salem	$50-60	71
523	Patricia	$50-60	71
524	Oxford	$125-145	71
525	Windsor	$95-115	71
526	Bellevue	$55-65	72
528	Surrey	$65-80	72
528A	Surrey Wall Model	$75-90	61
530	Nottingham	$140-150	72
531	Lorraine	$70-80	73
532	Standish	$60-70	73
533	not named	$135-160	73
551	Lexington	$35-45	74
552	Adams	$45-55	74
553	Belmont	$50-60	74
554	Miles Standish	$40-55	74
555	Burlington	$40-50	74
556	Virginian	$45-55	74
557	Lynnwood	$45-55	75
558	Geneva	$55-65	75
559	Durham	$55-65	75
560	Bennington	$55-65	76
562	not named	N/A	76
563	Huntington	$45-55	76
564	not named	$45-55	76
601	Normandy	$50-60	76
602	Castleton	$100-125	77
603	Jefferson	$110-125	77
604	Brittany	$65-75	77
605	Waverly	$75-90	78
606	Winchester	$65-75	78
654	Manchester	$55-65	78
655	Versailles	$45-55	79
656	Aristocrat	$75-90	79
661	Concord	$40-50	79
662	Magnolia	$55-70	80
663	Pilgrim	$40-50	80
664	Dorchester	$45-55	80
666	Norwich	$55-65	80
691	Madison	$90-100	87
692	Bullfinch	$50-60	88
694	Bullfinch	$60-65	88
1258	Banjo	$150-165	88
700	Electrolarm	$195-235	81
711	Telalarm	$60-75	83
712	Alarm Lite	$60-75	83
715	Telalarm	$60-75	84
716	Alarm Lite	$60-75	84
727	Alden	$45-55	84
728	not named	$45-55	84
AA	not named	$30-40	85
BB	not named	$35-45	85
AL	not named	$135-155	85
TM-2	not named	$55-65	86
TM-8	not named	$225-275	86
TM-19	not named	$35-45	86
TM-24	not named	$15-25	86
Unkn.	Washington Bi-Centennial	$100-125	87
Kitchen and Wall Clocks (Ch. 8)			
2B01	Priscilla	$60-75	89
2F01	Consort	$65-80	89
2BO2	not named	$55-70	90
2F02	New Hostess	$45-55	90
2F03	Kitchenguide	$45-55	91
2F04	Chef	$40-50	92
2F06	Kitchen Hostess	$55-65	93
2H07	Buffet	$40-60	93
2H08	Garcon	$45-60	94
2H09	Stewardess	$85-100	94
2H10	Domestic	$45-55	95
2H11	Café	$40-55	95
2HX12	New Chef	$35-45	96
2H13	Patron	$40-50	96
2H14	Pantry	$40-50	96
2H15	Kitchenguide	$35-45	97
2HX16	New Chef	$30-40	97
2H17	Minitmaster	$60-75	97
2H18	Chef	$30-45	98
2H19	Prudence	$30-40	98
2H20	Epicure	$35-45	98
2H21	Decorator	$40-55	98
2H22	Pantry	$25-35	98
2H24	Dinette	$25-35	99
2H25	Stewardess	$25-35	99
2H26	Gourmet	$35-45	99
2H27	Advisor	$35-45	99
2H28	Grille	$20-25	99
2H29	Pageant	$20-30	100
2H30	Clansman	$25-30	100
2H31	Jubilee	$15-20	100
2H32	Domestic	$15-20	100
2H33	Ivy	$30-35	101
2H34	Contour	$25-30	101
2H38	Helper	$15-20	101
2H39	Originality	$40-50	101
2H40	Carousel	$35-40	101
2H41	Butler	$10-15	101
2H42	Jackstraw	$25-35	102
2H43	Telemaid	$25-30	102
2H44	Topper	$25-30	102
2H45	Swirl	$25-35	103
2H46	Gay Wall	$15-20	103
2H47	Telechoice	$25-30	103
2H48	Ceramic	$45-55	103
2H49	Motif	$10-15	103
2H50	Dinette	$55-65	104
2H51	Shield	$75-90	104
2H52	Sunburst	N/A	104
2H54	Bordeaux	N/A	104
2H55	Colonist	$10-15	104
2H56	Marseille	$55-65	104
2S57	Inheritance	$45-55	104
2H59	Wallwood	$85-105	105
2F81	Swarthmore	$45-55	105
2H100	Gossamer	$45-55	106
2H101	Diameter	$90-105	106
2H103	Cupboard	$15-20	106
2H105	Illusion	$25-35	106
CF205	Matron	$60-75	92
CH203	Kitchenguide	$45-55	91
Shelf Clocks (Ch. 9)			
3A01	not named	N/A	107
3F01	Commonwealth	$50-65	107
3F02	Puritan	$45-55	107
3F03	Esquire	$45-60	108
3F04	Vivienne	$50-65	108
3A05	not named	$55-65	108
3H06	Pristine	$25-30	108
3H07	Gracewood	$35-45	108
3A51	Renault	$45-60	109
3F51	Duke	$70-80	109
3F52	Petite	$125-150	109
3F53	Daphne	$115-135	109
3F53T	Daphne (transprnt.)	$225-300	109
3F54	Little Hostess	$65-80	110
3F55	Newberry	$45-60	110
3F56	Vogue	$50-60	110
3F58	Secretary	$45-55	111
3F59	Squarart	$35-45	111
3F60	Fleet	$55-65	111
3F61	Tempo	$95-110	111
3F62	Unkn.	N/A	111
3F64	Wellfleet or New Fleet	$55-65	112
3F65	Iris	$65-75	112
3F66	Concord	$40-50	112
3F67	Pageant	$55-65	113
3F68	Longwood	$35-45	113
3F69	Nassau	$50-65	113
3F70	Park Avenue	$75-90	113
3F71	Coronado	$45-60	114
3F72	Brevet	$40-50	114
3H73	Domino	$45-55	114
3F74	Duncan	$60-70	114
3H76	Ithaca	$40-50	115
3H77	Advocate	$70-85	115
3H78	Basque	$115-140	115
3H79	Croft	$45-55	115
3H80	Morgan	$40-50	115
3H81	Virginian	$55-65	115
3H82	New Lotus	$90-105	116
3H83	Melbourne	$95-110	116
3H84	Monmouth	$40-50	116
3H85	Resolute	$55-65	116
3H86	New Brevet	$40-50	116
3H88	Farragut or World's Fair	$35-45	117
3H89	Bancroft	$70-80	117
3H90	Norfolk	$90-105	117
3H91	Glamour	$45-60	118
3H92	New Lorraine	$75-90	118
3H93	Investor	$35-45	119
3H94	Conway	$75-90	119
3H95	Snug	$60-70	120
3H96	Dartmouth	$90-105	120
3H97	Vassal	$40-50	120
3H98	Navigator	$45-55	121
3H99	Yachtsman	$45-55	121
3HX150	Briarcliff	$30-40	121
3H151	Pharaoh	$45-55	122
3H152	Sherwood	$50-60	122
3H154	Saddle	$70-80	122
3H155	Glamour	$40-50	122
3H156	Narcissus	$45-55	123
3H157	Yachtsman	$45-55	123
3H158	Gay	$50-65	123
3H159	Suave	$85-100	124
3H160	Rapture	$125-150	124
3H161	Somerset	$45-55	125
3H162	Thrill	$50-60	125
3H163	Swarthmore	$40-50	125
3H164	Bounty	$35-45	125
3H166	Nimbus	$30-40	125
3H168	Debutante	$40-50	126
3H169	not known	N/A	126
3H172	Candlelight	$45-60	126
3H176	Geneva	$45-55	126
3H178	Candidate	$35-45	126
3H180	Voyageur	$45-55	127
3H182	Designer	$40-50	127
3H184	Concord	$45-60	127
4A01	Bishop	$60-70	128
4F01	Maynard	$40-50	128
4A02	not known	N/A	128
4F02	not known	$45-55	128
4F03	Perry	$40-50	129
4F04	Lynnwood	$35-45	129
4A05	not known	$60-70	129
4F05	Gracewood	$80-90	129
4F06	Londonderry	$25-35	129
4B07	Harwich	$135-150	130
4H08	New Geneva	$55-70	130
4H10	Amherst	$45-55	130
4H12	Candlelight	$55-70	130
4A51	Pemberton	$45-55	130
4F51	Telart	$90-105	130
4F51A	Telart	$90-105	131
4F52	Debutante	$60-75	131
4F53	Colonist	$80-90	131
4F54	Stanwood	$45-55	131
4F55	Airlux	$45-55	132
4F56	not known	$40-50	132
4F57	Starman	$90-105	132
4F58	Lotus	$235-260	132
4F59	Attaché	$55-70	133
4F60	Dictator	$135-150	133
4F61	Pharaoh	$50-65	133

Cat.No.	Model	Price	Pg.
4F62	Blue Night	$115-135	134
4F63	Aztec	$75-85	134
4F64	Blue Night	$115-135	135
4F65	Luxor	$145-160	135
4F66	Blue Night	$115-135	135
4F67	Embassy	$45-60	135
4H68	Tuileries	$125-140	136
4F69	Traymore	$55-70	136
4F71	Casino	$165-180	137
4H72	Breton	$375-425	137
4F73	Smartset	$45-60	137
4H74	Chantilly	$40-50	137
4F75	Lido	$70-90	137
4H76	Samson	$55-70	138
4H77	Deauville	$145-170	138
4H78	Ballard	$50-60	138
4B79	Olympic	$65-80	139
4H80	Tuscan	$55-65	139
4H81	Statesman	$80-95	139
4H82	Quincy	$60-75	140
4H83	Naples	$65-80	140
4H84	Athens	$45-55	141
4B85	Cordova	$65-80	141
4H86	Nantucket	$40-50	141
4H87	Kirkwood	$45-55	141
4H88	Wareham	$65-80	142
4H89	Vagabond	$35-45	142
4H90	Ridgefield	$55-70	142
4H91	Finesse	$45-55	143
4H92	New Ballard	$50-60	143
4H93	Highland	$60-75	143
4H94	Ulysses	$45-55	144
4H95	Kendall	$45-55	144
4H97	Forum	$70-85	144
4H99	Knickerbocker	$40-50	144
4B151	Shoreham	$115-130	145
4B153	Barclay	$125-145	145
4B155	Hampshire	$125-145	145
4H157	Banker	$90-105	145
4H167	Wickford	$45-55	146
4H169	Resolute	$45-55	146
4H173	Woodmont	$50-65	146
5A01	Danforth	$40-50	147
5F01	Norwood	$65-70	147
5A02	not known	$70-80	148
5F02	Tampa	$45-55	148
5F03	Brandon	$125-150	148
5B07	Barrington	$45-55	148
5F50	Mirage	$325-375	149
5F51	Doric	$125-150	149
5F52	Mirage	$225-275	149
5B53	Sheffield	$50-60	150
5F54	Salon	$325-375	150
5B55	Congress	$50-60	150
5F56	Soiree	$325-375	151
5H57	Suave	$45-55	151
5F58	Ecstasy	$125-150	151
5F59	Satellite	$65-80	152
5F60	Ecstasy	$125-150	152
5H61	Fort	$70-85	152
5H64	Lorraine	$65-80	152
5H65	Outline	$175-215	153
5H66	Overseer	$50-60	153
5H67	Showpiece	$145-165	153
5H68	Caprice	$45-55	154
5H69	Illumitime	$75-90	154
5H70	Higgins Glass	$225-275	154
5H71	Panorama	$175-200	155
6H02	Alencon	$350-425	155
6H50	Jason	$65-80	155
CF363	Usher	$55-70	111
CH373	Domino	$45-55	114
CH387	Somerset	$75-90	117
CH399	not named	$60-70	121

Chime and Strike Clocks (Ch. 10)

Cat.No.	Model	Price	Pg.
201	Melody	$60-70	166
203	Harmony	$60-75	166
301	Concord	$325-400	176
303	Sussex	$425-475	176
305	Winthrop	$625-700	176
307	Middlesex	$625-700	176
309	Adams	$700-800	177
310	not named	$75-85	167
313	New Virginian	$475-550	177
350	Rhapsody	$85-100	167
352	Concerto	$95-110	167
356	Full Dress	$85-100	167
358	Campanila	$65-75	167
362	Orpheus	$65-75	167
364	Abbe	$45-55	168
366	Haverhill	$80-95	168
368	Lafayette	$90-105	168
370	Dorchester	$125-150	168
372	Hanover	$275-325	169
374	New Philharmonic	$135-150	169
376	New Rhapsody	$125-140	169
378	New Concerto	$115-130	169
380	Puritan	$350-425	177
382	Puritan	$350-425	177
384	Dowager	$350-425	177
386	Dearborn	$275-350	178
388	Winthrop	$375-450	178
400	Festival	$105-120	170
402	Serenade	$125-140	170
404	Joy	$80-90	171
406	Overture	$95-110	171
408	New Maestro	$85-95	171
410	Chorus	$95-105	171
412	Prelude	$125-140	170
414	Rhapsody	$135-150	172
416	Maestro	$115-130	171
418	Concerto	$85-100	171
420	Overture	$110-125	171
422	Prelude	$95-110	172
424	Philharmonic	$135-150	172
426	Chorus	$105-120	172
428	New Overture	$90-105	172
430	New Concerto	$95-105	172
6B01	Jubilee	$75-85	162
6B03	Seville	$60-70	162
6B04	Grafton	$55-70	162
6B05	Picardy	$60-75	163
6B06	Gloucester	$55-70	163
6B07	Minstrel	$40-50	163
6B08	Maestro	$55-70	164
6B09	Yachtsman	$50-60	164
6B10	Hearth	$70-85	164
6B11	Angelus	$60-70	164
6B12	Philosopher	$40-50	164
6B13	Magnolia	$80-95	165
6B14	Winthrop	$50-60	165
6B15	Wickford	$45-55	165
6B17	Resolute	$50-60	166
6B18	Nantucket	$60-70	166
6B20	Ridgefield	$45-55	166
701-S	Symphony	$60-75	172
R130	not named	$275-325	156
R150	not named	$200-250	157
R407	not named	$150-175	157
R602	not named	$45-60	158
R622	not named	$65-80	157
R624	not named	$55-70	158
R632	not named	$75-90	157
R634	not named	$55-70	158
R636	not named	$45-60	158
R638	not named	$95-110	158
R855	not named	$85-100	159
R857	not named	$95-120	159
R863	not named	$85-100	159
R865	not named	$75-90	159
R867	not named	$75-90	160
R869	not named	$80-95	160
R981	not named	$65-80	160
R983	not named	$65-75	160
R985	not named	$125-150	161
Unkn.	Haverhill	$90-110	157
Unkn.	Louis XVI	$300-350	161
Unkn.	Chippendale	$350-425	161
Unkn.	Louis XIV	$400-475	161
Unkn.	Cambridge	$550-625	175
Unkn.	Dawes	$625-700	173
Unkn.	Devonshire	$675-750	173
Unkn.	Hanover	$375-425	173
Unkn.	Mayfair	$375-425	174
Unkn.	Middlesex	$450-525	174
Unkn.	Plymouth	$375-425	175
Unkn.	Rosemary	$450-500	175
Unkn.	Roxbury	$425-500	174
Unkn.	Winthrop	$375-425	175

Alarm Clocks (Ch. 11)

Cat.No.	Model	Price	Pg.
7B01	Autolarm	$80-95	179
7F01	Announcer	$60-75	179
7B02	not known	$80-95	179
7F03	Clarion	$115-130	180
7H04	Repeater	$30-40	180
7H06	Drummer	$15-20	180
7H07	Everset	$10-15	181
7H09	Nocturne	$25-30	181
7F52	Morning Star	$80-95	181
7F53	Telebell or Telecall	$85-100	182
7F54	Deb	$40-50	182
7F55	Signalette	$90-105	182
7F56	Vedette	$50-65	183
7F57	Airlarm or Sportsman	$50-60	183
7F58	Lumalarm	$165-180	184
7F59	Squarlarm	$35-45	184
7F60	Morning Glory	$40-50	184
7F61	Vedette	$60-70	185
7F62	Englewood	$45-55	185
7F63	Quacker	$175-200	185
7F64	Utility Timer	$50-65	185
7F65	Deputy and Aladdin	$75-85	186
7F66	Dawning	$40-50	186
7F67	Carillon	$60-75	186
7F68	Beau	$45-55	186
7F70	Overseer	$50-60	187
7F71	Gendarme	$70-80	187
7F72	Heralder	$115-130	188
7F73	Meadowlark	$75-90	189
7F74	Heralder	$90-105	189
7F75	Mayfair	$45-55	189
7F76	Geneva	$70-80	189
7H77	Mirolarm	$75-90	190
7H78	Acorn	$65-80	190
7H79	Butler	$45-55	190
7H80	Julep	$115-140	191
7H82	Sophist	$95-105	191
7H84	Gladiator	$75-90	192
7H85	Attendant	$65-75	192
7H86	Warburton	$115-130	193
7H87	Mentor	$65-80	193
7H88	Dawning	$145-160	193
7H89	Guest	$75-90	193
7H90	Eldorado	$115-130	194
7H91	Secretary	$35-45	194
7H92	Circe	$375-450	194
7H93	New Telalarm	$65-75	195
7H94	Sergeant	$45-55	195
7H95	Colonnade	$70-85	195
7H96	New Gladiator	$75-90	196
7H98	Corporal	$35-45	196
7H99	Steward	$65-75	196
7H100	New Dawning	$45-55	197
7H101	Imp	$90-105	197
7H102	Ashby	$80-90	197
7H103	Conductor	$35-45	197
7H104	Hesperus	$70-85	198
7H105	Legislator	$90-105	198
7H106	Morning Glory	$70-80	198
7H107	Supervisor & Warden	$50-60	199
7H108	Serf	$75-90	199
7H109	Flotilla	$45-55	199
7H110	Orpheus	$55-70	199
7H112	Gallant	$45-55	200
7H113	Custodian	$50-60	200
7HX114	Norse	$60-70	200
7H115	Fortress	$75-90	200
7H116	Orderly	$45-55	200
7H117	Reporter	$65-75	200
7H118	Troubadour	$45-55	201
7H119	Governor	$35-45	201
7H120	Tweed	$50-60	201
7H121	Serene	$80-90	201
7H122	Informer	$55-65	201
7H124	Annapolis	$45-55	201
7H125	Dispatcher	$40-50	202
7HX126	Envoy	N/A	202
7HX128	New Lumalarm	$40-50	202
7HX130	not known	$95-105	202
7H132	Brisk	$55-65	202
7H133	Embassy	$60-70	202
7H134	Helper	$50-60	202
7H135	Telalarm, Jr.	$35-45	203
7H136	Gay Hour	$85-95	203
7H137	Little Tel	$35-45	203
7H138	Chipper	$65-75	203
7H139	Talisman	$35-45	203
7H140	Delegate	$30-40	204
7H141	Airlux	$45-55	204
7H142	Contact	$65-75	204
7H144	Nymph	$60-70	204
7HX146	not known	$60-70	204
7H147	Pinwall	$50-60	204
7H149	Sparkler	$25-35	205
7H153	Serene	$25-35	205
7H154	Chantilly	$40-50	205
7H155	Telebell	$35-45	205
7H157	Colonade	$30-40	206
7H159	Nocturne	$25-35	206
7H160	Heralder	$45-55	206
7H161	Tempo	$35-45	206
7H162	Gay Hour	$25-35	206
7H163	Kirkwood	$25-35	206
7H164	Beau	$20-25	207
7H165	Coronado	$30-40	207
7H166	Morning Glory	$45-55	207
7H167	Yachtsman	$35-45	208
7HA168	Chantilly	$35-45	208
7H169	Guest	$20-25	208
7H170	Morning Star	$30-40	208
7HP171	Bancroft	$15-20	209
7H173	Tel-A-Glow	$40-50	209
7H174	Informer	$35-45	209
7H176	Deb	$10-15	209
7H178	Orderly	$10-15	209
7H179	Tribute	$45-55	209
7H180	Chipper	$25-30	209
7H181	Mentor	$45-55	210
7H182	Twinkle	$65-75	210
7H183	Imp	$10-15	210
7H184	Warbler	$20-25	210
7H185	Tiara	$20-25	210
7H187	Personality	$25-35	210
7H188	Candlewick	$45-55	211
7H189	Aladdin	$20-25	211
7H190	Gay	$5-10	211
7H192	Wink	$5-10	211
7H194	Nudger	$5-10	211
7H195	Mirolarm	$35-45	211
7HA195	Parliament	$35-45	212
7H196	Heralder	$5-10	212
7H197	Illuminette	$20-25	212
7H198	Lumalarm	$15-20	212
7H199	Minstrel	$5-10	212
7H200	Cue and New Cue	$5-10	212
7H201	Telegrain	$15-20	212
7H202	Brisk	$4-8	212
7H203	Enhancer	$35-45	212
7H204	Tweed	$15-20	213
7H207	Lullaby	$5-10	213
7H208	Riser and PurrAlarm	$5-10	213
7H209	Gracewood	$20-25	213
7H210	Beau Alarm	$5-10	214
7H211	Dorm	$5-10	214
7H212	Woodsman	$25-35	214
7H213	Perspective	$35-45	214
7H214	Serenade	$25-30	214
7H215	Décor	$8-12	214
7H216	Brite Dial	$10-15	215
7H217	Telecrat	$5-10	215
7H218	Beckoner	$5-10	215
7H220	Starter	$4-8	215
7H221	Turnabout	$45-55	215
7H222	Boudoir	$10-15	216
7H223	Room-mate	$4-8	216
7H224	Partner	$35-45	216
7H225	Luminary	$6-12	216
7H226	Urban	$15-20	216
7H228	Architect	$20-30	216
7H229	Replica	$35-45	217
7H230	New Debutante	$15-20	217
7H232	Caller	$5-10	217
7H233	Circlewood	$35-45	217
7H234	Harlequin	$15-20	217
7H235	Fidelity	$25-30	218
7H236	Revelation	$35-45	218
CF705	not known	$50-60	180
CF769	Constable and Sheriff	$70-80	186
CH783	Kleertone	$105-115	191
CH785	Attendant	$65-75	193
CH797	not known	$70-85	196
CH7111	Semester	$115-130	200
Unkn.	War Alarm No. 1	$50-60	218
Unkn.	War Alarm No. 2	$50-60	218

Cyclometer, Day/Date, and Novelty Clocks (Ch. 12)

Cat.No.	Model	Price	Pg.
8027	Forecaster	$45-55	229
8030	Quartermaster	$50-60	229
8B01	Minitmaster	$110-125	219
8F01	Smug	$175-200	226
8B02	Executive	$110-125	219
8F02	Traveler	$45-55	227
8B03	Minitman	$80-95	219
8F03	Explorer or Globetrotter	$65-75	227
8B04	New Executive	$215-240	220
8B05	New Minitmaster	$145-160	220
8B06	Budgeteer	$70-85	220
8B07	Baron	$50-60	220
8B08	Executive	$60-70	220
8B09	Tribute	$65-75	221
8B10	Framingham	$85-95	221
8B11	Granada	$45-55	221
8B13	Register	$100-115	221
8H14	Almanac	$50-60	222
8H15	Instructor	$50-60	229
8H16	Barotime	$45-55	229
8H17	Registrar	$45-55	222
8H18	Bosun	$30-35	229
8H19	Prophet	$50-60	229
8B22	Executive	$35-40	222
8B23	Register	$40-45	222
8H24	Almanac	$20-25	223
8H27	Innovation	$150-175	227
8H28	Trixie	$45-55	227
8H29	Tele-jour	$50-60	223
8B50	Select-O-Switch	$60-70	223
8F50	Kitchen Timer	$50-65	223
8B51	Controlla	$75-85	224
8F51	Advisor	$80-95	224
8B52	Radio Traveler	$40-50	224
8B53	Organizer	$45-55	224
8B54	Radio Traveler	$40-50	225
8H55	Selector	$35-45	225
8H57	Lite-Call	$30-35	225
8H58	Select-O-Switch	$25-30	225
8H59	Musalarm	$60-75	228
8H60	Beam Alarm	$35-45	225
8H61	Switchalarm	$25-35	225
8H63	Minitmaster, Jr.	$15-20	225
8H64	Tune-A-Larm	$35-45	226
8H66	Little Chef	$15-20	226
8H67	Musalarm	$50-60	228
8S69	Videoclock	$25-35	226
8H70	New Tune-A-Larm	$40-50	226
8H72	Tune-A-Larm	$35-45	226
Unkn.	Minitmaster timer	$15-20	226
Unkn.	Minitmaster timer	$20-25	226
Unkn.	Fisk "Time to Retire"	$175-200	227
Unkn.	Monitor top	$200-235	227
Unkn.	75th Anniversary	$25-35	228